ALEJANDRO DABAT played a leading role in the Argentinian student movement in the early sixties, and was active in revolutionary and trade-union politics until his forced emigration in 1972. The author of numerous theoretical, political and historical articles, he is a member of the editorial collective of *Teoría y Política* — a journal based in Mexico City, where he has lived since 1975. A lawyer and economist by training, Dabat lectures at the Economics Faculty of the Autonomous National University of Mexico.

LUIS LORENZANO was a leading member of the Argentinian student movement in the early sixties and collaborated with left-wing union currents in Córdoba. After many years of political and theoretical activity, he was driven into exile in Mexico at the end of 1975. He is now a leader of the Argentinian group TYSAE, and a member both of the Argentinian Human Rights Coordinating Committee and of the *Teoría y Política* consultative committee. Lorenzano was trained in media sciences and now lectures at the Political Sciences Faculty of the Autonomous National University of Mexico.

Alejandro Dabat
Luis Lorenzano

Verso

Argentina:
The Malvinas and the
End of Military Rule

Translated by Ralph Johnstone

British Library
Cataloguing in Publication Data

Dabat, Alejandro
  Argentina: the Malvinas and the end of military rule.
  1. Falkland Islands War, 1982 — Influence
  2. Argentina — Politics and government — 1983
I. Title   II. Lorenzano, Luis
982'.064   F2849.2

First published as *Conflicto malvinense y crisis nacional,*
by Teoría y Politica, Mexico City 1982
© Teoría y Politica, 1982

This expanded and revised translation first published by
Verso Editions, 15 Greek Street, London W1V 5LF
© Verso Editions, 1984

Filmset in Bembo by
Swanston Graphics Limited, Derby

Printed in Great Britain by
The Thetford Press Limited
Thetford, Norfolk

ISBN 0 86091 085 7
      0 86091 790 8

Contents

1

Argentina
and the National Question

The Malvinas war was an extremely important political and military event for Argentina and Latin America, dividing the Left on the continent into two main groups. Some believed that Argentina was a semi-colonial (or neo-colonial) country waging a just war of national liberation against imperialism, regardless of the nature of its government, or of the reasons behind the war, or of the social and political costs to the Argentinian nation. Others believed that it was a conventional inter-capitalist war, sparked off by one of the most bloodthirsty and reactionary dictatorships in the world to consolidate its political position, which worsened living conditions for the masses and jeopardized the eventual recovery of the islands by the Argentinian nation.

Both groups recognize the legitimacy of Argentina's claim to the islands and vigorously condemn British colonialism. However, they substantially disagree not only about the advantageousness and nature of the war, but also about the character of Argentina itself and the role of the Malvinas and national questions in this characterization. In this broad range of disagreements, then, they have adopted different analytical perspectives and paths of political action in relation to the country's future.

In this chapter we will try to prove two central points: (a) that Argentina is a politically independent capitalist country which is inserted into the world market in a way that combines financial and technological dependence with its emergence as a regional power undergoing a profound process of militarization and economic and social disintegration; and (b) that Britain at present plays a completely marginal role in Argentinian political and economic life, and that its military control over the Malvinas Islands is one of the last significant legacies of its old colonial empire. We shall then argue, in the next chapter, that Argentina's legitimate claim for the return of the Malvinas is a non-essential point, less important than, for example, the recovery of popular sovereignty, the surmounting of the socio-economic crisis and the establishment of social and political democracy.

In support of these propositions, we shall begin by defining Argentina as a country and clarifying the form and nature of its national question. (The latter is essential if we are to determine the significance of the Malvinas war in the nation's development.) However, given the immense confusion among Marxists and socialists over essential theoretical concepts and the political significance of the so-called national problem, we think it necessary to include an introduction explaining our analytical framework.

1. The Nation in Marxist Theory

(a) *The Classification of Countries by National Type*

Marxist theory lends enormous importance to the so-called national problem by recognizing that the nation is the form adopted by human communities (territorial, cultural, economic) in the historical epoch of the development of capitalism. In this epoch the development of the social forces of production requires the formation of nation-states, as culturally homogeneous institutional – territorial spheres for the exchange of goods, and for the valorization and reproduction of capital.

The relation between the various nations and nation-states in the context of capitalist development determines two closely inter-related phenomena: the tendency to form nation-states as new spheres of rising capitalist development (which is implied by the awakening of national life, national movements and struggles against national oppression); and the tendency for all kinds of international ties to develop, pointing towards the destruction of national barriers. These inseparable yet mutually antagonistic processes are beset by internal conflicts, since they cannot develop without class struggle, revolutionary confrontations and wars.

To interpret rationally such conflicts, classical Marxism gradually established an objective method of analysis of the different types of nation and 'nationalism', progressive and reactionary, thereby making possible the education and organization, within a democratic, socialist and internationalist framework, of the working class and the masses exploited and oppressed by capitalism and imperialism. Following this methodology,[1] we must locate three fundamentally different levels of analysis, which then must be combined in a concrete analysis and fused with the remaining constituent features of a historically determined situation.

These levels are: (a) the degree of capitalist development in each country and the qualitative stage it has reached — the latter being directly linked to the political adequacy of the state to the needs of capitalist development at each stage; (b) the forms of economic integration into the world market at each stage of its development; (c) the nature of the state in each country, in relation both to other states (external relations of political dependence or subordination) and to different nationalities in the same country (in multinational states).

In the first category, the Marxist tradition distinguishes between *pre-capitalist* countries, in which the immense majority of the population works under non-capitalist relations of production; *semi-capitalist* countries, in which capitalist relations are widely developed but not dominant; *capitalist* or predominantly capitalist countries; and *monopoly-capitalist* countries. Monopoly capitalism is characterized by the sum of features analysed in the classical theories of imperialism. Here internal characteristics (a certain level of the concentration and centralization of capital, the development of finance capital, the corporate structures and work organization typical of Fordism) are indissolubly linked to external trends such as the export of capital and the 'broadening of economic space'. A particular level of monopoly-capitalist development corresponds to a sub-stage that Lenin and Bukharin call State Monopoly Capitalism. Whatever the name used, its essential feature is a higher concentration and centralization of capital under direct state management.

In the second category, classical Marxism establishes that one can characterize different types of country only after defining the stage of development reached by world capitalism, which implies a specific relationship between more advanced countries (colonial-manufacturing, industrial, monopolist-imperialist, according to the epoch) and the most backward. For the epoch of imperialism, Lenin distinguishes between *monopolist-imperialist* countries (capital exporters whose expanding economic space tends to develop politico-state spheres of influence broader than the original nation-state base) and *financially dependent countries*, whose processes of accumulation are based mainly on capital imports and which tend to be inserted into the world system as exporters of primary materials and importers of industrial products, and as segments of the political and economic space of one of the imperial powers.

Particularly since the Second World War, some aspects of the classic theory of imperialism have had to be modified.[2] Among the new features are the decolonization process (which opened previously colonial markets to the commodities and capital of all nations), the extension of industrialization to backward countries with the consequent formation of a 'new international division of labour', new types of rivalry between capitalist nation states, the growth of huge transnational companies and international regulatory agencies like the IMF, the World Bank and GATT, and the development of semi-autonomous economic spaces, both multinational (free trade areas, common markets, associations between states) and domestic (free zones). An essential facet of this new reality is the existence of state-directed economies integrated with the world capitalist market, whose fundamental nuclear grouping is the so-called Socialist Bloc revolving around the military and economic power of the USSR.

In the light of this new historical experience, we must conceptualize the phenomenon of recently developed capitalist-imperialist countries which, though still net importers of capital, have begun to acquire imperialist features at a regional level (export of industrial products and capital, the creation of regional spheres of economic and political influence, the structuring of state apparatuses, and military strongmen who back expansionist actions). Many of these features are similar to those found in Czarist Russia and are beginning to develop in many countries such as Brazil, South Africa, South Korea, Israel, Iran and Mexico.

Finally, in the third category, classical Marxist theory invariably distinguishes between *politically independent countries* (nation states) and *politically dependent nations or peoples*, whether it was examining national or pre-national societies subjected to an external state power, or multinational societies in which political domination was exercised by a majority or minority oppressor group. Supported by this analytical framework of Marxism, Lenin made another, exceptionally important distinction between *colonies* (or countries totally deprived of a nation-state and governed by officials of the oppressor state), and *semi-colonies*, or countries which, though possessing their own state structure, have been despoiled of essential functions needed to exercise internal sovereignty in line with the requirements of economic and social development (dismemberment of segments of the territory essential for a viable national economy, foreign control over the armed forces, foreign policy, customs, fiscal resources, etc.).[3]

The existence of an autonomous state is in no way a mere juridical formality. It implies, among other things, the formation of a unified national market under a single civil and commercial legislative code, and the circulation of a commonly used means of exchange (a national currency) which stimulates trade among producers. It also implies the construction of a military apparatus and a court system through which the state can wield coercive power, and the existence of a bureaucratic–administrative apparatus to manage national capital and to protect it from external capital through protectionist tariffs, subsidies, and so on.

The other essential component of a national political typology is the particular case of *oppressor multinational states*. Classical Marxism distinguishes between *nation-states* in the strict sense of the term, and *multinational states*. By *nation-states* it referred to culturally homogeneous societies organized as independent states, whatever the mechanism of the nation's formation or of its corresponding state organization (prolonged integration of different ethnic–regional communities, as in Western Europe; rapid assimilation of innumerable groups of immigrants from different nations, as in the USA and Argentina; progressive socio-cultural integration of a conquering oppressor community with several oppressed communities, as in Indo-American societies). In all these cases national unity was consolidated around a common language which eventually assimilated or subordinated all less dynamic languages and regional dialects. This yielded a unified system of social communication and a commonly held historico-literary tradition. In the case of *multinational states*, Marxism drew a distinction between federal or democratic variants (which group together separate national communities on an equal footing), and those which forcibly incorporate different oppressed nationalities in a strong unitary state governed by a dominant nationality, whether it is in a majority (the case of 'Great Russians' in Czarist Russia) or a minority (the case of whites in South Africa).

If we now combine and develop the categories outlined above, we can classify capitalist countries during the imperialist epoch as follows:

1. Imperialist countries. These may be further divided into: (a) great imperialist world powers in which a certain industrial and financial level is articulated with state and military force; (b) imperialist world powers that are second-rank by virtue of their decaying character, their smallness or relative backwardness, or the weakness of their state; (c) regional imperialist powers, which can only play a politically and economically expansionist role in a fixed area of the world. Here we would have to distinguish between regional imperialist powers with a tendency to become world powers (e.g. Japan before the 1960s), true regional imperialist powers (like South Africa) and regional capitalist powers which, though beginning to display clearly imperialist features, are to a substantial degree still financially and technologically dependent.

2. *Capitalist countries which are politically independent but economically dependent.* Here Lenin distinguished between what he called the 'Argentinian model' (a high degree of financial dependence expressed in diplomatic subordination) and the 'Portuguese model' (a weak capitalist country which could one day occupy an important international and even imperialist role with the 'protection' of an imperialist power, such as Britain was). However, any new classification, of the kind required today, would also have to take into account the level of capitalist development, the economic importance and strength of the state, and so on.

3. *Semi-colonial countries.* Lenin describes these only in very general terms and analyses only one particular case (Asian countries divided into 'spheres of influence', like China, Persia and Afghanistan) without looking at Latin American cases (Central America and the Caribbean) or Arab countries. Nowadays, for reasons we will analyse in chapter four, there are fewer truly *semi-colonial* countries.

4. *Colonial countries.* These are even rarer in today's world. It is more accurate to speak of colonial territories than of colonial peoples, since oppressed nationalities are today more a feature of multinational states.

Each of these four types may itself be either a *nation-state* or a *multinational state,* including, as we have seen, an *oppressor multinational state* governed by a dominant nationality (South

Africa, Iran, Iraq, Spain, Ethiopia, etc.).

Now that we have made these distinctions—which would have to be adjusted to capture aspects of world capitalist and imperialist development—we must turn to an examination of national struggle.

(b) *The Marxist Principle of National Self-Determination*

By national self-determination we mean the process of a nation's conversion into a politically autonomous nation-*state* endowed with all the attributes of political sovereignty, whether it is a question of colonies, semi-colonial states or oppressed national communities within a state. To the extent that the organization of national communities as states is a historical condition for the development of the productive forces in the epoch of capitalism, the principle of 'national self-determination' constitutes the fundamental political right of all nations as such, which is identified with the right to full development and self-organization as such. Marx and Engels fully asserted this right in their works on India, Poland and Ireland, and it marks a fundamental chapter in the development of the theory of imperialism. Lenin's contribution was to establish a clear *distinction between the concepts of economic dependence and political dependence,* and to identify national self-determination as a secondary part of the struggle for democracy.[4]

The basic political concept of national self-determination is inseparably linked to a broader concept: political sovereignty. *The right to national self-determination is thus only one aspect of the right of peoples to decide their own destiny* (that is, to be fully independent of any external state entity), just as another kind of demand (e.g. 'democratic government') expresses the internal aspect of the broader claim. This way of presenting the question of national self-determination is completely different from that of bourgeois nationalism, or even from that of bureaucratic socialism, since it links it more to the problematic of economic relations with other countries and to the state's economic policy.

For bourgeois nationalism the more protected a country's market is from 'penetration' by foreign goods and capital, and, in certain cases (the radical nationalism of the petty bourgeoisie), the more 'nationalist' or isolationist the economic policy and external relations of the state, the more independent that country is. The bourgeois idea of national sovereignty involves the separation of this principle from its democratic connotations, so that it is demoted to the level of the dictates of inter-capitalist competition in the national or world market.[5]

Bureaucratic socialism, inspired by the theory and practice of ruling parties in the 'Socialist Bloc', tends to subordinate the principle of self-determination to the reasons of state of the USSR, China, or whatever; to idealize the 'anti-imperialism' of friendly states regardless of their social and political complexion (for pro-Soviet tendencies, Argentina's terrorist dictatorship; for pro-Chinese tendencies, Pinochet's Chile); and vigorously to condemn all authentic movements of national self-determination which oppose their interests.

The notable influence in recent decades of bourgeois national-ism and bureaucratic socialism explains the widespread circula-tion of economist and pragmatic ideas about imperialism and the problematic of national self-determination. This has been expressed in the rise of new theories, among which the theory of dependency and the theory of neo-colonialism are the most prominent.

Dependency theory seeks to evacuate the degree of capitalist development and the economic and political variables of national subordination from theoretical analysis, reducing all these levels to the nebulous pair of 'dependent country' and 'underdeveloped country'. This groups together all countries which depend in some way on the economic and political centres of the world capitalist—imperialist system, whether they are pre-capitalist countries, semi-capitalist countries, capitalist or monopoly-capitalist countries with a tendency to export capital, or colonies, semi-colonies or politically independent countries. That is to say, the concept is sufficiently vague and anti-scientific to provide a basis for the historico-ideological concept of the 'Third World'.

The theory of 'neo-colonies', in turn, seeks to equate the financial and diplomatic dependence of politically independent countries and of semi-colonies by giving overwhelming priority to certain economic features, in particular the role of direct foreign investment by transnational companies. Direct foreign investment, associated with other forms of 'penetration', is supposed to turn the different countries into semi-colonies, although it is never clear which are to be included in the definition. (Would it apply, for example, to countries like South Africa, Canada or Spain, or only to 'Third World' countries?)[5]

According to this line of reasoning, bourgeois nation states would be progressive and anti-imperialist merely by opposing foreign investment, increasing customs duties and reducing the balance of external trade, or by linking themselves economically to the 'Socialist Bloc'. Marxism, however, regards such 'anti-imperialism' and such 'defence' of the principle of national self-determination as nothing more than an attempt to cover up competitive manoeuvres by capitals of different national bases, particularly by 'weak' monopoly capitals. (One thinks of the condemnation of Di Tella or Gelbard-type 'national' monopolies in Argentina.)

Insofar as the principle of the self-determination of peoples is related to their right to form an independent and fully sovereign state — which they must decide when and whether to exercise — there are a number of component parts: (a) the right of colonies and semi-colonies to full state independence; (b) the right to secession of national minorities oppressed within a multinational state; (c) the right to dispose freely of the national territory and to enjoy territorial 'integrity' (which implies the continuity and unity of national physical space and free use of natural resources for the development of economic and social life); (d) the right to recover basic state functions that imperialist powers have seized from weak countries, reducing them to the condition of semi-colonies; (e) the right to free development of the democratic and progressive features of each national culture, beginning with the free use of language and all those autochthonous expressions which facilitate the integration of peoples with more advanced forms of social co-existence; (f) the freedom of weak states from intervention in their internal life.

The above argument clearly shows that the right to national self-determination in all its implications is a *political claim of a democratic character which has nothing to do with economic or cultural nationalism*,[6] and which, therefore, must be part of the struggle for democracy and free organization of nations and of the exploited and oppressed masses. According to Marxist theory, the struggle for political democracy within the bourgeois state is a means by which the working class can educate and organize itself in the fight against capitalist exploitation and for the development of a proletarian-popular democracy leading to a socialist transformation of society. For this reason, Marxist analysis cannot limit itself to pointing out the progressive character of the struggle for self-determination or 'national democracy'; it also has to incorporate the precise link articulating the participation of the workers in this struggle with the development of their socialist class objectives.

We will examine this question as it relates to Argentina in the last part of chapter six. Here we should make the general observation that the struggle for 'national democracy' must never lead conscious workers and socialists to strengthen their internal class enemies; and still less to consolidate the repressive apparatus, militarism, and the paramilitary squads which murder workers and class fighters, or to bolster the conditions for a worsening of exploitation. For this reason socialists have always supported only just national demands — that is to say, quite simply, those which confront the masses with their internal and external oppressors.

2. The Evolution of the National Question in Argentina

One cannot separate analysis of the national question in Argentina from the formation and development of Argentina as a nation. Thus, we will adopt a historical perspective which embraces the main stages of capitalist development and of the Argentinian state, and of its particular insertion into the world market. We will draw a basic distinction between four great historical stages: (1) the formation of the Argentinian nation (1778-1881); (2) the development of an agricultural economy based upon integration with the world market (1881-1929); (3) industrialization, the shaping of a semi-autarkic economy and the birth of a welfare state (1930-1950); (4) attempts at capitalist modernization and reintegration with the world economy (1952 to the present).

(a) *The Formation of the Argentinian Nation*

This great historical stage stretches from the foundation of the economic base of the future nation (the regional spheres of exchange and social division of labour) to the definitive formation of the nation state. There are three sub-periods in this stage.

The first begins with the formation of the economic-geographical base on which the country will subsequently develop. It starts with the growth of a transport economy between the mines of Upper Peru (now Bolivia) and the port of

Buenos Aires in the final decades of Spanish colonial domination. During this time a market in surplus goods is set up between regions that were not previously linked (Upper Peru, the Salta–Tucumán periphery, the former Jesuit missions to the north-east, the Cuyo region split off from Chile, and the highway junctions of Córdoba and Sante Fe). It is stimulated by the English contraband trade geared to the dynamic centre of the River Plate. A strong bourgeoisie takes shape in Buenos Aires around the sizeable sector of illicit trade, and a drive begins to exploit the Pampas region. Previously a land full of *cimarrón,* or wild cattle, it now becomes linked to Europe as an exporter of hides. During this period, the emergent economic space adopts the Spanish vice-royalty form of state structure, extending its jurisdiction into what are now known as Bolivia, Paraguay and Uruguay and into mainly uninhabited regions, except northern mining centres and pockets of Indian settlement (Quechua and Aymara Indians in the north and Guarani in the north-east).

The second sub-period lasts from 1810 to 1852. The first form of independent state organization is now established under the hegemony first of the port commercial bourgeoisie, and later of the embryonic landowning class of Buenos Aires province. During this period, the vice-regal economic space is dismantled as a result of the mining crisis in Upper Peru and its subsequent secession, and the political–territorial space of the new nation is fixed. It is a period marked by the Wars of Independence, political anarchy and inter-regional civil wars, in which the economic centre of gravity increasingly shifts towards the River Plate region.

Commercial links with Britain are also strengthened in this period. English traders put down deep roots in Buenos Aires and other coastal settlements, becoming closely knit with the dominant creole class and eventually forming the nascent landowning bourgeoisie. The British also occupy the Malvinas Islands (1833) in the course of these years, and attempts by the British and French fleets to open the Littoral rivers to direct trade with Europe, bypassing Buenos Aires, are foiled.

The first cattle *haciendas* and salted-meat factories, producing for export, are set up in the Littoral region, particularly in Buenos Aires province. During most of this period, the states are organized politically under the 'Argentine Confederation', in which Buenos Aires province plays a completely dominant role because of its increased integration with the world market and its monopoly control over the port and customs houses, the nexus of all the new country's river and land routes. The 'march to the south' (the gradual occupation by the new landowning class of the extremely rich lands until then used by the Pampas nomads and *gauchos,* wandering whites and *mestizos* who hunted the wild cattle on the plains) begins now in response to the expansion of cattle-ranching in the Pampas region. Thus opens the creole epic and the conquest of the wilds, which, in economic terms, is nothing more than the specific historical modality of primitive capital accumulation on the Pampas plains (separation of lands and herds from the direct producers, development of private property, conversion of land and labour-power into commodities). This leads on the Pampas to the massacre of Indians and gauchos and the brazen seizure of land by the Buenos Aires military chiefs and traders.

The hegemony of the state of Buenos Aires over the rest of the provinces in the Confederation was expressed politically in its assumption of external representation, and economically in its monopoly control of Buenos Aires port. This would be the age of the rancher-general José Manuel Rosas, who not only fought the Pampas Indians and the 'Unitary' generals (the remnants of the old national army of the Independence wars, allied with the remnants of the old port commercial oligarchy excluded from the sharing-out of cows and land), but also temporarily assumed the interests of the nation when he defeated colonialist incursions by the British and French fleets in the 1830s and 1840s.

The laborious process of national organization begins with the defeat of Rosas's army by Urquiza's federal troops, continues with the passing of the first effective national constitution, and ends in 1881 when Buenos Aires becomes the nation's capital. During this period of time, a unified federal state structure is set up, the Buenos Aires customs houses are nationalized, the internal customs are eliminated, a single national currency is issued, a national legal code is established and a single army is organized. Simultaneously, under the progressive governments of Sarmiento and Avellaneda, a major boost is given to primary education, immigration, and the construction of new railways with public capital.

(b) Argentina Becomes 'The World's Granary'

Between 1881 and 1914 the unity and organization of the nation was consolidated, and the conversion of the Pampas into the 'world's granary' was speeded up. Argentina became the leading exporter of beef, maize, linseed, rye and oats, and the second largest exporter of wool, wheat and barley. The bases for this radical economic transformation were the growth of railway lines, the tidal wave of immigrants, bringing a new population of some three and a half million to Argentina (there were only one million native-born Argentinians in 1860), and a massive influx of foreign, especially British capital.

An exceptionally vigorous capitalist country develops on this political and economic base, with one of the world's highest per capita incomes and a highly developed financial system arising from huge, regular trade supluses. Land and immigrant labour — the primary sources of its wealth — are combined in large cattle ranches and family-run cereal farms, known as *chacras*, specializing in cereal exports and alfalfa pastures for cattle. The Argentinian capitalist class develops on the basis of land ownership: the enormous differential rent formed at an international level is capitalized in the export trade, commerce, finance, and the first large industrial investments (Bunge and Born, Torquinst, etc.). Although foreign capital has a crucial stake in this process of accumulation, it never displaces national investment as the main driving force.[7] At the same time, there is a major expansion of public capital, which becomes preponderant in banking (Banco de la Nación y de la Provincia de Buenos Aires) and oil exploitation (YPF) and plays a key role in the railway network, controlling 40 per cent of total investments right into the twentieth century. A very powerful 'middle class' of cereal farmers, *chacareros*, traders, professionals and artisans emerges beside the landowning bourgeoisie, and a sizeable and combative proletariat, mainly of immigrant origin, begins to take shape. The proletariat builds large revolutionary unions like FORA, and a very broad and combative movement develops around the principles of class solidarity and struggle against the bourgeois state.

This was also the most important period in the formation of the population base, involving the assimilation of millions of families from completely different national origins (Italians, Poles, French, Spaniards, Lebanese, Jews, Russians and Germans). The emergence of this new human and cultural medium was made possible by the inexhaustible supply of unexploited land, the very high level of wages (which even attracted huge flows of seasonal labour from Europe for the grain harvest) and the liberal legislation governing politics and civil life (the awarding of Argentinian citizenship). However, this process only affected the Pampas and Littoral regions, where two-thirds of the population lived. In the traditional north-eastern, central and eastern regions (Cuyo), the main population centres benefited from the immigrant influx to a much lesser extent. This economic and demographic explosion was extremely localized: only ten per cent of Argentinian territory, half of the country's cultivable land, was actually farmed in 1913-14. Enormous expanses of territory had not been incorporated into the economy at all, like the vast Patagonian region (half of the national territory) or the north-eastern Chaco region.[8]

Argentina's relations with imperialist powers in general and with Britain in particular, which commanded thirty per cent of the country's external trade and two-thirds of foreign investment, constitute the last fundamental feature of the period. Argentina at this time became integrated into the world market as a financially dependent agrarian capitalist society which could be considered, purely in an economic sense, to be part of Britain's informal empire. Although this financial dependence found expression in close political and diplomatic relations with the British government, Argentina's subsequent history never involved the loss of political-state independence. Argentina never granted Britain exclusive trade or tariff concessions: indeed, it maintained a permanent structure of relatively protectionist import duties.[9] The country went through short-lived anti-statist 'deviations' (like the sadly famous presidency of Juárez Celman, promptly corrected by the 'nationalist' regrouping of the dominant class behind Pellegrini and Roca after the failed 1890 revolution). Except for these brief periods, however, and in spite of its well-worn bourgeois-liberal ideology, the old Argentinian oligarchy encouraged state intervention in such important sectors as banking, railways and oil. The Argentinian state demonstrated its independence in the First World War, when Radical and Conservative governments adopted a policy of neutrality. Hence, there is no basis in fact for the opinion of certain authors that Argentina became a semi-colonial dependency of Great Britain, unless the concept is used improperly to denote commercial and financial dependence.

The expansion of agrarian capitalism and the integration into the world market slowed down with the outbreak of the First

World War, but they picked up again in the inter-war period, especially during the spell of very rapid growth from 1925 to 1929. However, the most important events of this sub-period were the introduction of free and universal suffrage, and the transformation of the political bases of the state by popular sectors grouped in the Radical Civic Union (UCR) party.

The dramatic rise of Radicalism at the level of state power reflected the political ascendancy of the emergent layers of cattlemen, traders, cereal farmers and professionals, who constituted the lower and middle layers of the Argentinian bourgeoisie. This spelled the end of the historic cycle of the 'Oligarchic state', which was the creation of the political and military elite of the landowning aristocracy. Such a sharp change in the political relations between different factions of the bourgeoisie, and in the bourgeoisie's relations with the people, was to have very important consequences. It led to a historical disjuncture between the most powerful and dynamic faction of the capitalist class and a newly emerging political hegemony whose popular base was beginning to express itself through a new type of liberal–democratic state.

Radicalism instituted a set of democratic and progressive transformations in Argentinian society, heralding the age of mass politics and consensus forms of domination. (This did not, of course, mean the end of the open repression of workers, when their struggles endangered the stability of the bourgeois state as such.) One landmark was the modification of the agrarian law favouring tenant *chacareros* and encouraging the 'farmerization' of the family producer and his integration into national life. The new state structure also favoured the transformation of the trade union movement, which, having emerged from its heroic stage, began to institutionalize itself in broader legal organizations after the bloody repression of striking workers in the *Semana Tragica* of 1919.

The main cultural development of this period was the spread of primary education, pushing literacy into all corners of the country and accelerating the socio-cultural assimilation of European immigrants and their descendants. This was also helped by the new political institutions and the growing popularity of the radio.

(c) Industrialization, 'Inward Development' and the Rise of a Welfare State

Argentina was profoundly transformed between 1933 and 1950. The year 1945 was in many ways an obvious point of rupture: the construction was begun of a new type of state with bureaucratic-paternalist features; the working class was fully integrated into political life; and the tendency towards nationalism sharpened at all levels of national life. Nevertheless, the structural processes which made possible the transformation of the 1940s date back to the preceding decade, when import-substitutionist indus-trialization began to convert the country into a semi-industrial nation, integrating the urban society of the coastal region with the ethnically mixed population of the pre-capitalist pockets in northern Argentina and the sizeable groups of Paraguayan, Bolivian and Chilean workers.

The Argentinian oligarchy reacted to the crisis of 1929 by ousting the Radical President Irigoyen from power. This ushered in an era of electoral fraud and political corruption popularly known, with good reason, as the *decada infame*. After the interim military government of 1930-32, the national economy began to shift under pressure from objective factors bound up with the Great Depression, which had closed external outlets for farm produce, and with the deliberate intervention of new 'Concordancista' governments. (This name was given to ruling coalitions between conservatives removed from power in 1916 and the so-called 'independent socialists' and 'anti-personalist radicals', who kept themselves in power by em-ploying electoral fraud.)

Between 1933 and 1942, the oligarchy's 'Concordancista' governments took the following economic measures: creation of a system of multiple exchange rates, imposition of parities favouring industry, raising of customs tariffs, creation of the Central Bank (BCRA), introduction of an expansionary fiscal policy (including a major boost to public construction), estab-lishment of an incomes tax, adoption of a policy to reduce interest rates by the BCRA, creation of the National Boards for Grains, Meats, Cotton and Yerba Mate; and of the Corporation for the Promotion of Trade; foundation of the first state industries (Altos Hornos Zapla, Fábrica Militar de Aceros), of the State Merchant Fleet and of several military armaments factories (B. Matheu, Río Tercero and Villa María); and creation of the Argentinian Corporation of Meat Producers (CAP). The intellectual architects of these measures were Federico Pinedo, one of the leaders of the fraudulent election-rigging oligarchy, and the young Raúl Prebisch, who was later to become one of the main exponents of independent industrial development in Latin America. An interesting fact is that the Argentina of the oligarchic and liberal periods was one of the first countries, if not the first, to adopt a frankly Keynesian economic policy, quite a long time before the publication of the *General Theory.*[10]

There were three main stages to industrial development. Between 1933 and 1939 industrialization proceeded very rapidly and employment in industry increased by fifty per cent, at a truly exceptional annual average of eight per cent. Between 1939 and 1945 growth slowed to half the previous rate, but was still high given world war conditions. Finally, between 1945 and 1949 there was another spurt in growth, which reached the first period's very high ceilings, and led to a hundred-per-cent increase in the industrial workforce in sixteen years and to the transformation of the country's social structure.

The new proletariat differed in two basic ways from its turn-of-the-century predecessor. Firstly, it had an Indo-American cultural base — apparent in its pejorative nickname *cabecitas negras,* or little black heads. It was therefore inexperienced in social struggle,[11] unlike the *cabecitas rubias,* or little blond heads, who had arrived from Europe half a century before, fresh from lessons in anarchism and Marxism. In other words, it was marked by two socio-cultural characteristics stemming from its pre-capitalist origins. Secondly, it was integrated into a properly industrial productive structure, which, despite its low level of centralization, reflected a fundamental change in relation to the artisan base of the early Argentinian workers movement. These two factors would have a decisive influence on the formation of a new workers movement that was larger and more centralized than the anarchist movement at the beginning of the century. It would be based on the industrial unions and adopt much more reformist and legalist procedures. Later still, this new economic, social and cultural base would considerably facilitate the rise of the Peronist movement and state unionism.

A major feature of the restructuring of Argentinian society around endogenous industrialization was the integration of new regions into the national market. Import substitution now spread to agricultural products like cotton, yerba mate, rice and apples, leading to the population and development of regions like

Misiones, El Chaco, some of Corrientes and the fertile Patagonian valleys. The rapid growth of the domestic consumer-goods
market, which expanded after 1945 under Peronism's redistributive policy, encouraged the integration into the new semi-
industrial society of previously related regions such as Tucumán,
a sugar producer, or Mendoza, a wine producer, leading to an
altogether more homogeneous Argentina, both socially and
economically. The obverse effect was a greater demographic
concentration in and around Buenos Aires and a few industrial
towns in the Pampas (Rosario), so that the Littoral eventually
came to hold eighty per cent of the population.

These processes were taking place at a time when the country's
relations with the world market and imperialist powers underwent radical change. The world crisis led to the closure of major
grain and meat markets, to the well-known flight of foreign
capital and the consequent autonomization of Argentina's
economic space. Argentinian exports, worth 2.3bn dollars a year
from 1928 to 1929, fell in 1933 to 1.1bn dollars, later recovering to
an average of 1.5bn dollars from 1938 to 1939. Only in 1944 and
1945, when the country's domestic product had grown by ninety
per cent, did they finally return to pre-crisis levels. Foreign
investment also fell from \$4bn before the crisis to \$3.2bn in 1939,
and only \$1.5bn in 1947 (see graph 1.1).[12]

The two most interesting developments were the
Roca–Runciman Treaty of 1933, believed by Argentinian
nationalists and most of the traditional Left to be the 'statute of
British colonial rule', and the nationalization of the railways.

The Roca–Runciman Treaty was an attempt by the ruling
oligarchy to defend itself in the British meat market against the
fundamental threat posed by the Ottawa imperial treaties,
through which Britain agreed to buy meat only from Commonwealth countries such as Australia, Canada and New Zealand. By
1933 exports had fallen to half the level of 1929, and closure of the
country's principal meat market would have dealt a devastating
blow to the upper bourgeoisie. In these circumstances, Argentina
signed a treaty with Britain granting it commercial and financial
concessions in return for access to the British meat market. The
treaty divided the Argentinian bourgeoisie, especially its agrarian
sector. The fatteners who pastured their cattle near Buenos Aires
— the most important fraction of cattlebreeders, intimately linked
to big financial and industrial capital — firmly supported the
treaty with the backing of the Industrial Union. The weaker

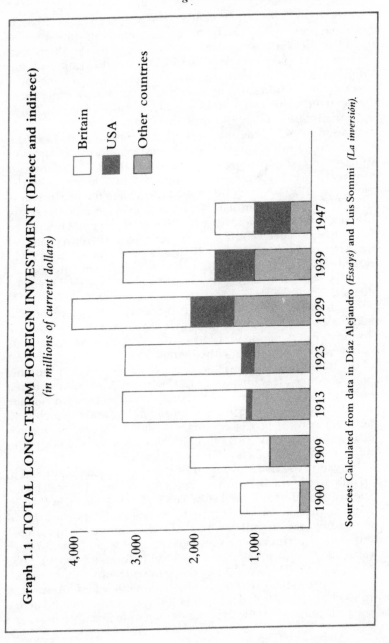

Graph 1.1. TOTAL LONG-TERM FOREIGN INVESTMENT (Direct and indirect)
(in millions of current dollars)

Britain
USA
Other countries

4,000
3,000
2,000
1,000

1900 1909 1913 1923 1929 1939 1947

Sources: Calculated from data in Díaz Alejandro *(Essays)* and Luis Sommi *(La inversión).*

fraction of southern cattlebreeders, who produced meat different from that preferred by the British, came out in opposition to the treaty, as did various agrarian sectors interested in alternative markets (groups represented politically by the UCR and the Progressive Democratic Party) and the crisis-fuelled nationalist currents. It is interesting that the main opposition came from forces which, over the next decade, would adopt an anti-industrialist, free-trade position.

Beyond these bourgeois and inter-imperialist clashes (the United States made a diplomatic protest against the treaty), the truth is that the famous treaty was based on precedents set immediately beforehand by the Irigoyen government (like the November 1929 treaty with Britain) which were the first attempts to forge a bilateral commercial policy ('buy from those who buy from us')[13] — an essential feature of Peronist external policy. The treaty had no adverse effect upon the rapid growth of national industry, which began precisely in 1933, the year the treaty was signed, with a vigorous drive to replace essentially British imports, like textiles. Nor did it lead to greater financial dependence upon Britain.

Just as the Roca–Runciman treaty was viewed by Argentinian nationalist mythology as the infamous pustule of colonial domination, so nationalization of the British railways 14 years later would be presented, rather paradoxically, by new exponents of the tradition as the declaratory act of the country's 'economic independence'. It is obvious to us that the nationalization of the railways was a progressive action, a step forward in the socialization of the country's productive forces which will facilitate control of the country's wealth once the people has assumed its own destiny. But this does not give a licence to disregard historical facts.

In reality, the nationalization of the railways corresponded to an initiative of the British companies themselves. Adopted by the apostle of conservative industrialism, Federico Pinedo, in 1940, its implementation was interrupted by the 1943 military coup. It was a measure that can only be understood in light of the profound crisis of British imperialism, devastated by the war, and its subsequent need to repatriate its saleable foreign investments.[14] Many authors have shown that the nationalization of the railways was unnecessarily onerous for the national heritage. And yet, it formed part of a broader nationalist-type perspective involving total cancellation of the external debt, nationalization of gas and telephones, and so forth.

The treatment of these two questions by the traditional left and by nationalists is only a taste of the method that a great number of Argentinian intellectuals use to explain the major political and economic events of national life. Always looking for a foreign conspiracy, British, North American or Soviet, behind every development, they set off in search of internal 'agents' and brush aside the factors which have a genuinely explanatory significance. In this surreal context, it was no accident that the Argentinian Communist Party (PCA), allied to the US embassy in 1945 and to the old oligarchy against 'Nazi-peronism', should have considered Perón in the 1950s to be an 'agent of US imperialism'.

Both Argentinian society and the state underwent considerable changes when the Peronists assumed power. One of the first new features was a near-total financial freedom for the country, together with a powerful boost to the development of state capitalism and import-substitutionist industrialization. In effect, this was only a continuation of the basic economic direction followed since the 'infamous decade'. Apart from those measures we have already mentioned (exchange control, strengthening of state enterprises, industrial protectionism, bilateral international trade), there were other notable continuities in policy from the 1930s to the 1940s. The IAPI, for example, one of the most loudly heralded Peronist institutions, had a direct antecedent in the Corporation for the Promotion of Trade. Similarities were also to be seen in policy on such territorial questions as the claim to Antarctica.

In the political sphere the major change was the formation of a new, benevolently authoritarian or paternalist state, based on an alliance of the army (half of the new government's first two budgets was devoted to it), the new labour unions and an emerging 'bureaucratic' industrial and commercial bourgeoisie ('bureaucratic' because of its structural dependence on state subvention and protection).[15] This *justicialista* state, as Perón would call it, combined three types of political mechanism in a concrete unity: (a) the recognition of universal free suffrage, inherited from Radicalism, in the context of traditional institutions of bourgeois democracy; (b) a new model of pyramidal integration of civil associations under government and presidential control (the CGE, CGT, CGP, suppression of the independence of the judiciary, the press, the universities, etc.) combining features from such different systems as Spanish Phalangism and the Mexican PNR; and (c) a direct appeal to the masses by the Chief of the Peronist movement and the state, through countless political festivals and calls to action. A very peculiar feature of this type of political organization was the association of Perón's wife, Evita, with the pinnacle of power through a kind of welfare agency (the Eva Perón Foundation) which linked Perón to the most disinherited masses.

Some of these elements, together with the military origins of the movement,[16] gave rise to the legend of 'Nazi-Peronism' — a term coined by the Argentinian Communist Party, the remains of the oligarchy and the old Liberal intellectuals. But although Peronism may be distinguished from fascist movements in many ways, it does resemble them in that it took shape only after the development of a broad mass movement. The military regime that seized power in 1945 could channel, control and institutionalize this movement, because of favourable economic conditions[17] and its own ability to develop policies that answered the demands of the masses.

As a result, it was the social base which underwent the most fundamental change. The existence of a powerful workers movement, emerging from the rapid industrialization of the previous twelve years, ultimately explains the Peronist phenomenon and the new relationship of forces at the workplace which took shape in advanced forms of democratic organization (shop stewards' committees, factory commissions, implementation of labour laws favouring workers, active strikes against employers, and so on). It also impelled the establishment of a *sui generis* Welfare Republic, which revealed itself in two different ideological discourses: the rough and primitive union message of a working-class base lacking independent leadership; and the authoritarian-bureaucratic and bourgeois-nationalist discourse of the political and union leaderships — the straightforward *justicialista* doctrine expressing the fusion of a new labour aristocracy (the union apparatus) with civilian-military state officials and the new bureaucratic bourgeoisie.

The second discourse formed the official ideology of the whole movement[18] and educated the workers politically in a tradition which combined progressive features, like unionism and the broad political unity of the workers and the people, with patently reactionary and demobilizing elements, such as confidence in the bourgeois state and the army, or belief in a substantive identity of interests between the different national classes, or the idea that political activity was the exclusive province of leaders ('from home to work, from work to home'). In the context of these new social and political class relations, very important changes took place in labour relations. The real wage (including the indirect wage) of various categories of workers rose by some eighty per cent between 1943 and 1949 — which translated into qualitative improvements in diet (greater consumption of beef, competing with export needs) and the emergence of new social needs such as housing, health, education and leisure activities. These developments may be summed up in Table 1.1, which demonstrates the extensive redistribution of income in Argentina during the period in question.

This process had very important social consequences for the country's future:

(a) It united the industrial proletariat with the working masses as a whole, in a dense network of economic and institutional solidarity (collective labour agreements, social security systems, etc.) and in a powerful social bloc of labour organized around the unions and the union confederation.

(b) It qualitatively raised the value of labour-power to a level that would later prove incompatible with the needs of the long-term valorization and accumulation of capital. To give some idea of the valorization of labour-power, in its international dimension, it is enough to recall that between 1950 and 1955 the average wage of an Argentinian unskilled industrial worker reached 45 US cents per hour (skilled workers earned about fifteen per cent more). This was three times less than the US equivalent, but higher than the average European wage of 35 cents.[19]

Table 1.1
WAGES AND SURPLUS-VALUE
TRANSFERS (as a proportion of GDP)

	A	B	C	D	E	F
	net wages	employers' contribs. to soc. sec. funds	workers' contribs. to soc. sec. funds	remittances of surplus-value abroad	real wages (1943= 100)	GNP per capita (1943= 100)
1935–36	38.3	0.8	8.0	5.2	—	—
1943–44	36.8	0.8	0.8	3.0	105	104
1945–46	37.0	1.6	1.4	2.2	109	106
1947–49	40.6	2.6	2.2	0.4	163	125
1953–55	43.7	4.1	3.0	0.1	161	112

Source: CEPAL and BCRA quoted in Díaz Alejandro, *Essays*, tables 2–20 and 65.

(c) It gave rise to a new conjunctural solidarity between the great mass of workers and consumers and the new bureaucratic bourgeoisie and the state, given that their interests seemed to be converging in the consumer goods market. This tended to express itself ideologically as a widespread 'national-popular solidarity' against imperialism and the landowning oligarchy, which lost the most as a result of this new pattern of income distribution. (In column D of Table 1.1 one can see the coincidence between rising real wages and the declining remittance abroad of profits, interest charges and other payments. Unfortunately, we have been unable to calculate the fall in agrarian income.)

These factors were an essential part of a pattern of capital reproduction which became increasingly incompatible with the logic of capitalist economic development and the special features of the Argentinian economy. Argentina's top economists, like Prebisch and Ferrer, have recognized that the economy under the Peronists was based on exaggerated growth of employment in relation to fixed capital and available labour reserves, and on a disproportionate subsidization of inefficient industry at the cost of the collapse of export agriculture,[20] which provided the foreign exchange indispensable for the technological updating of industrial plant and basic infrastructure. This group of tendencies could only lead to the stagnation and decline of labour productivity, and the collapse of capitalist profitability and the accumulation process itself. This happened when extensive capital accumulation began to exhaust itself as a spur to economic development — a process already apparent in the mid-1950s. The alternative now was an 'intensive' pattern of accumulation[21] centred on the development of heavy industry producing intermediate goods, plant and transport, the modernization of the energy, technology and communications infrastructure, and a continual rise in labour productivity. This was a pressing need, in order to meet both the internal demands of the Argentinian economy and the new exigencies of the world economy.

Here lies the explanation for the profound crisis which Peronism precipitated at the heart of the Argentinian political and economic system. Not only did it exacerbate contradictions inherited from preceding decades; it also generated a new conflict, deeper than all the others and insoluble in capitalist terms, between the living conditions that the working class considered to be beyond all question, and the imperative need for the capitalists to reduce popular consumption, to raise the level of

Table 1.2
CUMULATIVE ANNUAL GROWTH RATE OF
CAPITAL STOCK AND LABOUR EMPLOYED IN
ARGENTINIAN INDUSTRY (1935-1961)

	1935-45	*1946-55*	*1956-61*
Growth of capital stock	3.7%	1.8%	9.8%
Growth in Employment	3.4%	2.9%	0.4%

Source: Monica Peralta Ramos, *Acumulación de capital y crisis
política en la Argentina,* Ch. 1, Table I.

exports, and to augment the intensity and productivity of labour,
as the only way of sustaining the growth of Argentinian
capitalism. This crisis began to appear towards the end of Peronist
rule, when economic growth ground to a halt, exports collapsed
and real wages began to plummet dramatically. Then, despite the
voluble propaganda of the Peronist government, it became
obvious that Argentina had fallen way behind Brazil in economic
terms and was being overtaken by Mexico, and that Argentina was
turning into an increasingly provincial and backward country, as
the contemporary world made technological and cultural progress.

*(d) Monopoly-Capitalist Argentina: the Social Crisis and Reintegration
into the World Market*

The 1955 military coup[22] began a new historical epoch marked by
the fruitless search of the dominant class for a new national
balance between the needs of economic growth and technical
progress and the country's social and political stability. Since
then, eight different political projects (both military and civilian)
have succeeded one another, all of them failing to halt the
country's social, cultural, political and economic decline, and
only managing to exacerbate the class struggle and to unleash
increasingly murderous and irrational counter-revolutionary
forces.

In another part of the book we argue that the growing
deterioration of the bases underpinning Argentinian society
stems from the inherent limits of capitalism as a regime of social
organization, limits which hinder a society from surmounting a
crisis as deep as Argentina's without the murder and expulsion of
millions of people. It must therefore follow that a socialist
perspective is the only popular and democratic solution to the

country's ills, and not merely a theoretically convenient postulate. This conclusion is opposed to another argument, still dominant in Marxist intellectual circles, leftist organizations and the workers movement, which maintains that the Argentinian crisis is the result of imperialist penetration and the lack of economic and state independence. We shall seek to prove that this is an untenable position, and that the only alternative to a socialist solution is the deepening of monopoly-capitalist development by authoritarian and genocidal methods.

The main trends of Argentinian capitalist development over the past twenty-seven years may be summarized as follows:

(1) From 1960 to 1975 the economy recovered at a relatively rapid rate of growth, averaging four per cent per year. This new phase of expansion was marked by a radical shift away from the 'consumerist' direction of the economy under Perón, towards a pattern of reproduction in which priority was given to massive investment in infrastructure and in heavy industry producing plant and transport. The steel, electrical, petrochemical and automobile industries became particularly important as a result. But this was only made possible by the increase in the rate of accumulation, which in turn was the result of *important changes in the structure of capital and class relations.*

During this period the flow of direct foreign investment picked up again, peaking in the period 1959-1962 but later falling considerably to a more or less stable plateau. The rise in the rate of exploitation, the increased centralization of capital and the development of state capitalism and public enterprise (which took over the central role in the development of basic heavy industries) made possible major investment drives.

The state's attempt to increase accumulation can be seen not only in the drastic change in the investment profile (public investment gradually matching and then surpassing private investment) but also in the growth of the public internal and external debt, and in heavier fiscal burdens of all kinds. As to the structure of private capital, the rise in the levels of concentration and centralization was reflected in the emergence of new monopoly industries and financial groups, though less obviously than in Brazil and Mexico.

(2) The efforts made by different governments to further the integration of the economy into the world market bore relatively little fruit. Foreign investment followed an uneven course: it increased rapidly under Frondizi (1959–1962) with heavy invest-

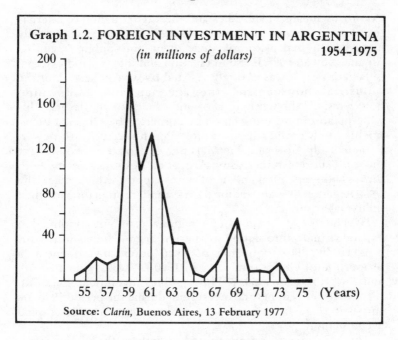

Graph 1.2. FOREIGN INVESTMENT IN ARGENTINA
(in millions of dollars) **1954–1975**

Source: *Clarín*, Buenos Aires, 13 February 1977

ments in the automobile industry and the oil sector; and then fell
off into a contradictory pattern, combining new periodic
investments with disinvestment in entire branches of the
economy (meat-packing, the electrical industry, and so on). After
1969, it tended first to stagnate and then to decline, while
advancing in almost every other Latin American country.

This same tendency can be followed in the expenditure of
transnational corporations (TNCs) on new plant and equipment.
Between 1976 and 1979 US transnationals spent an average of
US$790m in Brazil, $349m in Mexico, $282m in Venezuela, and
only $92m in Argentina.[23]

The attempt to integrate the economy into the world market by
substantially increasing exports also proved fruitless. Successive
efforts to boost production and agrarian exports were finally
abandoned just before the 1976 coup, in response to socio-
political pressure exerted by the bureaucratic bourgeoisie and the
union movement. During the Onganía dictatorship, the Krieger
Vasena Plan attached great importance to stimulating industrial

exports by means of subsidies and the strengthening of international competitiveness. But to the extent that the plan crucially involved an expansion of investment and public spending (financed by an overall rise in taxation and internal and external indebtedness), it was strongly resisted by weaker sectors of the industrial bourgeoisie, the agrarian and landowning bourgeoisie,[24] the working class and other popular layers. This widespread opposition eventually cornered the Onganía dictatorship and paved the way for Perón's return to power. Paradoxically, however, the Martínez de Hoz team would have the most success in increasing Argentina's export capacity, both through the encouragement of agro-exports, which made the USSR Argentina's main trading partner, and through the growth of industrial exports.[25]

(3) The role of the state in the national economy continued to expand virtually throughout this period. A good indication of this is given by the progression of fixed public investment as a proportion of GDP: from 5.3% in 1960-65, to 7.3% in 1973-75, and 7.4% in 1976-1980.[26] Thus, public investment made up fifty-three per cent of total investment during the period 1976-78, surpassing the contribution of private investment to capital accumulation.

This tendency to uninterrupted growth of the public sector continued despite the privatizations of 1966-69 and 1976-1981 (the 'liberal' economic plans of Krieger Vasena and Martínez de Hoz). Indeed, it is interesting to observe that such tendencies have always been accompanied by stronger counter-tendencies strengthening the state economy. The best scholar of Argentina's public economy has given an illuminating account of Martínez de Hoz's privatization drive: 'The state sold productive assets worth $80-100m and bought others for no less than $250m. Measured in terms of assets, the state productive apparatus is today greater than in April 1976, simply because of these transfers. The balance would be overwhelmingly in favour of the public sector if we included the huge investments made in the period 1976-79, which coincided with the contraction of private investment.'[27]

(4) The last major change in the structure of Argentinian capitalism was the growing tendency of capital to move abroad in search of higher profit margins and greater social and political stability. According to direct estimates based on the balances of Brazilian companies, the amount of Argentinian capital invested in Brazil easily surpassed $400m in 1974 (a figure which must have

Table 1.3
EVOLUTION OF DIRECT FOREIGN INVESTMENT
ACCUMULATED IN LATIN AMERICA *(in billions of dollars
at 1968 value)*

	1967	1973	1978
Argentina	3.8	3.8	3.4
Brazil	7.7	11.5	13.5
Mexico	3.8	4.8	6.0
Colombia	1.5	1.5	1.5
Chile	2.1	1.1	1.4
Peru	1.7	1.5	2.1
Venezuela	7.3	5.5	3.6
Panama	1.7	2.9	3.1
MCC (a)	1.3	1.4	1.1
Others (b)	1.0	1.5	1.7
Total	31.9	35.5	37.4

(a) Central American Common Market, comprising El Salvador,
    Guatemala, Honduras and Nicaragua.

(b) Bolivia, Ecuador, Paraguay, Uruguay, Haiti and Dominican Republic.

Source: E. Basualto, *'Tendencias a la transnacionalización de América
         Latina durante el decenio de los setenta', Comercio Exterior,* Mexico
         City, July 1982. (Constructed with figures from CEPAL, OCDI
         and the US Trade Department.)

at least doubled since then). At about the same time, Argentinian
finance capital controlled two of Paraguay's most important
corporations and had equally large investments in Bolivia,
Uruguay and Peru. Argentinian banks were also very active
abroad, especially in Panama, where their total assets roughly
equalled those of the North American banks, and where the
leading investor was the Argentinian Banco de la Nación, with
assets worth $7.5bn. More recently, Argentinian banks have
participated in syndicated loans on the eurodollar market,
lending to such countries as Peru, Brazil, Chile and Nigeria.[28]

These trends correspond to a series of contradictory phenomena expressed in an extension and deepening of capitalist
development on a state monopoly base. But not only did this fail
to resolve the major problems of Argentinian capitalism (e.g.
reintegration into the world market); it actually caused the
country's social and political problems to worsen.

Very important changes in the structure of the proletariat and
the mass of the working population matched the new pattern of

capital accumulation. The development of a new heavy industry, technologically far in advance of the traditional light industries of the preceding phase of industrialization, generated a new proletariat in the centres of the automobile, petrochemical and steel industries (Córdoba, the Paraná industrial region, the northern part of Greater Buenos Aires). Here, giant modern factories gave rise to Fordist labour processes and a new kind of workforce in which deskilled mass workers existed alongside new intellectual workers employed in design, maintenance and assembly. At the same time, there was a massive advance in the proletarianization of the traditional petty bourgeoisie (artisans, semi-artisans, liberal professionals, small peasants) and of the mass of white-collar workers, students and intellectuals.

These social tendencies made labour more intense and complex, while capital felt a growing need for state despotism and forced accumulation, on the basis of a rigid incomes policy. This phenomenon tended to strengthen the historic social contradictions of Argentinian capitalism, since it prevented capitalists from recognizing the new objective social expectations of the workers. This added factor of extreme tension, arising at a time when intra-bourgeois contradictions were also worsening, began to destroy the consensual bases of the Argentinian nation-state.

At the level of class contradictions, the labour movement adopted ever more hostile positions towards the policies of successive governments, including the last Perón government and that of his second wife, Isabel. From 1957-59 until the eve of the 1976 coup, the workers movement developed and enriched its methods of struggle, beginning with the recovery of the controlled unions. The process unfolded from the huge strikes of 1957-59, through the factory occupations of 1962-65, to the explosive, semi-insurrectional experiences like the *cordobazos* and *rosariazos* of 1969-1971. Class unionism followed in their wake in Córdoba and San Lorenzo, developing into a combination of general strike with acts of sabotage and the organization of the population to resist repression (Villa Constitución). Joined by revolutionary organizations, this great movement culminated in the Intersindicales of 1975-76 and the famous *Rodrigazo*.

This striking development of the revolutionary class potential of the Argentinian proletariat did not, however, take shape in a new general consciousness or a socialist political organization which could foster working-class or people's power and replace the old Peronist political and trade-union leadership.

It is true that there were breaks from the previous nationalist-reformist tradition, and sizeable sections of working-class youth moved towards revolutionary Marxism. But there was not a sufficient level of organic maturity[29] to cope with the adverse factors introduced in 1972-73 by the Great National Accord, the call for elections, the return of Perón, and the regrouping of the Peronist movement around its former leader. The immaturity of 'classism' and of the new revolutionary-socialist Left was evident in their inability to offer new political perspectives for the electorate and the mass movement, of a kind that would enable them to preserve and increase their forces and to develop their own political alternative. This failure accentuated their political fragmentation and heightened the vanguardist elements of some of the political currents that played a leading role in the movement. Later, from 1974 onwards, other factors would come into play and eventually disperse and destroy the movement. The first of these was the rapid growth of the Left's military apparatuses (the ERP, Montoneros, etc.); the second was the implacable deployment of state terrorism.

At another, partly overlapping level, the intellectual and student youth grew increasingly divorced from the older generation, and from the state institutions and traditions in general. While this phenomenon reflected the crisis gripping the country and its institutions, the historico-economic contradictions of Argentinian capitalism had also provoked this broad and highly active social sector to fight openly against the regime. From 1958-59 an increasingly radical student movement began to develop in Argentina, providing the social base for a new revolutionary Left directly influenced by the examples of the Cuban and Vietnamese revolutions.

As the chronic unemployment of social-science graduates worsened, and as the social and political crisis deepened, various politico-military organizations took shape and adopted tactics of struggle whose nature and political dynamic did not accord with those of the working-class and popular movement. Their basic mistake was to follow the Peronist characterization of the country and to identify the main enemy as US imperialism and its agents in the country. This led them to view Argentina's armed forces as 'forces of occupation', and to propose a frontal war that would involve commando assaults on police and military units and indiscriminate attacks on anyone wearing uniform. In the case of the *Montoneros,* there was even a policy of executing political and union leaders who, like General Aramburu and Augusto Vandor, were still respected by broad sectors of the people. Their calls for a 'second independence' or 'national liberation' not only expressed their misunderstanding of social conditions in the country, but served to confuse still more a working class which had not managed to match its objectively anti-employer and anti-government action with an adequate political consciousness.

These political and social tendencies were visible in the contradictions that emerged in the state. Onganía's dictatorship was effectively paralysed between 1968 and 1969, and its projects to set up a corporatist state came to nought. Thus, the only politically viable institutional dénouement was the return of Peronism to power. But although this happened at a time when international conditions were extremely favourable for Argentina, both politically and economically,[30] the three successive Peronist governments (democratic under Cámpora, Caesarist under Perón, proto-fascist under Isabel Perón) accelerated and deepened the economic, social and political contradictions of Argentinian society at a truly incredible speed. In less than three years the country was brought to an unprecedented economic crisis (yearly inflation rate of 600 per cent, collapse of output and wages, uncontrollable speculation encouraging contraband, black markets and unrestrained foreign exchange speculation); the mobilization of the working class reached its highest-ever level in the *Rodrigazo* explosion;[31] and Argentina underwent the most extreme state of political anarchy it has experienced this century, as a prelude to the stepping-up of the guerrilla war by the politico-military organizations.

For their part, the repressive forces of the state embarked upon a desperate effort to restore the social and political order of capitalism and its scale of values, essentially through the militarization of the state and society. This project was already apparent before Péron's death (with the creation of the 'Triple A' organization and the para-military terrorist apparatus linking the goon squads of the Peronist Right with the police and military commando units). It then became the main factor structuring power with the rise of López Rega and the subsequent 1976 military coup.

The tendency towards the militarization and fascization of the state openly appeared and developed during the chaos of 1973-76. In reality, however, it was the condensed expression of a much longer process of polarization, in which all the counter-revolutionary potentialities of the state's repressive apparatus, and the most reactionary sectors of the Argentinian bourgeoisie, acquired coherence within the country and were deployed externally to modify the very political bases of the state. The application of the CONINTES plan of the 1960s, the closer relations with the Inter-American Defence Board and the Pentagon, Onganía's military coup and his drive to restructure the institutional bases of the nation along fascist and corporatist lines — all these were but the antecedents of the López Rega death squads and the final systematic formation of state terrorism. Although a similar trend was visible elsewhere in Latin America, its main features, and its peculiar force, corresponded to the deep crisis of Argentinian capitalism, the power of the mass movement and the revolutionary struggle, the impotence of the political parties of the bourgeoisie, and the political errors of the revolutionary Left.

(e) The Military Coup and 'National Reorganization'

The return of the armed forces to power in 1976 should be seen as the logical outcome of a conjuncture which combined deepening economic crisis, ever sharper and broader social upheavals, and the unabating armed struggle of politico-military groups which, though badly dismembered by the fighting at Monte Chingolo, Tucumán and Chaco, were still a major source of political destabilization.

These factors led the bourgeoisie and most of the middle layers (including broad sectors of the union leadership) to support the coup as the only way to restore peace, social order and individual safety. This rightward regroupment enabled the military dictatorship to isolate the working class socially and the revolutionary forces politically, destroying the latter in a systematic campaign of extermination which did not leave the democratic movement untouched. This vast campaign of terror, known by the military as the 'dirty war', assailed vanguard worker activists and revolutionary and democratic intellectuals. The favourite targets were journalists, sociologists, psychoanalysts and lawyers who defended political prisoners. Its achievements are now widely known: more than 30,000 dead or missing, hundreds of thousands forced into exile, an impotent nation full of fear and loathing.[32]

The dictatorship's economic project (the Martínez de Hoz Plan) took the form of yet another offensive by big monopoly capital against working-class consumption, inefficient business and obstacles to full integration with the world market, while also doing battle with nearly four-digit inflation. But this time it went further, attacking on new fronts and with greater resolution.

The first of these fronts was the agro-export sector, where measures were introduced to restore profit levels. The new regime began by devaluing the peso, but it did not (as Krieger Vasena had done) appropriate exchange-dealing profits through fiscal deductions. Many commentators described this as a return to a 'pastoral Argentina', but its abandonment by the Martínez de Hoz team in 1978 showed that this was an incorrect assessment.

The second front was in the area of customs tariffs, where a drastic policy of liberalization removed the protective barriers from a domestic industry that had been seeking higher tariffs for its survival.[33] The subsequent over-valuation of the peso in 1978— a quite deliberate policy—cut the level of protection by a further twenty per cent and resulted in the devastation of the industrial structure.

The third front was the financial reform, where an attempt was made to foster a modern and efficient capital market that would accelerate the concentration and centralization of capital. This reform, imposed in June 1977, freed interest rates and stimulated the centralization of the banking system. There was an explosive rise of real interest rates to over ten per cent in some quarterly periods.

These new initiatives were part of the very ambitious public investment policy to develop the economic infrastructure (energy, transport, communications) and to build up a new armaments and iron-and-steel industry. The scarcity of foreign investment induced a series of powerful contradictions which, despite initial success, led to the eventual collapse of the plan.

The traditional nationalist-Marxist Left wrongly placed its emphasis on the 'anti-national', pro-imperialist nature of the Junta. Pointing to the numerous measures favourable to foreign capital (oil concessions, reduction of customs tariffs, etc.), it failed to grasp that the main trend in this period was *the consolidation of a national state-monopoly capitalism, based on a new military-industrial complex[34] and an attempt to modernize and rationalize the whole of the capitalist structure to make it more competitive on the international market.* (This explains the encouragement of agricultural exports, as the only conjunctural measure that could dramatically raise the ability to purchase strong currencies. It also explains the financial reform—which was a necessity imposed by the development of monopoly capital — and the reduction of customs duties to cut labour costs.)[35]

Blind to these realities, most of the Left could not see that the Junta was pressing its own form of bourgeois policy in the highly contentious areas of atomic energy, diplomatic and commercial relations with the USSR, and even participation in the Non-Aligned Movement. What was involved here was a totally pragmatic mixture of policies adjusting to the politico-military alliance with the United States and the development of a military and expansionist counter-revolutionary policy in the Southern Cone, Central America and the South Atlantic. We shall return to these points in chapters three and six.

One of the most crucial features of this policy was the Junta's attempt in 1978 to turn the conflict with Chile over an eastern access to the Beagle Channel and nearby islands into a fratricidal adventure. (For policy reasons of its own, the United States was opposed to such a war.) But although the Junta tried for the rest of the year to mobilize support for a war, the Argentinian Catholic Church strongly opposed it in a series of peace rallies. The difficulties of orchestrating this bellicose adventure, together with the brief political success of the country's World Cup soccer victory, encouraged the Junta to postpone the idea of a 'Patriotic War' for the purposes of internal consolidation and external expansion.

The main conclusion to be drawn from the experience of the military dictatorship of Videla, Viola, Galtieri and Bignone is that its oppressive and counter-revolutionary character derived not from subordination to US imperialism or any other foreign power, but from its unshakeable loyalty to the interests of national monopoly capital (associated with foreign capital) and to the military institution. This is the fundamental reason explaining state terrorism and its tragic consequences for the Argentinian nation.

3. Synthetic Characterization of Argentina

We can draw a series of conclusions from the preceding exposition. They will allow us to give an adequate characterization of Argentinian capitalism and the national question.

(a) The Internal Nature of Argentinian Capitalism

As we have seen, Argentina has been a capitalist country since the end of the last century. Its development has involved three main stages: agrarian capitalism (until 1933), non-monopoly industrial capitalism (until 1960), and the gradual formation of an integrated monopoly capitalism (since 1960). The development of monopoly capitalism as a general phenomenon was *preceded* by state capitalism, which began to play a key role in the 1930s. From the 1960s onwards both features tended to fuse, thus allowing us to define the present socio-economic formation as one of conversion into State Monopoly Capitalism.

Unlike most Latin American countries, Argentina no longer has any major pre-capitalist relics. Its agriculture is clearly capitalist, combining a farmer-type economy in the production of food grains and industrial crops with modern 'meat factories' on the vast Pampas haciendas (although in cattle ranching we must distinguish between an advanced export sector and a more backward sector geared to the internal market). As to processing, the ascendancy of modern heavy industry is almost complete, and the handicrafts have been dying out since 1960, when their production levels began to fall in absolute terms.

Despite the growth of its markets and output, Argentinian capitalism continues to show signs of a relatively backward economic structure in three main areas. First, its relative technological backwardness is the result of a highly protected industrial structure, and of extensive agrarian production based essentially on the fertility of the soil and, except in export cattle-farming, a low level of capital investment. Secondly, the relatively weak centralization of capital (above all in trade, and to a lesser extent in industry, where small and medium-sized family capital is still strongly present) combined with the characteristics of agricultural production to make Argentina a significantly 'petty-bourgeois' country. Thirdly, the delayed formation of a modern financial system can be seen particularly clearly in the weakness of the banking system and an inadequate articulation with industry. Taken as a whole, these features relegate Argentinian capitalism to a place behind Mexico and Brazil. However, an exact assessment of this lag will have to await a serious study of the objective consequences of the Martínez de Hoz plan.

In terms of the structure of civil society, all this implies that the bourgeoisie as a whole is the dominant class and that its most powerful fraction is now the modern monopolist-finance bourgeoisie (which articulates big agrarian, industrial and commercial capital) fused with state capital and the civil-military bureaucracy. Contrary to the analysis of the traditional nationalist and reformist Left, the 'landowning oligarchy' no longer exists as a clear-cut class fraction, for the big cattlemen, cereal farmers, sugar producers or vine-growers are now associated with big industrial and commercial interests. The only truly 'agrarian' sector, distinct from other forms of capital, is that of small and medium producers. Similarly, the 'national bourgeois' class fraction (that is, the 'bureaucratic' sector producing consumer goods and the small to middle-sized industrial bourgeoisie) totally disintegrated under the onslaught of monopoly capitalism and state capitalism (bankruptcies, subordinate integration with modern finance capital, sub-contracts from industrial state monopolies, and so on).

(b) The Place of Argentinian Capitalism in World Economy and Politics

It is universally accepted that the Argentinian economy is dependent on the capitalist world market in the three forms of existence of capital: commercial, financial and technological. But this obvious point must be understood in terms of an *active* dependence — which implies relations of interdependence, association and contradiction, and not just passive elements locating an object of 'penetration' by, and 'subordination' to, international finance capital.

Argentina is a net importer of capital and of the goods (including technology) that it needs for expanded reproduction and intensive industrialization. But from the 1960s onwards, as it increased its technological and financial independence, Argentinian capitalism began to develop an export industry and to strengthen its role as a regional exporter of capital. Since 1966, it has also managed to resume its role as a major grain exporter, while its powerful state-military machine has extended its sphere of operations into the Southern Cone, Central America and the South Atlantic. These active phenomena should be seen as expressing the 'external' interests of Argentinian capitalism — that is to say, a stage of externally oriented expansion in which commercial, financial and military factors are substantively unified.

It is thus possible to characterize Argentina as an emerging regional capitalist power, combining financial, commercial and technological dependence with the development of a capitalist–monopolist economy with regional imperialist features. In this sense, the 'dependence' of Argentinian capitalism on international finance capital is located on a completely different plane from that of pre-industrial and pre-monopolist capitalist countries, having more in common with the position of other Latin American countries like Brazil, Mexico and Venezuela, and well-known historic cases like Czarist Russia.

This has a number of political implications, particularly for the appreciation of Argentinian nationalism. Given that 'national' interests are inseparable from those of the dominant class (for the same reason that they are an inseparable part of the bourgeois nation), Argentinian nationalism is basically different from that of the 1930s and of the 1943–45 period, when the tasks of the Argentinian state and bourgeoisie did not oppose the national interests of other countries and peoples, as they do today on so many issues.

(c) The Character of the Argentinian State

It clearly emerges from this historical exposition that the Argentinian bourgeoisie has been able to rely upon a politically independent state, already endowed with a national form through the process of unification and political integration that lasted from 1852 to 1881. Broad integration into the world capitalist market and massive inflows of foreign capital did not prevent the oligarchy from controlling the state and implementing 'national' policies (in the sense of favouring the valorization and reproduction of capital in the national economic space). In this way, the Argentinian oligarchy maintained diversified trade (seventy per cent of it with countries other than Britain), imposed relatively protectionist customs tariffs, nationalized vital branches of production like petroleum, kept tight control of the greater part of the banking system, and remained neutral in the First World War. When the world crisis obstructed the continuity of the 'primary exporter' pattern of accumulation, it rapidly and decisively switched to a pattern of reproduction based upon substantive industrialization and the development of state capitalism.

From the mid-1940s the country stood up to the diplomatic

and economic offensive of US imperialism. As the big corporations moved into its industrial sector, the country signed a series of international treaties consolidating the new, US-led inter-American order (the Rio Treaty, the setting up of the IATRA, creation of the OAS, formation of the Inter-American Defence Board, etc.). Adherence to these treaties did not, however, imply that Argentina had reverted to the status of a semi-colony, as part of the Argentinian Left (especially the current of Trotskyism led by Nahuel Moreno) persistently maintained. Perón's government decided to join the Inter-American system in 1947-48, yet it went on to support the 1952 Bolivian Revolution, backed Arbenz against the US invasion of Guatemala in 1954, and tried to set up an independent trade-union confederation, the CIOLS. Similarly, despite Buenos Aires's support for the blockade of Cuba, never once did an Argentinian government accept the installation of military bases on its territory. The Radical Illia government — with the Peronists, the most 'anti-imperialist' of this century — was in reality the most favourable towards North American imperialism, as it proved by supporting the Dominican Republic intervention in 1964. The most slavish government towards the transnational corporations, the most susceptible to participation in the military alliance system of US imperialism, the only one on the point of granting a military base, was the 1976 Military Junta. Yet it was this same government which made the USSR the country's principal trading partner and assumed the task of 'recovering' the Malvinas Islands, thereby entering into conflict with the United States and its main world ally.

The Argentinian nationalist and Marxist Left could see only the repeated surrender of the national heritage, the association of interests with the imperialist bourgeoisie, the diplomatic servility towards the United States and the US Marines. These it confused with political dependence (a colonial or semi-colonial status, a puppet government or armed forces), whereas the reality is much simpler. The fact that all governments in relatively weak capitalist countries (however independent their state structure) are necessarily 'conciliatory', 'capitulatory' and 'servile' is but a stratagem for obtaining other kinds of concessions from imperialist governments or corporations — whether in order to satisfy the bourgeoisie's economic needs, to consolidate alliances or subordinate associations with imperialist powers, or merely to pocket juicy commissions by acting as middlemen in all kinds of 'dirty business'. Such activity is of the very essence of all bourgeois governments, however nationalist they are thought to be. Considered in isolation, it does not affect the state structure or its relationship to the valorization and reproduction of capital on a national scale. For the state remains a direct expression of the interests of dominant national classes, and not of the imperialist states and bourgeoisies of other countries.

(d) British Imperialism and Present-Day Argentina

It is a long time since British capital and British markets were the dynamic force behind the Argentinian economy. Since the Second World War Britain has steadily lost its importance for the national economy, and at present it controls no more than eight per cent of total direct private investment and 3.5 per cent of Argentina's export trade — ten times less than during its heyday. It is true that British banks are centrally involved in administering the external public debt: they directly absorb some fifteen per cent of Argentina's debt obligations and participate in most of the syndicated loans. Royal Dutch Shell also had a stake in the oil programme of the military dictatorship, playing a major role in the exploration of the Magellan maritime basin. Even in these two areas, however, British capital was allowed to play such a role as a result of the Junta's irresponsible lack of foresight in preparing for the occupation of the Malvinas.

Since Britain's declining role is also expressed at the level of arms deals (where the United States, France and West Germany are all larger suppliers) and of diplomatic relations between the two governments, it is clear that the significance of the old imperial power for Argentina centres on its presence in the South Atlantic and the resulting conflict over sovereignty. Nevertheless, broad sectors of the Argentinian Left continue to see British imperialism as an oppressor of the nation, the biggest robber, along with the United States, of national resources and of the popular masses.

(e) Concluding Remarks on the Argentinian National Question

Our historical exposition, together with the analysis in the preceding section, point to a clear conclusion: Argentina is a politically independent and nationally integrated capitalist country, inserted into the capitalist world market as a semi-industrial dependent economy in the process of becoming monopolized, statified and militarized, which is itself generating secondary imperialist tendencies. Furthermore, the development and deepening of Argentinian capitalism has coincided with a profound social and political crisis that is tending to destroy the very bases of civil society and national life. This is expressed in the social and cultural disintegration which the Argentinian monopolist bourgeoisie has tried to arrest by militarizing society and establishing a regime of state terror.

The crisis tearing Argentinian society apart is the result not of dependence upon the imperialist powers, but of inner class contradictions and of the incapacity of the capitalist system to solve such a crisis without resorting to terrorist methods. It is impossible to understand the role of imperialism in the Argentinian economy except through a correct analysis of the underlying process, in which imperialism appears as a contributing but not determinant factor.

2

The Significance of the Malvinas for the Argentinian Nation.

1. Historical and Geographical Aspects

The Malvinas, South Georgia and South Sandwich Islands are the archipelagos at the south-eastern tip of the American continent and of the Andes mountain range. They form an arc beginning some 500 kilometres from the Argentinian shoreline (Malvinas) and ending about 2,000 kilometres away (Sandwich), in the inhospitable region bordering the Antarctic. Since the archipelagos do not constitute a unified geographical mass, and since they have neither the same history nor the same economic importance, we will examine each one in turn.

The Malvinas Islands are by far the most important in the region, both in size (12,173 km²) and in economic significance (extensive sheep breeding, major reserves of fish, especially krill, and a probably rich oil-bearing shelf). Nor should we overlook their location: they are close to one of the most important sea lanes in the world, linking the Atlantic Ocean to the Pacific. Geographically, they are part of the American continent, since they lie on the continental shelf which stretches out from Argentina at less than 200 metres below the surface of the ocean. The archipelago comprises two main islands and several smaller ones, with rocky, hard soil and an extremely cold climate, lashed by hurricane-force winds and surrounded by deep seas to the east and swift, turbulent currents to the west.

According to historical records, they seem to have been uninhabited until the second half of the eighteenth century, when English, French and Spanish seamen began to contend for them as a base for fishing operations and interoceanic travel, sporadically establishing fixed settlements there. The Viceroyalty of the River Plate tried to enforce respect for the rights of the Spanish

Crown, citing Pope Alexander VI's papal bull of 1493 and the Treaty of Tordecillas; and from time to time it managed to secure effective occupation of the islands. Once independence was won, the new Argentinian government laid claim to Spain's former rights and, in spite of its own weakness, proceeded to set up a political and military command there. In 1829, it appointed the Hamburg fisherman and trader, Luis Vernet, as governor of the islands. After further military incidents also involving North American fishermen, Britain seized the islands by military force in 1833, in an action which could well be described as colonial piracy. The Argentinian government condemned this British usurpation, and since then successive governments in Buenos Aires have tried to claim their rights at various international fora. In 1964 Argentina obtained from the United Nations a partial resolution in its favour, supported in 1966 by the General Assembly (Resolution 2065), which agreed to include the Malvinas situation as part of the decolonization process.[1] It invited the two disputants to begin bilateral talks to settle the issue of sovereignty, taking into account the interests of the islands population. However the UN resolution did not recognize the Malvinas 'kelpers' as a 'nation' — which could have implied their right to self-determination — but only as simple inhabitants of the territory.

Secret negotiations between the two countries began in 1966, just after General Onganía's military coup and during the term of Wilson's Labour government in Britain. By the end of 1967, the so-called 'Agreed Position' seemed to indicate that a conclusion was in sight. The Foreign Office acceded in principle to the Argentinian demand, believing that this would help to improve commercial relations with all of Latin America. But the dominant economic interests on the islands (the Falkland Islands Company), together with the most colonialist faction of the Conservative Party, aborted the agreement by mobilizing the islanders against it. They denounced it publicly with the support of the quality press and even the BBC, drawing much of parliament along behind them. This development 'politicized' the conflict in Britain and directed it along new paths. Argentina began to talk of buying out the Falkland Islands Company, although without any success, while the idea of a military occupation was mooted in the armed forces.[2] The British government in turn adopted a new position, aimed at sidestepping the core of Argentina's claim in favour of gradual accords to win the islanders' consent.

This stage coincided with the return of the Tories in Britain and the weakening of the Argentinian dictatorship in the face of explosive working-class and popular resistance (the governments of Generals Lanusse and Levingston). Agreements were signed in 1971 to allow direct air and postal links between the islands and the mainland, and a wide range of commercial, social and cultural relations began to develop (study tours, health care, tourism), awakening the 'enthusiasm' of particularly the younger 'kelpers'. During this period Buenos Aires continued to press its claim to the islands and presented a special petition to the UN group of Twenty Four to reopen the case before the United Nations. This led to the passing of Resolution 3160 at the end of 1973, which only repeated the terms of Resolution 2065.

Argentina's position hardened considerably with the return of the Peronists to power, especially after Cámpora was replaced by General Perón in a significant swing to the right. After justly denouncing Whitehall's evasiveness on the question of sovereignty, Argentina's ambassador to the UN stated that 'unless there is a solution to this dispute within a brief and reasonable time, we will begin a profound re-examination of the policy followed up to now' (letter to the UN Secretary-General, dated 15 August 1973). At the same time, a major campaign in the *Cronica* and *Mayoría* newspapers called for a speedy end to foreign occupation of that part of Argentinian territory. The climax was marked by a series of notable actions: the *de facto* annulment of nearly all communications agreements; the ending of the situation whereby islanders were free to emigrate to Argentina and obtain citizenship; and the attack by the warship *Almirante Storni* on the British oceanographic vessel *Shackleton* at the end of 1975.

The last stage began with the advent of General Videla's terrorist regime. On the British side, the Shackleton Report argued that it was impossible to hold the islands without an agreement with Argentina. For its part, the Argentinian dictatorship contemplated two apparently contradictory policy options: the search for an agreement with Britain to exploit oil resources in the South Atlantic, encouraged by Minister Martínez de Hoz and his team of economists; and the plan for a drastic military solution or 'Goa Option', already proposed by the Navy after the 1976 coup and the 1978 World Cup victory, but shelved on both occasions for fear of British nuclear submarines.

The Thatcher government inherited from Labour the search for a negotiated settlement with Argentina, in the spirit of the

Shackleton Report and the quest for investment opportunities in Argentina and the South Atlantic. This policy was pursued by her man in the foreign office, Mr Ridley[3]; but towards the end of 1981 the Tory government began to develop what Anthony Barnett has termed a 'South Atlantic Spirit', which deliberately excluded the possibility of agreement on completely anachronistic and reactionary colonialist grounds.[4]

This choice to continue occupation of the islands cannot be explained simply by reference to their economic value. With a total population of 1,800 humans and half-a-million sheep, they had paid no more than £1.9m in taxes in the 22 years from 1951 to 1973: some £14,000 a month. Proof of Whitehall's slight interest in the islands was its treatment of the 'kelpers' (whom it did not recognize as British nationals unless they or their pa ·nts or grandparents had been born in Britain) and the paltry sums invested in the interests of the islanders.[5] Since, moreover, London had to pay a political cost in terms of its relations with Latin America, its desire to maintain the colonial situation has to be explained by a mix of other factors, beginning with the islands' potential economic and strategic importance.

The South Georgia and Sandwich Islands, which are almost uninhabited, are two substantially smaller archipelagos totalling 4,132 sq.kms. Located more than 1,500 kms. off the Argentinian coastline, and a long way from the American continental shelf, they are nevertheless related to the continent to the extent that they lie on the underwater extension of the Andes mountain range. They are less important economically, being covered by ice for most of the year, and are used intermittently as bases for scientific expeditions. There is very little that can be said of their history.

2. The Economic and Strategic Importance of the Malvinas, Georgias and South Sandwich Islands

There are a number of reasons why the islands are economically and strategically important, such as the probable existence of oil deposits, the looming discussions on rights in the Antarctic (1991), and the growing commercial and strategic role of the interoceanic route through the South Atlantic. Let us examine these points in turn.

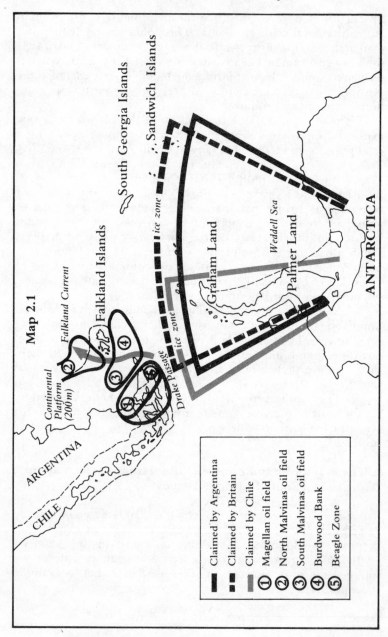

Map 2.1

ARGENTINA

CHILE

Continental Platform (200 m)

Falkland Current

Falkland Islands

South Georgia Islands

Sandwich Islands

ice zone

ice zone

Drake Passage

Graham Land

Weddell Sea

Palmer Land

ANTARCTICA

② ③ ④ ① ⑤

Claimed by Argentina
Claimed by Britain
Claimed by Chile
① Magellan oil field
② North Malvinas oil field
③ South Malvinas oil field
④ Burdwood Bank
⑤ Beagle Zone

(a) Oil

At least three oil fields have been tentatively identified in the Malvinas region in the past few years. One of these, called the Magellan Field, stretches over the mainland, Tierra del Fuego and the surrounding channels and islands, including the Beagle zone that has been the subject of a Chile-Argentina border dispute. Exploitation of this field will prove relatively easy, since it covers dry land and shallow waters, although some parts cannot be drilled until the outstanding border problems are finally resolved. The second field, called Malvinas North, is located in the north and west of the islands and lies mostly in quite deep and rough waters. The third, Malvinas South, lies to the south-east of the islands, partly in the rough sea over the continental shelf and partly to the south, off the continental shelf, in the shallow waters of the Burdwood Bank.

The existence of oil here has been the object of long debate. It seems clear that the region is *potentially* rich in oil.[6] However, three specific points must be made in this respect. First, the true extent of the fields has not yet been confirmed, since the first Argentinian assays in the Magellan field have proved inconclusive.[7] At the least, a further four or five years of exploration would have to precede any substantive commitment of resources. Secondly, extraction costs could be very high, especially in the Malvinas fields, since part of the oil lies in deep water and another part in the rough seas of the Falkland current, one of the swiftest in the world. Cost factors are, of course, especially significant in the present medium-to-long-term conjuncture of declining oil prices.[8] Thirdly, given that the Malvinas fields would require massive injections of fixed capital in the form of huge, complex ocean-going rigs, everyone accepts the conclusion of the Shackleton Report that the problems of sovereignty and regional stability would first have to be resolved.

(b) The Struggle for Antarctica

The Antarctic issue is directly linked to the conflict over the South Atlantic islands, for their geographical proximity provides a possible legal basis for claims to the last uninhabited and unexplored continent on earth. Despite expeditions by several countries since the last century, and the establishment of scientific-type bases by most of them, it is only in recent years that technological developments have made it possible to exploit the region economically or to utilize it for military purposes.

The Antarctic is exceedingly rich in fish resources (especially in krill, a small crustacean high in protein content), minerals and oil. Of the countries with rival claims, Britain, Argentina, Chile, Norway, Australia, New Zealand and France have staked out an interest in large, well-defined areas, employing arguments based upon discovery, geographical proximity, presence of scientific bases, and so on; and more recently, Brazil and India have added themselves to the list. The United States, the USSR, Japan, South Africa and Belgium do not recognize such claims, even though they have set up their own territorial bases and reserve their own future rights. Argentina and Britain are tussling over the huge, mineral-rich peninsula formed by Graham and Palmer Land, and over the potential oil wealth of the Wedell Sea and its surrounding territory. In both cases, moreover, Brazil is also beginning to assert an interest, basing its position upon a southward projection of the 39th and 53rd meridians.

The Georgias and Sandwich Islands are important for two reasons. First, they are the only areas of dry land situated in the most important krill reserves. Possession of these islands would therefore allow any country to control a major part of this biological wealth, which may account for as much as ten per cent of the international shellfish market. Argentina does not suggest that it has historic rights to these islands, as in the case of the Malvinas, but it does advance a geographic claim stemming from their location on an underwater prolongation of the Andean mountain range. This argument directly links the question of the South Georgia and Sandwich Islands to the conflict with Chile over the Beagle Channel. For if Chile succeeds in asserting its rights to the Atlantic part of the Channel zone, it would be in a strong position to claim the south-western side of the underwater mountain range. (See Map 2.2).

On the question of krill fishing, however, it should be added that we are dealing with a species that has still to be exploited commercially. Some sources argue that it would not be competitive to do so for some time, and that a new type of fishing vessel would have to be developed. Even then its commercial value could not be compared to that of oil, and it would be of only marginal significance for the Argentinian and, *a fortiori,* the British economy.

The second reason for the importance of these archipelagos is that they provide a legal basis for claims to the eastern part of the Antarctic. The Sandwich Islands are the starting-point for a southward projection of the line that marks out the two rival claims — a line which extends westward thanks to the successive presence of the Georgias and the Malvinas. There are other archipelagos to the west which are crucial to the dispute: above all, the South Orkneys, where Argentina has had a meteorological station since 1902, and the South Shetlands, currently occupied by Britain but also the object of Chilean and Argentinian claims. However, only the Georgias and the Sandwich Islands are involved in the present conflict, since both are under British colonial jurisdiction based in Port Stanley.

(c) The Interoceanic Route and the Military-Strategic Importance of the South Atlantic

When we come to the interoceanic route (Drake Passage), it is important to bear in mind a number of fundamental points: (i) the growing role of the South Atlantic route, as the Panama Canal becomes less firmly controlled by the USA, less able to cope with the draught of giant oil tankers, and more vulnerable to attack from modern weaponry; (ii) the striking growth of the USSR as a seapower during the 1970s, after its development of a major long-range nuclear submarine fleet; (iii) the quest of the Argentinian dictatorship for an agreement with South Africa and the United States to form a South Atlantic Treaty Organization (SATO),[9] allowing it to adjust the strategic role of Argentinian capitalism as a regional sub-power within the Western world; (iv) the rise to power of Ronald Reagan and Margaret Thatcher, with their hard-line military–strategic policies favouring direct control of key geographical areas.

For all these reasons, the South Atlantic islands have acquired a major significance for the organization of a broad counter-revolutionary alliance in that zone. But this in turn poses a further problem: will Argentina or Britain be the lynchpin of the war machine in the area of the Drake Passage?

As we shall see, this appears to be one of the fundamental issues of the conflict, and it must be carefully distinguished from the questions of oil and the Antarctic. For, whereas the exploitation of oil and the utilization of Antarctic territory are progressive claims which benefit the Argentinian nation, control of the southern passages with counter-revolutionary objectives in mind poses a tremendous danger to both the Argentinian and other Latin American nations, whether Argentina plays a leading or a subordinate role in SATO or in any military pact that might materialize.

3. Britain and the Islands

(a) The British Empire Today

Britain possessed the largest colonial empire in the world until the post-war period. It began to crumble quickly after 1946, when Attlee's Labour government initiated a decolonization programme, subsequently applied by all Labour and Conservative governments. This policy had the character of an inevitable political process, given Britain's inability to contain the powerful independence movements in Africa, Asia and the Caribbean, and the growing influence of Communist parties in Asia. Decolonization was also part of a new capitalist–imperialist project: namely the re-establishment of Britain's financial and industrial role in a free world market, ready to compromise with inevitable social reforms and the emergence of new nations, in the context of a world capitalist system regulated by international institutions like GATT, the IMF and the World Bank. The British bourgeoisie also accepted, as part of this policy, that it had been relegated to the role of a secondary imperialist power, a minor partner and key ally of the US bourgeoisie.

As the 1980s witnessed the independence of Belize, the 'Falklands' and their dependencies (Georgias and Sandwich Islands) made up ninety per cent of Britain's remaining colonies, alongside an assortment of geographically and demographically insignificant islets and outcrops in Europe, the Caribbean, the Pacific and Indian Oceans, the Atlantic Ocean and Antarctica, (See Table 2.1). We have omitted Hong Kong because this important Asian financial and industrial centre, with a population of five million on a territory of 1,000 sq.kms., is administered by Britain by virtue of a leaseback contract with China imposed by force in 1898 for a duration of 99 years. We have also omitted the Associated States of the Antilles (Antigua, St Christopher and others), since these are *sui generis* colonies with an autonomous administration. Britain only has one colony of any economic importance, excluding Hong Kong, and that is the Virgin Islands (a financial centre). It also has secondary international tourist centres and three military bases rented to the United States. The

Table 2.1
THE BRITISH EMPIRE'S COLONIAL
DEPENDENCIES AT PRESENT

Name of dependency	surface	population	economic importance
EUROPE			
Gibraltar	5.5 km²	30,000	Tourism
ANTILLES			
Bermudas	53.0 km²	60,000	Tourism
Montserrat	102.0 km²	11,500	Minimal (tropical produce)
Virgin Islands	153.0 km²	11,000	Tourism
Turks and Caicos	430.0 km²	7,200	None
Cayman Islands	259.0 km²	30,000	Financial centre
ATLANTIC OCEAN			
Saint Helen	122.0 km²	5,200	Tourism
Ascension	88.0 km²	1,000	Military base
Tristan Da Cunha	201.0 km²	300	Military base
INDIAN OCEAN			
Changos archipelago (Diego Garcia Island)	52.0 km²	—	Military base
OCEANIA			
Pitcairn	4.5 km²	100	None
ANTARCTIC			
South Shetland Islands	n/a	—	None
South Orkney	n/a	—	None
Graham Land	n/a	—	Potential
TOTAL	1,559.0	155,300	

Source: *World Atlas 1982* and other sources.

official explanation for keeping these colonial relics is that most of them (except perhaps Bermuda and the Cayman Islands, which, together with Gibraltar, have 80 per cent of the population) do not have sufficiently viable economies to constitute independent states. The military bases installed on uninhabited islands (or islands evacuated expressly for that purpose, like Diego Garcia) are in an interesting category of their own.

Belize, the last colony to be granted independence, in 1981, had oil reserves and a more powerful neighbour claiming its territory (Guatemala). Nevertheless Britain agreed to grant it independence, handing power to a social-democratic government entertaining relations with Cuba and Nicaragua. Belize was a viable nation, with a territory of 22,195 sq.kms., a population of 160,000, a GDP of \$17.4m, and a per capita income of \$900. In 1975 its exports were a quarter of total Guatemalan exports.

We are faced, then, by an 'empire' which only retains insignificant scraps of what it once owned — scraps claimed neither by itself, nor by the inhabitants (where there are any), nor by bordering countries. Almost all of them are semi-deserted islands, luxurious playgrounds or semi-private business concerns. If we exclude Gibraltar, justly claimed by Spain, the Malvinas Islands are the last imperial residue of any importance now in dispute, which Britain obstinately retains by force, against opposition from the international community and the unanimous condemnation of Latin American countries.

Before considering the fundamental reasons for this intransigence, we should examine the official British position on the islands, and in particular on the alternative of 'self-determination'.

(b) Britain's Attitude to Self-Determination

The official British position on the Malvinas Islands is thoroughly ambiguous. It has done nothing at all to improve the living conditions of the islanders or to develop their natural resources. Nor has it yet encouraged any concrete plan for oil exploration. One particularly striking indication of the British attitude was the attempt in 1981 to sell the only British icebreaker supplying the islands, *The Endurance,* to the Brazilian government. It was not until a few months before the war that the Minister of Defence finally vetoed the deal. This major ambiguity is expressed in the fact that London has made no serious move to implement a policy of self-determination for the islanders, despite the rhetorical statement made by parliament, nor to reach an agreement with the Argentinian government.

On the issue of self-determination, British policy was based until now on the recognition that the islanders did not have a viable economy or an independent state able to withstand Argentinian pressure. The Shackleton Report makes this absolutely clear. Not only are the Malvinas Islands practically uninhabited — more than half the population is based in Port Stanley — but they lack their own social classes as such. The only important capitalist enterprise on the islands (the Falkland Islands Company) owns most of the sheep and 47 per cent of the land. It monopolizes external trade, controls 80 per cent of retail trade, and employs the bulk of the workforce. Most of the wage-earning population (civil servants, office staff, manual workers) are paid by the British Treasury or the FIC. Finally, the local proletariat combines its tasks of shepherding and shearing with trips to Australia and New Zealand as a migrant workforce for seasonal agricultural tasks. Whereas the employees and officials are British citizens, and are paid the highest wages, the mass of labourers and small producers are natives of the islands.

For these reasons there is nothing resembling an independence movement from Britain. Instead there are dynamic forces, still in a minority, who support closer links with Argentina in order to gain access to work, study, healthcare and holidays, in considerably more advantageous conditions than they could enjoy in Britain, New Zealand or Australia. The 'independence project' recently floated by Mrs Thatcher's government cannot therefore be taken any more seriously than its alleged respect for the islanders' desire to remain British. (It is enough to recall that in 1966 the British government expelled 1,300 inhabitants from Diego Garcia, against their will, in order to lease the territory to the United States for a military base.)

(c) The British Attitude to a Negotiated Settlement with Argentina

As we have seen, an agreement with Argentina is absolutely necessary if the oil reserves off the Malvinas are to be exploited. It is common knowledge that the Argentinian dictatorship was quite prepared to grant concessions to British and US transnationals (Shell and Exxon), as it had done in 1980 for the Magellan Basin, in conjunction with the new 'national' bureaucratic monopolies, such as Pérez Comanc, Bridas and Cadipsa. There were also powerful technological motives for such a deal: namely, the adaptability of the offshore platforms in the North Sea to the conditions of the South Atlantic,[10] and Argentina's lack of expertise in seabed exploration in very deep and rough waters. Logically enough, the oil transnationals and the big bourgeoisie in Britain do appear to have been in favour of a negotiated settlement with Argentina. It also seems clear that Britain could only obtain Argentinian recognition of its rights in the Antarctic by offering substantial concessions over the Malvinas. Britain had other cards up its sleeve in the struggle for the frozen continent: it had effectively occupied the South Orkney and South Shetland Islands, and a large part of Graham Land (all claimed by

Argentina). Yet the British government made no attempt to link the two issues, and remained completely passive on this whole aspect.

It is quite evident that the Argentinian military dictatorship wanted more than anyone else to set up a South Atlantic equivalent of NATO, firmly aligned with the United States and the 'free world'. Thus a resolution of the Malvinas question favourable to Argentina would not have essentially affected the strategic interests of the West. Indeed, the SATO project was not feasible without Argentinian participation.

In this historical context, Mr. Ridley proposed three options in 1980–81: postponement of a settlement for an indefinite period (obviously unacceptable to Argentina); joint ownership of the islands (also unacceptable to public opinion); and a 'Hong-Kong' type solution (recognition of Argentinian sovereignty and leaseback of islands to Britain). But despite the Junta's initial favourable response, this last proposal was not even seriously discussed, owing to the change in the position of the British parliament, the Thatcher government, and most of the conservative interests on the islands (certainly including the FIC and the islands' administration).

How can we account for the British change of course? How can we explain such a stance on the part of an extremely lucid bourgeois class which had had the sense to withdraw in time from rich and important countries like India and Nigeria, and which had just granted independence to oil-rich Belize? Why was a conservative and counter-insurgent regime ready to cede power to Price's left-wing government in such a sensitive area as Central America, and yet adamantly opposed to the idea of handing over some semi-deserted islands to as close an ally as the Argentinian military?

The answers are not simple or one-sided, but involve a mix of essentially political factors, together with the survival of colonialist sentiments in broad layers of the British ruling class and population.

Firstly, the British military high command, and at least part of the Pentagon, were very probably convinced that the Argentinian dictatorship was an unreliable force on which to base a military presence in the South Atlantic. (As Barnett has shown, the Royal Navy carried particular weight in the development of a hard-line British position.) These military strategists used three types of argument: (a) that the Argentinian dictatorship lacked political stability; (b) that the Argentinian navy did not have the technological sophistication to discharge a leading role in defence of the South Atlantic; and (c) that the Argentinian dictatorship was so discredited in the eyes of world opinion that it had become a less than desirable ally, obstructing the policy quest for an international counter-revolutionary consensus endowed with certain reformist features. The indecisive attitude of Britain (and also, in our view, of the United States) was therefore bound up with the factors that made it difficult to reach a decision on the SATO project. That is to say, influential sections of the British and US high command wanted to sit out the crisis of military rule in Argentina before engaging in a bitter and troublesome debate on strategy in the South Atlantic.

The second factor, of a strictly political and even electoral nature, was the strong opposition of the British Labour and Liberal leaderships to the idea of handing the long-forgotten 'kelpers' over to a dictatorship which, for much of the British electorate, was a symbol of corruption and fascist terror. Paradoxically, it was the Opposition that had hoisted this banner as the Conservative government sought a compromise with the Junta. The situation then changed dramatically when the Thatcher government launched an ideological and political crusade in defence of the eternal principles of the British nation — one that allowed her to consolidate her position in an extremely difficult economic and social conjuncture.

This combination of factors (together with the traditional resistance of the nostalgic Victorian right to a 'surrender' of any part of the former Empire) led the British government to support a myopic policy, with no long-term future, that cannot be explained in terms of the historic or conjunctural interests of British or world capitalism. But it was the even more blind and irresponsible policy of the Argentinian dictatorship which crystallized this array of forces, turning a problem that had previously met with popular indifference and government indecision into a question of deep national feeling. Incapable of combining diplomatic activity and international pressure with a search for solidarity with the British people and the deepening of cultural and economic ties with the more progressive and dynamic 'kelpers', the Junta managed to produce a tragedy which further complicated the recovery of the Malvinas by the Argentinian nation.

4. Argentina and the Malvinas: Pointers for a Marxist Analysis

Argentina's claim to the islands must be analysed in two ways. Firstly, we have to examine the geographical and juridical bases for the claim, as well as the economic and political significance of the reintegration of the islands, while simultaneously taking into account the principles of social progress, democracy and international solidarity. Secondly, we have to determine the exact place of the Malvinas in the general development of the Argentinian nation and its social and political needs. This last aspect is essential for any adequate account of the current conflict, and of its location in national and international politics.

(a) Bases of the Argentinian Claim

There are numerous historical, geographical and juridical arguments on which the legitimacy of Argentina's claim is based.[11] Many substantial contributions have already referred to such basic points as the original seizure of the islands at a time of political anarchy in Argentina; the systematic reiteration of Argentinian protests; the geographical connection of the Malvinas with the American continent, and their location in Argentinian waters; and, above all, the obvious illegitimacy of the British occupation of islands situated more than 10,000 kms from the metropolis. This last point was fully recognized by the UN when, as we have seen, it included the Malvinas within the problematic of decolonization.

Despite their correctness, however, these reasons are not convincing in and of themselves: none, for example, succeeds in demonstrating that reversion to Argentina would be economically more progressive or politically more just and more democratic than a solution involving self-determination for the islanders. The case outlined above has much in common with Guatemala's claim to Belize, or Venezuela's to the Essequibo region of Guyana. There, too, the history is one of colonial plunder, diplomatic protests, territorial contiguity, and illegitimate British occupation in the eyes of international law established over long decades of struggle against colonialism. But it is also true that, in both cases, the process of decolonization allowed a nation to exercise the right of self-determination in forming a new, independent state.

At present the Guatemalan and Venezuelan bourgeoisies are

trying to whip up popular feeling against the new Caribbean nations. Together with historical, juridical and geographical arguments, they seek to strengthen their own claims by citing the Argentinian precedent, and to cover up their political and military preparations for what could turn out to be tragic and criminal fratricidal wars. The peoples of Latin America should raise their voices loudly and clearly in support of the right of nations to self-determination, fully defending Belizean and Guyanese independence and territorial integrity, whatever the historical and juridical titles the aggressor may invoke. But what about the Malvinas? So long as the Argentinian Left remains at the level of discourse of its bourgeoisie, it will be in no position either to legitimize its policy before the peoples of Latin America, or to assist the working class to adopt an independent, class perspective, or to express a consistently internationalist and democratic point of view. It is therefore crucially important to consider, in a calm and principled manner, whether the proposal of self-determination for the islanders is a just and feasible solution. First, however, we must answer some even more fundamental questions. Are the 'kelpers' a nation? Can they constitute an independent state? Have they developed their own political expressions for· obtaining independence? And finally, which political solution would allow them to develop their natural resources and productive forces to achieve more advanced forms of life and social coexistence?

The 'kelpers' are not a nation, because they lack their own economy and national life. They have no national classes to speak of, and their destiny is directly linked to Britain, Australia or Argentina. Employees of the state and the FIC think only of returning to Britain. Labourers must travel thousands of miles in harsh conditions (to New Zealand and Australia) to find employment during the long dead months after shearing — and to know something of the world. The virtual absence of young women clearly demonstrates the impracticability of constituting not just a nation but even stable families. Currently there are four to six British soldiers for each adult islander.

The 'kelpers' are unable to develop a viable economy, given their thin population and scant resources, If, for instance, they wanted to extract oil for their own use, how would they go about it? Evidently with British capital and technology, and with British (or Argentinian) workers. If this were to happen, the foreign population would immediately swamp the islanders, generating a completely different economy and another kind of society. It would turn the Falk*lands* into a puppet-state, unable to make any of its own decisions.

The most tangible proof of this is that the 'kelpers' have not even tried to develop a nationalist movement, and that internal political differences developed between those who wanted to stay under British colonial rule[12] and the younger, more 'cosmopolitan' inhabitants who wanted some sort of link with Argentina. What sense is there in trying to resolve this by a vote, when the voters would be mainly officials of the British state or the FIC, and when British governments can ensure the right decision by using their ample economic resources to enrich the entire population? If we accept that the colonial situation is politically and economically anachronistic (because of the enormous distance involved and Britain's inability to develop the islands for its own benefit), and that an independence solution is not practicable, then it is obvious that the only progressive alternative is integration into Argentina. The islands' natural resources could then be exploited; the economy could be incorporated into an incomparably larger economic and commercial space; and more human forms of life could be developed in a more advanced social and cultural environment, with a very rich tradition of immigrant assimilation.

This is the most correct and progressive solution. But can it be done by a murderous military dictatorship which does not even respect the human rights of its own people? Can a government hated by its own population deserve the respect and loyalty of other peoples? We do not believe it can. This obstructs the development of a bold and successful national policy towards the British people and the Malvinas population.

(b) How the Significance of the Malvinas Question Differs for the Argentinian People and its Oppressors

The claim to the archipelago has different meanings for the people, the bourgeoisie and the military government. In the popular consciousness, it objectively involves the reintegration of a region whose economic wealth is potentially very great; the encouragement of national links with the Antarctic and the extension of the limits of self-determination over its wealth and geographical space; and the prevention of big-power exploitation of its land and adjacent regions for counter-revolutionary military purposes. It also means the fulfilment of a long-awaited objective that would allow the people to redress an unjust seizure, the memory of which dates back more than a century and a half and has become a matter of national pride. Thus the claim to the islands is inseparably linked to improvement of the rights and living standards of the Argentinian people, and can in no case imply their future deterioration.

For the bourgeoisie, and the armed forces which govern in their name, the claim has a quite different meaning. Firstly, it is related to a reactionary, anti-popular project for regional capitalist development, based upon a military strengthening of the state and the opposition of the country's interests to those of other Latin American nations. According to this project, which will be further discussed in the next chapter, the Argentinian nation must work more intensively and suffer greater privations to make Argentina a power that really counts. Secondly, the military rulers want to exploit legitimate popular feeling in order to re-establish their bases of political support, to shroud their own crimes and 'betrayals', and to drag the working-class and popular masses behind projects and adventures which run directly counter to their interests.

The existence of these two meanings is expressed in the distinct characterizations of the Malvinas question. It is a vital problem for the bourgeoisie, arising at a time when it urgently needs a way to avoid answering the people's most pressing social needs and to resist their demands of unconditional democratization and punishment of the crimes of the dictatorship. Hence it has to convince the masses that the Malvinas question is the nation's top priority. Very broad sectors of the Argentinian Left have opportunistically latched on to this bourgeois option. At the same time, however, they are trying to cover their lack of principle with a completely spurious analysis. In their view, British occupation of the islands, in conjunction with Argentina's financial and technological dependence, is enough to define a colonial-type situation that is supposed to be the principal obstacle to the development of the Argentinian nation. Since the country is a semi-colony (or neo-colony, according to taste), any attempt to end its present status is necessarily correct, whatever the cost to the nation and whatever the wider political consequences.

In the last chapter we tried to demonstrate that Argentina is not a semi-colony, either of Britain or of any other imperialist

power, but a monopoly-capitalist country with regional imperialist features; and that the principal exploiter and oppressor
of the Argentinian people is its own bourgeoisie and armed
forces (associated with US and British capital). British military
occupation of the Malvinas is fundamentally an unpleasant
after-taste of colonialism, not crucially obstructing the development of Argentina as a country. It is a simple and obvious fact
that the hunger, unemployment, fear and despair suffered by the
Argentinian people have not been essentially caused by the
British bourgeoisie, military or government, but by the Argentinian bourgeoisie, military and government, during decades of
offensives against their own people.

In the pages that follow we shall try to make this idea more
precise.

5. The Malvinas, Argentinian Territorial Integration and National Sovereignty

Our argument is that the recovery of the Malvinas by the
Argentinian nation is a non-essential democratic claim which,
though still unresolved, does not decisively affect any sector of
the Argentinian population. In practice, the British occupation
has had no major impact on either the evolution or the life of the
nation. The status of the islands does not limit the political
independence of the state, but only the amount of geographical
space over which it exercises sovereignty.

It is precisely this aspect that we must now clarify. For Britain's
colonial rule in the Malvinas has been cited as proof that
Argentina itself is a colonial, 'semi-colonial' or 'neo-colonial'
country, and that the war plans of the dictatorship had an
anti-colonial character. The 'Malvinas situation' has now been
equated with the 'situation of the Argentinian nation'. And,
indeed, if this were actually so, it would have been a just war,
whatever kind of people General Galtieri and his Junta were.

In order to pose the problem correctly, we must try more
concretely to assess the significance of Argentina's territorial
claim for the development of the nation. The first step is to
consider in general terms how the problematic of territory is
related to the national question.

Clearly, in the development of a nation one essential factor is
the possession of territory, of a space in which to unfold its

economic and social life. Three kinds of obstacle may hinder the development of a nation: (a) expulsion from its natural-geographical space, as in the recent case of the Palestinians; (b) the forced breaking-up of a country, implying the seizure of territory vital for economic development (the case of an outlet to the sea for Bolivia)[13]; and (c) the control by foreign powers of territory vital for national development, as in the case of the Panama and (before 1956) the Suez Canal, or of the 'spheres of influence' and extra-territorial zones in Imperial China. We can see this process at work when a state cannot be formed (case a), or when a state is substantially weakened (case b), or when a state is reduced to a semi-colonial status (case c).

It may often be true that a territorial claim is intrinsically just, and yet not sufficiently strong to constitute a vital need for national economic development. For example, there is the Spanish claim to the rock of Gibraltar, or the much more important Cuban demand for the return of Guantánamo, or the simple inheritance of forcible redivisions of territory which litter the history of Latin America, Asia and Africa. However, the justness of these claims cannot be treated abstractly or from a strictly national point of view (since all 'reason of state' is unilateral and exclusive by definition), and we should cede to more important principles, such as the right of the people in those territories to self-determination and to use of the soil on which they live. Moreover, even if the claim is just, it cannot override more vital national-democratic objectives. For the right to self-determination is a democratic right of peoples as such, not something to be used by the exploiter and oppressor classes against the people.

In the case of the Malvinas, we are faced with a just *territorial* claim,[14] but one that is secondary to other social and political demands of the nation. The reintegration of the islands cannot solve any vital national needs in the long term, and much less so in the short term. It could mean, in six or eight years, a major boost to oil production and, quite possibly, export surpluses. However, this remains uncertain, not only because of the difficult location and inconclusive quantification of the oil reserves, but also because of likely trends in the world oil market. From every point of view, a realistic oil policy would lend priority to the territorial waters in Patagonia and the Magellan Basin (which are endowed with the same potential), rather than encouraging political and military adventures that threaten the country's economic situation and the living standards of the people.

As to the southern passages, military control is not necessary for Argentina's national development. What is needed is an actively neutralist and pacifist policy, including demilitarization and internationalization of the inter-oceanic route among its essential points. This, in turn, is a major aspect of the broader search for a democratic agreement with Chile and Brazil on utilization of the South Atlantic resources.

We have argued that the principal obstacle to the progressive development of the Argentinian economy is found today in the social relations of production. With regard to physical space, the problem lies not in the lack of territory and territorial waters (since the country's resources are already among the largest in the world), but in the failure to undertake adequate prospection and exploitation of that territory. This is itself closely linked to the historical crisis of Argentinian capitalism and its extremely strong tendency to expel capital and labour to countries offering better labour-market conditions and opportunities for valorization or simply survival. Certainly the Malvinas are important. But of much greater importance is the recovery of the national territory for the people's use.

3

The Junta's Decision
to Occupy the Islands

The decision to reoccupy the Malvinas cannot be explained by psychological factors such as the supposed megalomania of Galtieri (that 'majestic general', as his Pentagon colleagues called him), and still less by his choleric outbursts under the influence of drink. Nor was it due to a sudden surge of patriotism in the ranks of the armed forces, or to their continual assertion that 'the Malvinas are Argentinian'. Similarly, the Junta did not act in response to a strong wave of popular demands. Although there was a broad popular consensus on the problem, the mass movement did not pose it as a priority, and in recent decades it is difficult — if not impossible — to find a single instance of a mass mobilization that has centred on the Malvinas.

The landing on 2 April 1982 did, however, answer the specific needs, both domestic and international, of one sector of Argentinian society. It was not an arbitrary adventure, but served objectives which the military, in common with the expanding national forces of monopoly and finance capital, considered to be an essential priority. That the military chose to use this traditional claim as a cover caused confusion in the country and abroad, masking the real significance of the manoeuvre. Even some layers of the Argentinian masses found themselves carried along by it.

1. The Situation in Argentina on the Eve of the War

As we have seen, Argentina still had a long diplomatič road to travel before it could assert its incontestable right to the islands. If the Juntas rejected such a procedure, opting instead for a military solution that provided in effect a *casus belli*, its decision has to be explained in terms of the internal situation in the preceding months and the position of the dominant class in the world capitalist order.

(a) The Economic Crisis

The Junta's economic programme, as outlined in chapter one, led in just over a year to a crisis affecting all orders of society that deepened and spread with striking rapidity. The attempt to restructure the bases of reproduction of Argentinian capitalism and its insertion into the world market resulted in a partial triumph and a signal failure. Without doubt, it involved the strengthening of the financially strongest elements of the monopolist bourgeoisie and, in particular, of sectors linked to the production of the means of production for the state sector and the military–industrial complex.

This entailed the virtual dismantling of entire branches of production, bankrupting many firms in the mass consumer goods sector. This process was particularly violent in textiles, in the agricultural consumer-goods branches of the metal industry, and in major regional employers of labour such as the Mendoza wine industry and the fruit farms of the Río Negro Valley.[1] It affected big enterprises in financial difficulties (like Celulosa and Sasetru), and also hit the automobile transnationals because of the contraction of the domestic market and the high costs in relation to international markets.[2] The number of bankruptcies and receiving-orders rocketed by seventy-four per cent in the period from 1979 to 1980 alone — against a background of debt sluggishness in the productive sectors and liquidation of financial and banking institutions such as the Banco de Intercambios Regional. As Table 3.1 demonstrates, this trend became more acute in 1981 and the first months of 1982.[3]

The worst-hit sectors were textiles, foodstuffs, beverages, tobacco and metallurgy, excluding steel — precisely those which played a decisive role in the previous phase of import-substitutionist industrialization. A comparison of output in certain consumer goods industries and in basic metallurgy affords a more precise overview of the situation. (Table 3.2 shows a fall in the first three columns between 1976 and 1980, alongside a recovery of basic metallurgy).

Now, if we bear in mind the importance of the consumer sector in the formation of the 'populist' bourgeoisie, it becomes clear not only that the previous phase of Argentinian industrial

Table 3.1
CIVIL AND COMMERCIAL BANKRUPTCIES

Activities	Total 1978-1980 (in dollars)	Percentage structure %
1. Farming	18,309,254	1.31
2. Mining	5,375,164	0.39
3. Commerce	264,810,920	19.02
4. Manufacturing Industry, of which:	815,147,737	58.57
(a) Foods, beverages and tobacco	235,019,766	16.89
(b) Textiles	260,894,010	18.74
(c) Wood	4,386,278	0.32
(d) Leather and footware	84,072,850	6.04
(e) Paper, printing and publishing	13,355,534	0.96
(f) Chemical products, rubber & plastics	41,055,094	2.95
(g) Non-metallic minerals	8,740,528	0.63
(h) Metallurgy	167,623,377	12.04
5. Construction	29,178,634	2.10
6. Services	250,019,190	18.61
TOTALS	1,391,840,899	100

Source: Ministry of Economics, November 1981.

Table 3.2
**INDICES OF EVOLUTION OF OUTPUT IN SELECTED
INDUSTRIAL BRANCHES (1974=100)**

Year	Foods, drinks, tobacco	Textiles, clothing, leather	Wood and furniture	Basic metals
1974	100	100	100	100
1975	99	104	87	98
1976	99	98	63	74
1977	96	98	56	85
1978	89	85	49	83
1979	91	88	52	96
1980	93	80	51	90

Source: FIDE and the magazine *Mercado*, based on official figures.

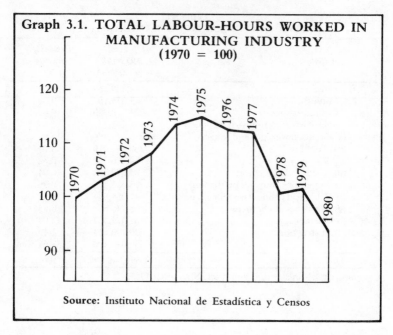

Graph 3.1. TOTAL LABOUR-HOURS WORKED IN MANUFACTURING INDUSTRY (1970 = 100)

Source: Instituto Nacional de Estadística y Censos

development was being dismantled at an ever faster pace, but also that the political groups which had been their traditional representatives (whether in their 'Peronist–redistributive' or 'Liberal–Radical' form) were rapidly losing their material base for affecting the political and economic options of the country.

Furthermore, these had been the crucial sectors for an earlier distribution and concentration of the labour force. In conjunction with the 'rationalization' of industry, their massive collapse precipitated a huge decline in working hours throughout manufacturing industry, and even an absolute fall in the numbers employed in industry. (See Graphs 3.1 and 3.2.)

As we might expect, this process had near-catastrophic effects on the population: unemployment in sectors where labour had been most in demand, internal migration, an increase in the number of self-employed workers (according to Schaposnik-Vacchino, from eighteen to twenty-five per cent of the economically active population). There was also a spectacular increase in

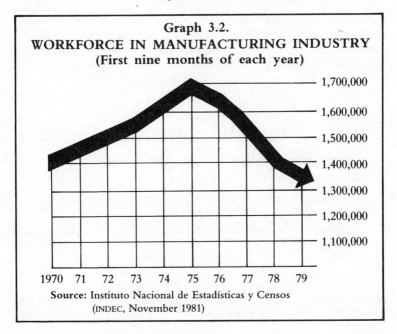

Graph 3.2.
WORKFORCE IN MANUFACTURING INDUSTRY
(First nine months of each year)

Source: Instituto Nacional de Estadísticas y Censos
(INDEC, November 1981)

the ranks of 'travelling salesmen' and various home-based workers, particularly in the repair of domestic electrical appliances.

Unemployment soared among wage-earners proper, especially from 1980 onwards. Thus, in 1980 the Textile Workers Association condemned the laying off or under-employment of 80,000 of its 129,000 members; and in June 1981 the Automobile Mechanics and Allied Workers Union (SMATA) recorded a similar situation for 40,000 of its 135,000 members. In January of that year a director of the Argentinian Chamber of Commerce of Construction calculated that there were 400,000 unemployed in the industry. In addition there was a dramatic fall in consumption levels — estimated at twenty-five per cent of global demand for goods and services.[4]

The destructive effect of the crisis could not stimulate the hypothetical productive effects, mainly because of the long depression gripping the world economy, and the conflicts within the ruling bloc that expressed themselves in a contradictory application of the Junta's plan.[5] For want of productive outlets, a vast mass of monetary assets looked to speculation as a means of reproduction, chiefly being converted into value-conserving

Table 3.3
GENERAL INDICATORS OF THE ARGENTINIAN ECONOMY

Growth Rate	1976	1977	1978	1979	1980	1981	1982
Gross Product	−0.2	6.0	−3.9	6.8	1.1	−6.1	−5.7
Consumption	−7.0	1.7	−3.2	11.0	4.6	−5.2	−7.1
Gross investment	8.2	19.8	−9.7	8.9	8.4	−21.9	−20.5
Wages	−36.2	−12.0	−7.5	13.0	10.3	−10.0	—
Inflation	444%	178%	175%	160%	100%	131%	165%

Sources: BCRA, Ministry of Economics, UADE.

physical assets or drawn out of the country by the massive rise in world interest rates.[6] The results are there for everyone to see in Table 3.3

However, despite the years of negative growth, GDP did rise during the period 1974-1982, at an average rate of approximately one per cent. As is shown in Table 3.4, there was significant growth in certain sectors of the economy, while consumer goods sectors were in sharp decline. The principal growth areas were agricultural exports, energy and major infrastructural works. Even in the industrial sector the category of 'machinery and plant' grew by twelve per cent from 1976 to 1980, despite a sharp recession in 1978 (according to Central Bank figures). This is also evidence that new priorities were being set in that sector. In general terms, popular consumption fell, but investment rose strongly until 1980. Or, to put it another way, the Argentinian economy was being restructured at the expense of formerly subsidized and tariff-protected sectors and of working-class consumption levels.

This reconversion could not advance without enormous social costs to the nation, including the colossal burden of military expenditure. These costs were already sharply felt towards 1980, and they became even more apparent in 1981 and 1982. Thus, GDP fell 5.7 per cent in the first half of 1982, while industrial output

Table 3.4
EVOLUTION OF GDP IN SELECTED SECTORS (1974=100)

Year	Agriculture	Electricity, gas and water	Construction
1974	100	100	100
1975	98.4	106	105
1976	102	109	118
1977	104	115	135
1978	105	118	136
1979	111	130	142
1980*	115	136	141
1981	116	135	136
1982	120	140	100

Sources: BCRA and *El Economista*.

* The figures given are for values. Volume figures would be at least double, given the fall in prices since 1978.

plunged by 16 per cent in 1981 (9.4 per cent in the first three months). Between 1957 and 1981, the share of industry declined from 29 per cent to a mere 22 per cent of GDP, the worst-affected sectors being plant and machinery, metalworking and assembly, chemicals and textiles. At the same time, imports of consumer goods, particularly in the luxury bracket, soared by 183 per cent in 1979 and 140 per cent in 1980.

One aspect that should be stressed is the enormous growth of the external debt. This swelled from approximately $3.2bn in 1975 to $39bn in 1982, bearing down heavily on the workers who had to produce the means of repayment and turning the country into one of the largest per capita debtors in the world. A major part of this debt consisted of loans that were raised to speculate on high domestic interest-rates and to cover military expenditure of already $12bn.

Within the bourgeoisie itself, these phenomena accorded prime importance to those who could efficiently compete on the world market (the landowners monopolizing the Pampas and the differential rent extracted from it), to the financial groups that provided a link between internal sources of finance, and to the few industrial sectors (such as steel) that were competitive on South American and world markets. In addition, there were those who knew how to exploit the heyday of the 'speculative economy', or to gain contracts for the supply of means of production to the state – military sector.

The Martínez de Hoz team really began to lose control of the economy in the middle of 1980, when a financial crisis and flight of capital combined with a soaring external debt. It then became obvious that the anti-inflation policy had failed to achieve its aims. Despite the extremely rigorous use of exchange instruments (overvaluation of the peso), which badly hit production and created an uncontrollable balance-of-payments deficit, the government failed to stabilize the value of the peso or significantly to check the explosive growth of speculation. The rapid increase of military spending neutralized any anti-inflationary effects by adding to the budget deficit. It also diverted investment resources and massively raised the external debt at a time when the Central Bank's exchange reserves were flooding out of the country.

Such a course could not fail to provoke a deep crisis within the dominant class. Already in March 1981 the Sociedad Rural Argentina (the main institution of the landowners) urgently protested at the financial plight of Argentinian firms and the aberrant state of the exchange and finance markets. The Argentinian Industrial Union called for steps to halt 'the destruction of the productive apparatus' and for an emergency programme including medium-to-long-term measures to salvage the productive economy.[7] Similar or more radical plans were proposed by the Argentinian Agrarian Federation and the National Business Assembly.

(b) The Political Crisis

In a country like Argentina, marked by complex and diversified development, all this was equivalent to an economic and social catastrophe. It caused the fragmentation of the bourgeois concord, which had not only tolerated but supported the Junta's terrorist policy. *The monopolist and financial pinnacle grew increasingly isolated, even from its own class.*

The onset of political crisis was heralded by a wave of protest actions from regional producers and chambers of production and commerce ('black-outs' of shop windows, shut-downs and demonstrations promoted by business groups). Party leaders gradually began again to make public declarations, questioning for the moment only the economic programme rather than the 'process of national reorganization' as a whole.

The bourgeois sectors affected by the crisis fought for their survival as a class, without passing political or ideological judgement on the new order of finance and monopoly capital.

From this 'state of mind', the *Multipartidaria* alliance was formed by the (Peronist) Justicialist Party, the Radical Party, the Movement for Integration and Development, the Christian Democrats and the Intransigent Party. It proceeded to issue moderate demands for a change in economic policy and a degree of political democracy for tolerated bourgeois parties. *But the leadership of these parties represented political and economic opposition within the system.* Their economic limits will be extensively documented in chapter six. As to their political role, the fact that they 'forgot' other forces within the so-called popular camp, in their call for political legality, had the effect of marginalizing the democratic aspirations of broad sectors of the nation, and particularly of the Mothers of the Plaza de Mayo and similar groups. The Multipartidaria's first public declaration, and the totality of its activity during subsequent months, are a sign of all this.[8]

The Multipartidaria, then, proposed to become an oppositional negotiator with the dictatorship. As a matter of fact, its component parties could have achieved this a long time before: already in the last period of Videla's rule — the first of the Junta bosses — the Minister of the Interior had planned a 'political dialogue' that might have allowed him to negotiate from a position of strength with dissenting sectors of the bourgeoisie, without questioning the control of the state by the finance—monopoly sector.

When, as expected, the reins of power were removed from Videla (and the Martínez de Hoz team of economists), the new regime of General Viola made fleeting attempts in March—December 1981 to reconstruct the solid bourgeois front. An agreement was to be reached with the bourgeois opposition through the opening of a dialogue with the political parties and the partial fulfilment of various economic demands. But although a new team of economists under Sigaut, including representatives of the employers' institutions, put an end to the three-year overvaluation of the peso, this did not satisfy any section of society and actually fanned the flames of opposition. The politicians demanded the suspension of military rule and the organization of elections, reflecting the fact that the perspectives of the different capitalist groups were quite incompatible. The workers movement also took advantage of the general political chaos to make considerable advances in rebuilding its organizations and defending its economic interests.

At the same time, the Catholic Church began to distance itself from the regime — an event of enormous symptomatic importance, since the Church tends to represent the general interests of the system and to support its preservation. In May 1981, after five years of silence, tolerance and complacency, the Conference of Argentinian Bishops issued a document ('Church and National Community') criticizing the excesses of repression and pointing out the dangers of 'usury, anathematized in the Bible'.[9] Following this statement by the ecclesiastical hierarchy, some bishops with a record of democratic and humanitarian positions began to engage in open activity, and 'worker priests' re-emerged in working-class dioceses like Avellanda, Villa Dominico and Landus (all in the Buenos Aires industrial zone). Their sermons played an important role in preparations for the peaceful march of 7 November 1981.

A strong sign that the crisis was beginning to corrode the monolithic state-military apparatus, was the appearance of open contradictions among the official spokesmen and between Viola and the Military Junta. One might even say that he was a president who suffered a *capitis diminutio* from the very moment he took office. For the Junta took the opportunity to affirm that it was the real holder of power.

These open contradictions were accompanied by others, more secret and difficult to detect, which blossomed at the very heart of the armed forces. Indeed, the spectre of a new military coup began to emerge, as the spotlight was trained on various active or retired military chiefs: above all, the former commander-in-chief of the army and dictator from 1966 to 1970, Juan Carlos Onganía. Viola's government was paralysed by this pell-mell accumulation of problems which, in the end, led to his bloodless and legal ouster on grounds of illness. The time came for Galtieri to inaugurate a new stage of military government. His twin tasks were to see the ruling-class project through to the end, and to restore the legitimacy of the state and the dominant fractions of the bourgeoisie. He tried to accomplish the first by appointing Alemann Minister of Economics, the second by undertaking the Malvinas adventure.

(c) The Social Crisis

In the second half of 1980, the resurgence of mass action went so deep that it pushed the Multipartidaria to the 'left' — particularly certain currents within its constituent parties. It was never the leading representative of the people's aspirations, but was dragged along behind them. All this accentuated the isolation of the groups in power, indirectly sheltering the mass movement.

The state apparatus was increasingly incapable of controlling or repressing these developments. On several occasions it proved too weak or indecisive to enforce the ban on public assembly. Different police forces and commanders did not know whether to authorize rallies or not, and it gradually became the rule that the stronger the tone of opposition, the more successful were the acts of protest. More profoundly still, the economic crisis, the splintering of the bourgeois bloc and the contradictions at the heart of the state apparatus facilitated the reactivation of a very experienced and conscious working class, whose organizational tradition could not be totally destroyed by repression.

As early as September–October 1976 the dictatorship had had to cope with major strikes by automobile workers, electricians, bank employees and telephonists. But it had then been a question of sporadic, even desperate, actions unlikely to ignite wider support. From 1979, influenced by an upturn in the economy, the tide of factory conflicts began to rise, acquiring greatest force in the Buenos Aires industrial heartland, but spreading to virtually the whole of the country.[10] The working class began to regroup and resist by sections and departments, and partly recovered its former wage levels. This process gained further momentum in 1981, spurred on by the inter-bourgeois conflicts. Sectors of the Peronist union bureaucracy reconstituted the dissolved General Workers Confederation (CGT). And although this was led by old foes of the militant Left, without consultation with the base, it did begin to serve as a point of reference for workers who wanted to fight the dictatorship.

In June 1981, the automobile workers started marching again, with a general strike and assemblies at which street demonstrations were proposed. The dictatorship reacted by hugely increasing its military presence and jailing some 4,000 workers (according to *El Dia* and *Uno Mas Uno* newspapers). On 22 July, however, the Federal Police reported that more than one and a half million workers had answered a general strike call issued by the CGT. The response was particularly strong among workers in food, metallurgy, automobiles, textiles, the docks, the railway workshops, and certain train lines, and it spread out from Buenos Aires to the main industrial conurbations. Many small and medium-sized traders shut up shop in support of the strike.

On 7 November a mass commemorating Saint Cayetano, patron saint of labour, was used by the unions as a vehicle for a peaceful, 50,000-strong march for 'Peace, Bread and Work', which brought together employed and unemployed, blue-collar and white-collar workers. This highly significant action, though still of a defensive character, pointed to the beginning of the transformation of the anti-Junta resistance.[11] For the first time since the 1976 military coup, the workers and the exploited made their presence felt not only by making specific demands, but also by raising slogans that questioned the regime's policy in its entirety.

In February 1982 a small event pregnant with consequences suggested another step forward: a column of unionists joined the protests of the Mothers of the Plaza de Mayo outside the presidential palace, signalling the way for a broad worker–popular front *led by the base* to confront the dictatorship. In the first half of the year, the protests generally intensified, and the atmosphere grew thinner and tenser. The factory strikes and workers' actions spread rapidly to nearly all branches of industry, and it became clear that the organs of immediate struggle of the workers' movement were being partially restored (shop stewards, factory committees, etc.). At the same time, the bureaucratic summit was gradually hardening its stance and drawing up more limited plans of action.

The struggle of the Mothers had a growing resonance at home and abroad. Even the Multipartidaria began to see that it had to recognize their incessant demands, declaring that it constituted a priority problem although no mention had been made of it in the founding document of the alliance. Thousands of women carrying pots and pans led the street demonstrations in Buenos Aires and Rosario against the government's economic policy, the high cost of living and unemployment. The university students also began to recover from the ferocious repression and organized rallies and demonstrations in Buenos Aires, La Plata and Córdoba against the high fees, entry quotas and the whole range of anti-democratic measures applied against young people in the centres of learning.

Intellectuals and artists, who until 1981 had accepted almost with docility the regime of censorship and self-censorship, even the death of some of their comrades, now began to denounce the cultural fetters and repression, the fate of the *desaparecidos,* and the general climate of authoritarianism. The second declaration in this vein was signed by the Writers Union, the Actors Association, the Plastic Arts Society, the organization of Argentinian Film Directors, and the Pen Club — that is to say, practically all the corporate bodies of the 'humanist' intelligentsia. Traditionally pliant groups such as the Buenos Aires Lawyers Association publicly condemned the practice of torture, and even the civil and criminal courts began to hand down sentences that were out of line with official policy. All these developments were a clear sign that the professional, intellectual and middle layers who had supported the need for 'peace and order' in 1976 were growing ever more exasperated with the military dictatorship.

Finally, on 30 March 1982, some fifteen thousand demonstrators confronted a terrified repressive apparatus all along the roads stretching from the working-class suburbs to the city centre. From eleven o'clock in the morning until seven o'clock in the evening, they fought and demonstrated under such slogans as 'Peace, Bread and Work' and 'The Military Dictatorship is Near Its End', relying on their experience of street combat and the tactic of rapid dispersal and regroupment. There were also violent clashes in Mendoza, and thousands demonstrated peacefully in Rosario. In Córdoba columns led by ten assault tanks took charge of the city, while the police broke up assemblies at the Renault, Ilasa, Transax and other factories. The Mothers of the Plaza de Mayo took part in the day of action, supported by various political parties and human rights groups. At least one person was killed and many wounded by bullets, and more than two thousand were arrested by the repressive forces.

If the march of 7 November showed how widespread and unified the resistance had become, the mobilization of 30 March saw the working masses beginning to fight the dictatorship for control of the streets. Such was the internal situation when the military embarked upon the Malvinas landing: an uncontrollable worsening of the economic crisis; contradictions in the armed forces and disintegration of the bourgeois front; isolation of the military, monopolist and financial pinnacle from the rest of society; and great advances in the mass movement and the struggle for democracy. This whole process set the country on the road to a social explosion, and the declarations made by various sections of the dominant class increasingly warned of precisely such a danger. One of its 'organic intellectuals', Roberto Roth, baldly described the situation as follows: 'Argentina is on the brink of a serious convulsion, due to unrestrained corruption and the official economic policy. Society will tolerate Galtieri even less than it did Viola.'[12]

2. Internal Political Significance of the Malvinas Initiative

Against this background, the main objective of the Junta in 'recovering' the Malvinas was to forge a new basis for consensus and to relegitimize the state and the monopoly–finance fractions controlling it.

The reintegration of the archipelago after 149 years of British occupation did allow the Junta in the first instance to unite around itself the principal fractions and parties of the bourgeoisie, including those hardest hit by its economic policy. The Multipartidaria's response from 2 April onwards clearly showed, that the assessment of the armed forces had not been mistaken. At the same time, the men in uniform were able to cease appearing as the oppressors of the nation, the economic agents of the monopolies, and to become again a liberation army garbed in the shining colours of San Martín.[13] From being the army of the 'dirty war', they would turn into patriots bent on recovering for the nation a portion of territory under imperial occupation. And having risked their lives in defence of the nation, they would become the dispensers of reward and punishment. All dissent would constitute an outrage against the architects and guarantors of national integrity, who would be in a position to choose their allies and judge their enemies. No one would feel able to discuss its leadership merits or to question the course it charted in the economy, polity and society.

This perspective naturally implied that any continuing movement for democracy would itself become isolated and deprived of moral and political support. Morally, the Mothers of the Plaza de Mayo would be branded as the parents of 'reprobates' who had died or disappeared for offending the guardians of the nation. Politically and socially, they would stand alone on the side of the 'traitors'. The 'war against subversion' would be sanctified as the necessary prelude to the war for the Malvinas.

In a strategic sense, however, the main result would be to strengthen the most opportunist currents within the mass movement, so that the working class could be demobilized and infected with the chauvinist virus of the big bourgeoisie. For reasons relating to Argentina's social and political history — the importance of the Irigoyenist 'national-democratic' movement in the first decades of the twentieth century, the role of the 'national-reformist' Peronist experience in shaping the consciousness of very broad sections of the masses — the agrarian-based monopoly–finance sector had never been able to achieve the necessary consensus within civil society. In successive elections its parties had never won more than five to ten per cent of the vote — indeed, the governments which expressed its interests had had to impose themselves through coups d'etat, proscriptions and sensational frauds. Now, in the early months of 1982, they had even less support than during the *decada infame* of the thirties: any attempt by the military to organize pseudo-democratic elections would inevitably result in an overwhelming victory for rival bourgeois factions. Thus, a successful recovery of the Malvinas would make it possible to construct a nationalist current directly linked to the armed forces — one that would acknowledge them as the 'national leadership' and draw along sizeable sectors of the mass movement. A spectacular reversal of the country's political history would finally consolidate the naked, exclusive and direct rule of monopoly–finance capital and its military agencies.

This had also become a crucial necessity because of the level of development reached by Argentinian capitalism, in which fractions geared to the world market occupied the dominant position. By strengthening itself internally, the Junta hoped to build a platform from which to launch Argentina as a major world power, with a decisive weight in South America.

3. The Dream of Becoming a World Power

The ideology of *Argentina Potencia,* Argentina as a 'great power' 'at the level of the most advanced countries', has been present as a possibility or an illusion in most of the substantive historical projects of the national bourgeoisie — from the generation of '37 (Echeverria, Alberdi and, to a degree, Sarmiento) until the so-called eighties generation, from the diplomatic campaign of the liberal-conservative Saavedra Lamas and the tenacious resistance of both conservatives and radicals to US-led pan-Americanism, right up to the militarist conceptions inspired by

Clausewitz's theory of 'total war'. In more recent years (1973-74), Perón and Gelbard specifically referred to the task of making Argentina a great power, basing themselves on a multi-class accord between the state, national businessmen and union bureaucrats, yet preserving a relative autonomy from world capitalism. Paradoxically, the plan introduced by the Junta and Martínez de Hoz also invoked such an idea, although now it was to involve full integration into the international economy, a radical transformation of the productive and financial economy, and the crushing of the popular and working-class movement.[14]

Advances in the concentration and centralization of capital, and in the formation of an autonomous finance capital, gave the dream of *Argentina Potencia* an objective material base that squared with the pretensions of the Argentinian bourgeoisie to play a leading (or even hegemonic) role in the region.[15] In the economic sphere, the development of an arms industry (Pucara aeroplanes, VAM tanks, VCI combat vehicles, etc.), and of a nuclear programme enabling it to process the plutonium required for an atomic weapons capacity, form part of the same tendency. In the political-military sphere, Viola launched his 'doctrine of continental security' at a conference of army commanders-in-chief in Bogota in 1979. This expressed not only Argentina's willingness to offer the services of its armed forces to other countries, but also the hope that Argentina would play a major role within the counter-revolutionary alliance.

The new profile took shape in Argentina's direct planning and execution of the Bolivian military coup of 1980, and with even greater force in its widespread involvement in Central America. (See the appendix to this chapter.) It is important to understand that this did not express a relationship of practical subordination to the United States, as the Malvinas War would so strikingly demonstrate.[16] Rather, it marked the onset of an all-round counter-revolutionary alliance with the United States, to share, as minor partner, in the 'tutelage' of less-developed bourgeoisies.[17] This, of course, provided the illusion that the Junta was a privileged ally of the Yankees, and that they would give their backing to its Malvinas initiative.

In turn, the attempt to 'recover' the Malvinas formed part of the Junta's regional great-power ambitions and was a 'logical' consequence of its intervention in Bolivia and Central America. The military were not driven by a sudden patriotic impulse to take the Malvinas, but by the need to strengthen their national and international position.

Possession of the archipelago undoubtedly boosted the claim of Argentinian monopoly and finance capital to have a major stake in the distribution of the world market, and hence in the oppression and exploitation of proletariats other than their own. From an economic point of view it would greatly strengthen the hand of the dictatorship in the coming struggle for the Antarctic; while the control of oil and krill resources, combined with the projected privatization of major areas of the soil and subsoil, would give it a powerful lever in negotiations with the transnationals. At the military–strategic level, the Malvinas would offer an immediate base for US forces in the South Atlantic,[18] free of the problems that a similar British presence would pose for Latin American public opinion. Above all, however, this would give the Junta a massive lever in negotiating a deal that would extend its role in the Southern Cone and enhance the opportunities for big capital in Central and Southern America. Finally, Argentina would be able, together with South Africa, to exercise strict and effective supervision over the South Atlantic and the southern passage, so that any future South Atlantic Treaty Organization would be securely founded upon two highly anti-revolutionary regimes unhampered by democratic constraints.

With regard to the Southern Cone (Chile, Bolivia, Paraguay, Uruguay, and also Brazil and Peru), occupation of the islands would more than compensate for the possible loss of the Beagle islets, reinforce Argentinian dominance over the bourgeoisies of those countries, counter-balance advantages acquired by Brazil in the age-old rivalry with Argentina, and offer a more solid base for the traditional alliance between the Argentinian and Peruvian armies.

In all respects, then, the characterization of the Malvinas conflict as a reactionary war with reactionary aims is fully confirmed. The worst favour that could have been done for the Argentinian people and the peoples of central and South America would have been to support this desperate, though objectively rooted, attempt of the military–terrorist regime of monopoly–finance capital to consolidate itself nationally and internationally.[19]

Appendix: The Interventionist Military Policy in Latin America

The record of external intervention by the Argentinian military dictatorship may be examined under three broad headings.

Intervention in the Bolivian coup of 1980. The participation of the Argentinian armed forces in the García Meza coup of July 1980 came to light almost immediately after the event. Indeed, General Videla admitted as much in August of that year, at a press conference in Córdoba: 'Between a formally correct option (electoral determination) and a formally incorrect one (military coup), we have viewed the second with greater sympathy because of the degree of risk faced by the Argentinian government. It is worth saying what the risk was: we do not want to see in South America what Cuba has become in Central America.'

Argentina's participation in the coup had many facets: (a) creation of a suitable psychological climate through assassinations and so forth; (b) the supply of military hardware; (c) the supply of food for the Bolivian Army, against the possibility of a strike; (d) technical training in intelligence, coordination and execution of the coup; (e) command of the military and paramilitary commandos that seized the COB union federation and assassinated Marcelo Quiroga Santa Cruz; (f) management of the torture centres to which captured militants were taken; and (g) the granting of a $200m loan after the coup.

In January 1982 three lieutenant-colonels of the Argentinian Army were decorated in Bolivia for their services to the local armed forces. Lt. – Col. César Durand said at the award ceremony that 'today, as before, a group of Argentinian soldiers are present within the Bolivian army, fighting to preserve freedom'.[20]

Intervention in Central America. In mid-1981 the presence of Argentinian officers in several Central American countries became public knowledge. Journalists have since reliably reported the following events: (a) the conversion of the Argentinian embassy in Panama into a huge intelligence and logistics centre, staffed by more than sixty 'military attachés', and the appointment as ambassador of the man responsible for Argentina's Joint Chiefs-of-Staff intelligence; (b) the establishment of a similar centre in Honduras; (c) the training of more than 200 Guatemalan officers in 'interrogation techniques' (torture) and repressive methods, at Argentinian military bases; (d) participation in the training at US military bases of officers and elite troops of the

Salvadorean army; (e) training and combat leadership for incursions by Somocista bands based in Honduras; (f) logistic and economic support for the 'Nicaraguan Democratic Force' in its plot to overthrow the Sandinista regime; (g) the despatch of at least fifty more officers to Honduras as para-military troops to intervene in counter-revolutionary activities throughout the region, particularly against Nicaragua; (h) the supply of arms and ammunition to the Guatemalan regime; (i) direct participation in torture sessions in Guatemala,and — together with Israeli officers — the creation of an 'intelligence centre' in that country; (j) the organization of para-military bands along the lines of the Triple A in Costa Rica, repeated attacks on Radio Noticias del Continente, and a press campaign of intimidation of democratic public figures in that country; (k) training, advice and leadership of combat troops in El Salvador (the FMLN has revealed that more than 120 Argentinian military advisers have been killed in El Salvador, including one killed in combat in the uniform of the crack Atlacatl counter-insurgency batallion). This review, obviously incomplete, is based on data made public by sources in the US Congress, US and Argentinian newspapers, the Sandinista government and the FMLN.

In the political sphere, the key role of Argentinian diplomats in the 'Declaration of the 9' — which condemned The Franco-Mexican communiqué as 'interference' in the Salvadorean conflict — is by now notorious. Economic aid to the Salvadorean Christian Democrat Junta is certainly not less than 15m dollars.

The political prospects envisaged by the military regime in Argentina are clearly expressed in the declarations of its ambassador to Washington: 'The Argentinian government considers itself to be a friend of the United States. We have given strong support to many US initiatives in the hemisphere. We recognize the dangers of the campaigns organized to undermine the forces of liberty in the hemisphere, because we ourselves have experienced a subversive war. In the name of my government, I can assure you that we look forward to a sustained period of cooperation with the United States' (4 February 1982).

It should be added that the 14th Conference of American Armies held in Washington in November 1981, at which Galtieri played a central role, adopted three basic policy decisions: to define everything 'revolutionary' as 'terrorist'; to use all means at their disposal to combat Marxist subversion; and to set up an integrated intelligence centre.

Counter-revolutionary Police and Military Operations in the Southern Cone. The Argentinian Junta developed a substantial repressive apparatus outside its borders as one of its first steps in police and military expansionism. Its accomplishments include: (a) the kidnapping and 'disappearance' of exiles in Uruguay, Paraguay, Brazil, Venezuela and Peru (witness the hair-raising case of Sra. de Molfino, kidnapped with her four companions in Peru and found dead in Madrid); (b) the signing of counter-insurgency intelligence treaties with Brazil, Chile and Uruguay;[21] (c) the free supply of arms to the Paraguayan and Uruguayan military regimes, 'with the aim of achieving a real and effective integration of Latin American countries';[22] and (d) the exchange of political prisoners with all countries of the Southern Cone, under the terms of the so-called Condor Operation to exterminate all opposition in the region.

4

The War for the Malvinas

The sense of shock which the Malvinas conflict caused in the Argentinian and Latin American Left was due to the fact that many currents saw it as a 'just' war, yet could not deny that it was being conducted by one of the bloodiest anti-working-class and anti-popular dictatorships on the continent. In addition, it pitted against each other two of the closest allies of the United States. Since these sectors nevertheless supported the Junta's initiative, and not merely the justness of the claim to the islands, it is important to understand why they arrived at that position.

In the course of the twentieth century, humanity has suffered two major imperialist wars designed to redivide and dominate the world, as well as a number of liberation wars for full national independence (e.g., Algeria, Angola, Vietnam) which also evinced the features of a class war between the nationally dominant classes and the exploited and oppressed masses. Basing themselves on this historical reality, however, many currents began to act — at the level of international politics — as if these were the only possible forms of military conflict. In particular, they tended to identify any confrontation between a small country and one of the great capitalist powers as by definition a just and progressive conflict, even viewing diplomatic and economic contradictions in the same light.[1] Thus, the confused typology of nations that we discussed in chapter one was carried over, in the military sphere, into the characterization of wars and conflicts.

We can see this mechanism operating very clearly in the case of the Malvinas. The fact that the war was fought between a power which has rightly aroused the hatred of oppressed humanity, and a country which 'third worldists' still see as belonging to their camp, led to the condemnation of Britain's war-like response as a rebirth of old-style imperialism, or as a 'colonial expedition' comparable to those mounted against Argentina itself in the nineteenth century (the invasions of 1806 and 1807 and the conflicts of the 1830s and 1840s). What was absent from this analysis was any differentiation of the 'Third World' in terms of economic development and class structure. Economic dependence was simply conflated with political subordination, and the Malvinas War was accordingly interpreted as a conflict between an 'oppressed' and an 'oppressor' nation.

Our position is radically opposed to such ideological conceptions prevailing in broad democratic, progressive and even revolutionary circles. Their scant understanding of the basic tendencies of the contemporary world prevents them from developing a policy that will effectively encourage mass struggles against exploitation and oppression. Moreover, they find themselves helpless to provide a clear orientation in the Malvinas-type conflict that is becoming increasingly common.

1.The Revolutionary Marxist Attitude to Wars

In order to assess the various positions taken on the Malvinas War, we must first analyse the elements which revolutionary Marxism has regarded as essential in defining the character of any given war. Quite clearly, Marxism does not offer an indiscriminate apology for peace, and still less for war.[2] The fundamental task is to determine the objective conditions and the precise nature of the conflict, according to Clausewitz's famous principle that 'war is merely the continuation of politics by other means'.[3]

This implies that before deciding on the justness or unjustness of a military confrontation, *we must make an analysis of the nations involved and of the classes which have a direct interest in its pursuit.* We must specify whether it is a question of imperialist powers, politically independent countries, colonies or semi-colonies, whether the war aims are those of progressive or reactionary, exploited or exploiter classes, and whether any of the combatant nations is the object of subjugation or aggression.

In general, it is possible to say that a war is just and progressive whenever it serves to combat national, political or social oppression, and to foster the emergence of higher, more democratic forms of social and political organization. There are three main types of such a war. The first encompasses national—revolutionary or national—democratic wars, which express movements of national self-determination, in a broad sense of the term, against a foreign power and its internal agents, or against an oppressor nationality within a multinational state. The second type is the bourgeois–democratic or popular–democratic civil war[4] against an autocratic, reactionary state or government (the first phase of the Mexican Revolution, the Russian revolution of February 1917, or the Nicaraguan and Iranian revolutions of 1979). The third is the revolutionary civil or class war against social exploitation by capitalists or landowners.

As regards wars between independent countries, the only ones we can consider just are those in which a weaker country legitimately resists an economically and politically more powerful country that is seeking to conquer it, to break it up or to extract economic or political concessions by force. In such cases, the rights of the weaker country are based upon democratic principles: non-intervention in the internal affairs of another country, peaceful settlement of international disputes, and respect for the self-determination of peoples.

Now, it is an established historical fact that just and progressive wars have always involved forms of widespread popular mobilization or participation. *The more reactionary and regressive the political motives for a conflict, the more it tends to assume the form of a conventional war under the strict control of the possessors of 'the martial art', without any significant mass participation or mobilization. Thus, the content conditions not only the character of the war, but also the general nature of the military methods employed.*[5]

If we take the wars of the French Revolution as an example, it is clear that a 'nation in arms', liberated from the feudal yoke, confronted mercenary armies generally recruited by press-gangs and led by absolutist princes. (Napoleon's army, although a perfectly hierarchical war machine, reflected this moral and political superiority.) Even in the Spanish-American wars of independence, which were often led by conservative military men like San Martín and O'Higgins, the general tendency was to combine conventional armies and forms of warfare with expressions of popular war such as Güemes's *montoneros* and their counterparts in Upper Peru (now Bolivia), Páez's *llaneros* and the radical wing of Hidalgo and Morelos.

Wars for a just cause, even when waged under reactionary generals, have always aroused the fervour and active participation of the masses, and have tended to spark off deep popular mobilizations for social and political objectives. Twentieth-century examples would include: the Ethiopian national resistance—led by none other than the feudal Haile Selassie—against the Italian invasion in 1935; the support of the Hindu masses for the bourgeois leadership of Gandhi and Nehru; and the massive support for the Kuomintang during the 1924–27 revolution and 'march to the north'. The fervour of the masses for a just war has even compelled reactionary leaders to reach a compromise, albeit unstable and contradictory, with the unfolding popular mobilization. Once again China provides a clear illustration of this, with the agreement between the Kuomintang and the Communist Party during the anti-Japanese war.

By contrast, the two world wars had the conventional military characteristics of a reactionary war, while the French and US campaigns in Indochina further elucidate the opposition between conventional wars with reactionary aims and popular wars with revolutionary goals. It was precisely the conceptualization of this distinction which led Mao Tse-tung and Ngyuen Giap to develop a new military theory adapted to the conditions of an agrarian society. This contains aspects applicable to all truly popular wars that must be incorporated into the Marxist theory of revolutionary wars and popular insurrections.

2. The Changing Content of Wars

(a) The Post-War Period

The period after 1945 was dominated by movements of national liberation in the old colonial and semi-colonial countries. The popular masses were the leading historical protagonists in this process, paving the way for the emergence of new nation-states and the consolidation of those already in existence. Ho Chi Minh's famous statement, 'Independence is the supreme good', powerfully captures the thinking not only of the intellectuals and upper strata of oppressed societies, but above all of the millions and millions who constituted the popular forces of the liberation struggle.

It was precisely this period — from the anti-Japanese national war in China, through the liberation struggles in South-East Asia and Algeria, to the victories in Mozambique, Angola and Guinea-Bissau — which created the false impression that any conflict whatsoever with one of the major capitalist powers was a struggle for national liberation. This was true in many cases, where a colonial or semi-colonial country confronted the metropolis and the indigenous masses entered into battle against their mainly foreign oppressors. However, the state and class structures of these countries were radically reorganized as a result of their successful struggles. Whereas only a small minority of politically independent nations existed at the beginning of the period, some ninety-five per cent of the post-colonial world was divided up into sovereign states possessing their own constitution, currency, army, civil service, commercial and penal legislation. They were recognized internationally as autonomous entities, with a place of their own at the United Nations; and their internal markets were undergoing various degrees of development.

Within this new reality, pre-capitalist relics generally became less and less significant and the remaining colonial territories ever more marginal.[6] At the same time, two new types of conflict came to prominence: the economic, military and political contradictions between the 'socialist bloc' and the imperialist system led by the United States; and revolutionary civil wars of a class character.

The first of these tendencies involved the presence of a global East—West conflict within the clashes between particular countries. For its part, the USSR, as the practically undisputed head of the 'socialist bloc',[7] tended to support movements of national liberation, especially those which challenged US imperialism and were led or strongly influenced by the local Communist party. The clearest illustration of this was the prolonged Vietnam war. But in the case of struggles for self-determination against colonial powers with which the Soviet Union was not in open conflict, its policy was ambiguous, wavering and even hostile. Examples here would be the early attitude of Moscow and the PCF to the Algerian FLN; the abandonment of Patrice Lumumba to his fate at the beginning of the 1960s; the initial policy of the Cuban CP (the Popular Socialist Party) towards the 26th of July Movement; support for the creation of the Zionist state in 1948, and the long delay in establishing relations with the Palestinian revolution. In the case of the Sino-Indian frontier dispute, Moscow even gave its support to a cause which cannot in any sense be regarded as progressive.

On the other hand, the reactionary and oppressive character of US policy was demonstrated by its clashes with liberation movements, above all when these specifically challenged US interests (the Phillipines), or were seen to be developing in an anti-capitalist direction (Vietnam) or tending to side with the

Soviet Union in the 'global contest' (Angola). Where none of these factors came into play, however, Washington was quite capable of adopting a more nuanced position — witness its good relations with the Indian and (initially) the Indonesian liberation movements, or its crucial diplomatic support for Nasser's Egypt against the Anglo–Franco–Israeli aggression.

Two myths have arisen on the basis of post-war history: one is the 'unstinting' support of the socialist bloc for just wars; the other is the unvarying frontal opposition of the United States. Both myths are part of the growing ideologization of the contemporary world and, with respect to the Left, form part of the Stalinist inheritance from the Cold War. The truth is that each of the major powers has formulated its policies and lines of action as a function of its own national interest. Although the USSR and the United States have a different social nature, their mere alignment with one or another party to a conflict is not a *sufficient* criterion to characterize it as 'progressive' or 'reactionary'. This can only be determined by an analysis of the countries in conflict, and of the classes that stand to gain from its pursuit.

The second new tendency in the modern world which concerns us here is *the advance of class struggles by the oppressed and exploited against their internal and external subjugators.* Again the Chinese and Vietnamese liberation struggles are the clearest case in point, both having increasingly combined the features of a struggle for national self-determination with those of a social war against the internal exploiting classes. In Latin America, the first such development in the post-war period was the Bolivian revolution of 1952, in which the mining proletariat and armed workers' militias played a leading role. Although it was in essence a bourgeois–democratic revolution, it had greater real significance than distant precedents like the insurrections led by Farabundo Marti in El Salvador or the Prestes Column in Brazil. In 1961 the Playa Girón was the arena of a new step forward, when the Cuban masses inflicted a crushing military defeat on the coalition formed by US monopoly capitalism and Cuban capitalists affected by the revolution. Five years earlier, a national–democratic movement with an essentially proletarian base and orientation had thrown up organs of direct popular and working-class power in the struggle against Soviet intervention in Hungary. This was another high point in the unfolding process of class war — however paradoxical that judgement may appear to those on the left with fashionable views.

(b) New Types of Civil and Inter-State Wars

New types of conflict have developed in recent years which express the economic and political changes in the world. The main operative tendencies are as follows: (i) the emergence of deep-seated contradictions among the imperialist countries within a context of continuing internationalization (weakening of the United States vis-à-vis Japan and the EEC); (ii) deepening of the crisis within and among the countries of the 'socialist camp'; (iii) a significant maturation of capitalism in the so-called Third World, with the rise of new regional capitalist powers and the intensification of contradictions between capital and labour; (iv) a drift of the whole world capitalist system towards crisis, beginning in the mid-1960s and gaining momentum since the early 1970s.

As we have seen, the conflict between colonies or semi-colonies and the metropolitan powers has lost most of its former prominence. The appearance of newly independent capitalist and non-capitalist countries, together with the rise of struggles between the oppressed and dominant classes, has tended to generalize the tendencies of the earlier period and to produce a new complex of political and military confrontations. First, we should mention *the armed conflicts within the 'socialist bloc'*. Although we cannot dwell on these here, since they would require a broad historical and political analysis of their own, we can state that there is no possibility of recovering the communist perspective without a balance-sheet that rises above national interests and subordinates them to the interests of the international proletariat. From the point of view of the world working class, and even of general democratic principles, all such wars have a reactionary content which involves the primacy of the narrow limits, interests and conceptions of the nation-state.[8]

Secondly, *a new type of revolutionary – democratic civil war has emerged* from the post-colonial advance of capitalist industrialism, the strengthening of the nation-state and politico-military bureaucracies in the backward countries, and the development of an explosive world crisis. The signs of this were already apparent in the turbulent events of 1968, but the years since then have witnessed a succession of mass struggles. In Latin America the Argentinian workers rose to the heights of the Cordobazo in 1969 and the Rodrizago in 1975; the Chilean masses threw up a chain of *cordones industriales* and launched a wave of factory occupations in the early 1970s; a movement of workers, students and peasants thwarted the Natusch Busch coup in Bolivia; the Brazilian proletariat developed its organizational strength and strike activity; and the Nicaraguan and Salvadorean peoples took the road of full-scale civil war against their ruling oligarchies. At the same time, there have been unprecedented strike movements and semi-insurrectional explosions in Asian and African countries such as Egypt, Turkey and South Korea; while in the eastern bloc the Prague Spring was followed by a series of working-class upsurges in Poland that culminated in the formation of Solidarnosc.

Most of these movements have not directly ignited revolution-ary or proletarian–popular civil wars. But they destabilized the existing regimes to such a point that the bourgeoisies could only respond by unleashing counter-revolutionary military coups and installing a system of state terror — for example, in the Southern Cone of Latin America, and in Guatemala and El Salvador. The emergence of state terrorism in Turkey also seems to have been largely due to the power of the mass movement.[9] These developments, to which should be added the popular mobiliza-tions against the war in Vietnam and the current peace movements in Europe, Japan and the United States, brought about the gradual collapse of the bureaucratic–reformist and national–populist structures that corresponded to the previous phase of social and political struggles in the world.

The third important trend of recent times is *the multiplication of 'new' inter-capitalist wars* between politically independent countries.[10] Their essential protagonists are not state-monopoly powers of the first order, but capitalist groups fighting to extend their influence in various regions and, in many cases, rapidly advancing towards 'their own' state-monopoly capitalism and autonomous finance capital. Such wars were already a feature of the end of the decolonization process: for instance, the struggle between India and Pakistan for Kashmir and Bangladesh, or between Greece and Turkey for control of Cyprus and the Aegean Sea. Even the so-called 'football war' between Honduras and El Salvador in 1969 expressed not only the break-up of the Central American Common Market, but the rivalry of two bourgeoisies to extend or protect their economic space. The conflicts between Iran and Iraq, Peru and Ecuador, Ethiopia and Somalia, as well as the tensions between Guatemala and Belize, Venezuela and Guyana, Chile and Argentina — all these correspond to a stage at which regionally strong bourgeoisies are trying to strengthen themselves at their neighbours' expense. The confrontation between Morocco and Algeria over the ex-Spanish Sahara represents a specific case in which a national liberation movement (Polisario) is combated or supported as a function of the particular interests of two local bourgeoisies.

In general, therefore, we can say that these wars between newly independent capitalist countries do not constitute a progressive phenomenon. On the basis of fully constituted nations and states, *they tend to reinforce the interests and positions of the most developed sectors of capital, which are able to compete for regional dominance or hegemony through the expansion of emergent national monopoly capital.* Much of the democratic and revolutionary left has been confused about the true nature of these wars because some of the countries in question achieved their final independence under the aegis of democratic wars and strong national liberation movements (Algeria, India, Iraq, Egypt, and so on), and because their expansive thrust has often generated frictions and conflict with old imperialist powers. The tendency is to theorize them as a kind of prolongation of national liberation movements, as if they were anti-colonial or anti-imperialist struggles to liquidate the remnants of a bygone age. However, almost the exact opposite is true: they are wars whose function is to consolidate the national exploiter class; and any contradictions with the old imperialist powers bring into conflict different capitals with different origins and national bases. The whole process essentially favours the monopoly-capitalist classes of the contending countries.

Once the cycle of national struggles had reshaped the capitalist world on the basis of independent political entities, the only 'just' inter-state wars were those in which a weak country resisted the attempts of a stronger power to impose by force disadvantageous conditions that negatively circumscribed its sovereignty. Outside such cases, however, the only just war is one waged by the popular masses against an exploitative or oppressive regime, whether in the West or East, the North or South.

After this survey of the changing content of war, we must now examine certain elements of the Malvinas War and draw some conclusions about the problems which these new tendencies pose for the democratic and revolutionary movement.

3. The Military Expedition and the Causes of Argentina's Defeat

The landing of the Junta's troops on the Malvinas on 2 April 1982 caught virtually everyone by surprise—including the Argentinian people and its democratic and revolutionary organizations at home and in exile. The British government was also taken unawares, despite the reports of its habitually competent intelligence services.

It cannot be said, however, that the action came as a bolt from the blue. Several Argentinian newspapers had for some time been discussing the possibility of 'recovery', and in late January Iglesias Rouco, a columnist on *La Prensa,* had indicated that Buenos Aires was preparing to deliver an ultimatum and 'might consider a forcible solution'. The fact is that although the eventual decision was taken in response to the general worsening of the crisis of the regime, preparations had already been under way for a long time.

(a) Political Preparations for the War

In the internal politics of Argentina, the choice between a diplomatic and a military solution already seems to have played a role in the replacement of Viola by Galtieri in December 1981. According to serious journalists such as Selser of *Le Monde Diplomatique* and E. Riva Palacio of *Excelsior,* Viola had wanted to continue negotiations on the basis of Britain's alternative proposals; but when a recomposition of the Junta brought in the heads of the navy and air force (Jorge Anaya and Basilio Lami Dozo), he suddenly found himself without support. Anaya had a reputation as the most consistent 'hawk' on the problems of the Beagle Channel, the Malvinas and Antarctica, and he was known as co-author of the 'Goa Plan' which had envisaged an occupation of the islands in the late 1960s. Lami Dozo, on the other hand, had failed in his diplomatic efforts to reach agreement with Chile, and was now also in favour of a definitive solution to the disputes. Finally, Galtieri himself, whose extremist temperament had been displayed as head of repressive operations in Rosario, was much more prone than Viola to 'predictable courses of action'. If he retained command of the army, this was not only for internal political reasons but also to assure a unified leadership in the impending crisis with Britain.[11]

In the international sphere, as we have seen, the Junta had

accentuated its belligerently interventionist policy. Galtieri further proposed to withdraw from the Non-Aligned Movement, agreed to raise Argentina's participation in international counter-revolutionary activities, and opened talks with Washington on the establishment of US bases in Patagonia, so that the North Americans could control navigation around Cape Horn and the Magellan Straits. There is quite strong evidence that the Malvinas were also the subject of discussion between US and Argentinian officers during this period.[12]

Such services to the 'Christian West' were the objective basis for the Junta's belief that it could count on full US support for a Malvinas operation — hence the extremely rapid acceptance of Alexander Haig as a mediator in the first phase of the conflict. The Junta also probably calculated that Washington would not allow a confrontation between two of its closest allies, and that it would press Britain, after an initial show of force, to react only in the diplomatic field. Naturally this incorrect assessment would have serious repercussions for the eventual course of the war.

In these two areas of war preparation (reorganization of the Junta and strengthening of links with the main reactionary power in the world), the Argentinian people were in no way associated with government policy. Indeed, Galtieri's assumption of presidential office was greeted with hatred and contempt, while the turn towards the United States was decided in the secret world of embassies and military conclaves and covered up with disinformation.

(b) Military Preparations for War

The Junta's massive arms programme was a crucial accompaniment to its internal and external political orientation. In Latin American terms, the number of officers, NCOs and privates on permanent duty or training, together with the relative sophistication of war matériel in all three services, has undoubtedly made Argentina a major military power. In order to obtain ultra-modern equipment, the Junta invested some US$13bn during the period from 1980 to 1981. (Even in 1978, as Table 4.1 shows, Argentina had been one of the world's largest per capita spenders on arms.)

In addition to imports, Argentina has a well-developed military industry of its own, inherited from the 1930s, which sells weapons to Chile, Mauritania, Pakistan and Uruguay, as well as providing

Table 4.1
THE COMPARATIVE SIZE OF ARGENTINIAN MILITARY
EXPENDITURE (in current US dollars per capita)

Country	1 Military spending	2 Education	3 Health	Col. 1 as % of Cols. 1-3
Argentina	55	54	11	45.83
USA	499	565	341	35.51
Brazil	18	55	27	18.00
Sweden	365	927	883	16.78
Venezuela	44	149	83	15.94

Source: *World Military and Social Expenditures, 1978.*

Bolivia, Paraguay and Uruguay with free equipment under the terms of tacit pacts of repression. The chief products are TAM tanks (similar to the German Leopard), warplanes like the Pucara (specially designed for anti-guerrilla operations), naval destroyers, light and heavy firearms (rifles, machine-guns, mortars, artillery), and all kinds of ammunition. We should add that there is a crash nuclear energy programme, one aim of which is clearly to fabricate atomic weapons in the near future.[13] This was not a factor in the April–June war, but it demonstrates the level reached by sectors of industry with a military capacity.

In terms of personnel, the Argentinian army, navy and air force are now almost as large as the armed forces of the most developed industrial countries. 185,000 men serve in the three branches, including some 50,000 career officers and NCOs. There are also 43,000 members of the *gendarmeria* (the militarized frontier police), the coastguard and the federal police (which had its trained elite units during the struggle against 'subversion').[14] Had this total force of 230,000 men been equipped with a correct stategy and the fervour of a just national cause, their prospects for victory in the Malvinas would have been far from negligible. For a number of reasons, however, the high command failed to develop a rational strategy and to take the necessary minimum precautions.

First of all, given Britain's naval power and its possession of nuclear submarines, it was easy to foresee that Argentina would be at a distinct disadvantage in any sea battle. The Argentinian navy had benefited the least from the huge rise in arms spending, since the army and airforce had been in the front line during the tensions with Chile over the Beagle Channel. As a result, its equipment had not reached the level of sophistication of the two other branches.

As the sea would therefore be dominated by the British, one of the first battles would inevitably be for the control of air space, to keep open the lines of communication with the Malvinas. The main requirement was for a plentiful supply of mechanics and maintenance services, and an improvement in the network of landing strips and other facilities, particularly in the region of southern Argentina closest to the war zone. There is absolutely no indication, however, that the Junta paid any attention to these points in the months preceding April 1982.[15]

Similarly, it was common knowledge that Britain's professional army was highly trained as a component of NATO and could rely upon various commando and mercenary forces such as the Gurkhas. But instead of pitting against them its best long-service battalions, or even units specially formed from members of the military apparatus and career staff, the Junta sent a mass of barely trained conscripts to defend the Malvinas. On one of the few occasions when it had an elite unit at its disposal—Captain Astiz's 'Lagartos' on the South Georgia Islands — the result was a shameful capitulation.

We may conclude that despite the numerical strength and sophisticated weaponry of the army and air force, the Argentinian high command demonstrated a prodigious incompetence and lack of foresight in embarking upon a military adventure that was condemned from the start.

(c) The Forces in Conflict

As Table 4.2 shows, the British armed forces had an obvious superiority in numbers and matériel, in addition to their better training, organization and technological sophistication. Within the geographical and political limits of the Malvinas War, however, none of these factors provided an overwhelming advantage, and there were some areas in which Argentina had a countervailing pre-eminence.

Firstly, because of international political conditions and the need to avoid a total collapse on the 'American front' of world capitalism, Britain could not threaten to bomb the mainland with its submarine-launched nuclear weapons. In fact, the submarine did not even play a major conventional role, since Argentina did

Table 4.2
THE MILITARY BALANCE OF FORCES

	Britain	Argentina
Army:		
forces	176,248	130,000
tanks	1,414	185
Navy:		
forces	74,687	36,000
submarines	34	4
aircraft-carriers	2	1
cruisers	—	1
destroyers	14	9
frigates	46	—
minesweepers	38	6
patrol boats	25	10
fighter-planes	20	11
helicopters	90	19
Air Force:		
forces	92,701	19,500
bombers	132	9
fighters	325	145

Source: International Institute of Strategic Studies

not mobilize its war fleet or find it necessary to maintain a naval supply route.

Secondly, the long lines of communication (15,000kms from London, 5,000kms from the Ascension Islands) prevented Britain from employing its full military strength in the war theatre. This was a particularly strong obstacle in the case of air activity, where the political veto on bombardment of the mainland bases was compounded by the presence of only two aircraft-carriers. The British Harrier jets, despite their great manoeuvrability, were relatively inferior to the Argentinian Mirages and Skyhawks and had a much shorter operational radius (460kms, against 2,000kms). Thus, during the second phase of the war Britain did not at any time manage to establish air superiority. If the Junta had been able to resolve its problems of maintenance and bomb-priming, it could have inflicted a crushing defeat that would have wiped out the core of the British fleet.[16]

Thirdly, Argentina's three-or-four-to-one superiority in ground troops was only outweighed by the better training and

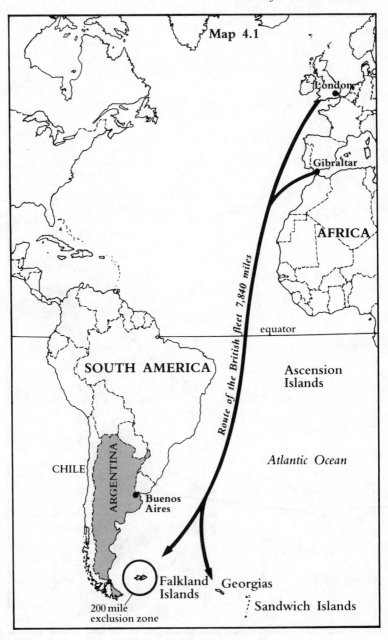

Map 4.1

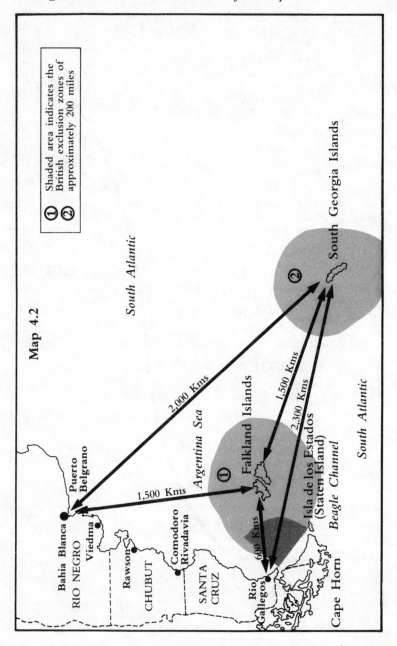

Map 4.2

leadership of the British infantry — a relationship which confirms that the outcome would have been much more problematic if the Junta had adopted a correct strategy and employed the key professional units of the army.

(d) The Three Phases of the War

It appears quite easy and convenient to divide the Malvinas conflict into three distinct phases: (i) the period from the landing of 2 April to the British recapture of the Georgias on 25 April and the declaration of US support for Whitehall on 30 April; (ii) the aerial battle, lasting from the beginning of May until the San Carlos landing on 22-25 May (when the British had very weak air cover and lost a number of landing craft, planes and helicopters); and (iii) the land offensive, stretching from the consolidation of the San Carlos bridgehead through the capture of Goose Green and Port Darwin to the final encirclement and occupation of the capital.

The first phase was dominated by the massive despatch of Argentinian troops and supplies to the islands, the departure and approach of the British 'task force', and the well-reported diplomatic efforts of the US Secretary of State, Alexander Haig. Contrary to the Junta's expectations, the UN Security Council condemned its seizure of the Malvinas — the only opposing vote being cast by the representative of Panama; while the EEC blocked all economic and financial exchanges with Argentina and embargoed further arms supplies. Paradoxically Cuba was one of the first countries to express support for the Junta's military initiative, and this was soon echoed at a meeting of the OAS. In hard political terms, however, Buenos Aires was drifting into war at a considerable disadvantage.

The chief military operation of this period was Britain's recapture of the Georgia Islands. The dictatorship had sent there an elite naval commando unit, known as the 'Lagartos', which was composed of officers and NCOs supposedly steeled in the 'internal war'. At some time between 1976 and 1979, all of them had performed duties at the navy's notorious College of Mechanics, one of the main organizing centres of torture and 'disappearances' through which at least four thousand political and social prisoners had passed. This cream of the navy was ordered to 'resist until death'; and before its departure the commanding officer, Captain Alfredo Astiz, had boasted: 'Officers die on their feet. We will give our last drop of blood in defence of the Georgias.'[17] Yet, on 25 April, after the purely token firing of a few shells at British ships, these men surrendered unconditionally. As Admiral Sanguinetti, ex-inspector of the French Navy, had explained a few days before: 'Killing women, unarmed men and children, torture and rape, are not the same as killing Englishmen in combat.'[18] The officers of the Junta's army, even those most hardened by war, had received the major part of their training in torture chambers. Without the political, moral or professional capacity to sustain a just war, they proved to be lacking in any real combat discipline.

The second phase of the conflict, which began on 30 April, was the battle for the skies. One might have expected that in this high-technology form of warfare Britain would demonstrate an overwhelming superiority. But that was not what happened. The 'task force' suffered its harshest setbacks at this point, losing ultra-modern ships like the *Sheffield,* and sustaining damage to as much as sixty per cent of the fleet, possibly including its key aircraft-carriers, the *Hermes* and the *Invincible.*[19] The Argentinian Mirages were at least a match for the Harrier, and towards the end of the war the British were forced to withdraw their fleet beyond the reach of enemy aircraft and to undertake the landing with precious little air cover.

Military experts throughout the world paid the closest attention to the duel between modern electronic equipment (Exocet and Tigerfish missiles, advanced radar, communications systems and ballistic guidance technology).[20] The balance-sheet is that the two sides tended to stay level, although the position of the British became critical at certain times.[21] This completely undermines the Junta's explanation of defeat in terms of Britain's 'technological superiority'. For even if Argentina lost a greater number of warplanes, there were compensating losses and damage to British ships, aircraft and helicopters.

The real turning-point came with the British landing at Port San Carlos, when they were able to assert their pre-eminence in arms and equipment (extra-light sub-machine-guns, durable and fully adequate ration packs, thermal clothing, night-fighting equipment, etc.), and in battle readiness and military strategy. After the speedy consolidation of the San Carlos bridgehead, the mobility of Britain's helicopter-borne troops contrasted starkly with the lack of transport facilities on the Argentinian side. Soon the combination of all these factors produced the surrender of the

Goose Green and Port Darwin garrisons, and then the collapse of the beleaguered defences around Port Stanley after three days of sporadic fighting. General Menéndez, in command of nine thousand Argentinian soldiers, signed the act of surrender to a British force numbering no more than three or four thousand men.

The British advance had been preceded by two weeks of positional manoeuvring in which there were virtually no major battles. Finally, on the night of Friday, 11 June, the British troops used artillery cover to sweep over the hills to the west of the capital. The fiercest fighting took place on Mount Longdon, where at least sixty young Argentinian soldiers lost their lives. The next day, the Argentinian airforce carried out its last strike, causing little damage to British positions and losing one aeroplane to a Sea Dart missile. That night, the British resumed their advance and captured the remaining high ground. With the first rays of sun, the Argentinian soldiers abandoned their defences and began to retreat in ever greater disorder. As the British moved into the outskirts of Port Stanley, with orders not to fire unless attacked, the first white flags made their appearance. The final battle simply did not happen.

(e) Why the Junta Lost the War

Apart from the lack of logistical and technical preparation, which we have already discussed in some detail, the Argentinian defeat was essentially due to a faulty strategy on the part of the Junta. The military men had thought that they could simply despatch a sizeable force to the islands, deploy it in fixed positions, and passively await an enemy landing. There seem to have been no plans to concentrate forces and launch a vigorous counter-attack at the site of such a landing. The British were therefore able to seize the initiative, dictating the general course of operations and achieving numerical superiority at any point they chose. Their powerful surprise attacks gave them a huge psychological advantage and intensified the demoralization of the Argentinian forces.

The British general Jeremy Moore is reported to have said that the Argentinian generals 'were guided by US combat tactics: a show of force, underestimation of secondary objectives, premature concentration of forces, and a certain lack of scruple in risking losses'. The British, on the other hand, preferred 'a gradual approach to the objective, careful planning of actions, the use of tactics to throw the enemy off balance and produce psychological effects, and a general effort to save their men's lives.[22]

Furthermore, the highly bureaucratic nature of the Argentinian military apparatus had bred a generation of officers with an inflexible command structure, slaves to routine and parade-ground discipline and lovers of needless paperwork. Although this may seem a purely formal defect, we should not discount its significance for the lack of cohesion, initiative and fighting morale of their subordinates. Every order had to move slowly and inefficiently along a rigid chain, while the authoritarian and even arbitrary character of the order generated feelings of hatred and contempt, rather than political identification, on the part of the ordinary soldiers. Not surprisingly, they were quite unwilling to act in the absence of the appropriate authorization.

The background in the 'dirty war', with its torture, looting and kidnapping, had given rise to widespread corruption and moral perversion among the commanding officers. Most of them therefore showed overriding concern for their own comfort, security and personal gain, rather than preparations for combat. General Menéndez, for instance, used a supply plane to transport his luxury LTD car to the islands, and ordered personnel under his direct command to fit new carpets and tapestry in his 'governor's residence'. It is also well known that the military would collect chocolate bars from schoolchildren to smuggle to the Malvinas garrison, and one can easily imagine that this was repeated with higher-value commodities such as petrol and tools. As far as personal safety was concerned, there are many reports that officers commanded their troops by radio from a distance of several kilometres. Such displays of moral corruption and brazen cowardice naturally made a deep impression on the young conscripts, who in the middle of their one-year compulsory military service suddenly found themselves left to face the expertly trained professionals of the British army. Nor is it likely that they were deeply convinced about the justness of the war and the necessity of their involvement.

A further demoralizing factor was the deficiency or absence of such crucial items as thermal clothing, communications systems, ammunition and everyday provisions. The contrast was stark indeed between the diet of the average conscript and that of his officers.[23]

All these features of the corrupt, incompetent and authoritarian Argentinian army explain why so many soldiers decided to abandon their trenches around Port Stanley. This was not a sign of cowardice: the officers were generally the first to run; and there is even evidence of sharp conflicts between them and the ranks. Disoriented by the corruption and strategic blundering of the generals, badly clothed, undernourished and exposed to a harsh climate, the mass of soldiers took the only reasonable course of action and brought to an end the adventure launched by Galtieri, Anaya, Lami Dozo, Menéndez and their whole blood-soaked mafia.

(f) 'New Inter-capitalist Wars' and the Malvinas Conflict

We should now summarize our conclusions on the character of the war for the Malvinas and its relevance for national and international politics. Argentina achieved self-determination in the last century and is a politically independent country. It has a high degree of capitalist integration which not only fully constitutes the 'bourgeois nation' but is impelling, at an ever faster pace, the formation of a state monopoly capitalism. The dominance of the highly concentrated and centralized monopoly—finance sectors is combined with the enormous power of the army—state machine over civil society. This capitalist structure has strong expansionist tendencies, cloaked in the ideology of 'Argentina as a great power', which express themselves in the export of capital and an interventionist policy against other Latin American countries (above all, their democratic movements). Argentina's just claim to the Malvinas is a non-essential demand, and British occupation of the islands has in no significant way affected the formation of the state. The classes and class fractions directly interested in a struggle for their recovery were the bourgeoisie and, more specifically, the monopoly—finance sector and its murderous armed forces.

The war, then, was a continuation of the Junta's anti—democratic internal policy and its expansionist external thrust. Although it was waged against British imperialism for a historically legitimate claim, it was neither an anti-colonial conflict nor a struggle by an oppressed against an oppressor nation. The contending parties were an emergent capitalist country with regional and continental imperialist features,[24] and a long-standing imperialist power which, though in marked decline, is still a powerful force. There was not a progressive and a reactionary camp. Both the Junta and Margaret Thatcher represented, and were seen to represent, highly retrograde anti-democratic and anti-working-class sectors of their own society, as well as of the 'Christian West' as a whole. One reactionary side was bent on extending its influence, while the other was concerned to retain the last wisps of its former empire and to establish a pecking order among the national components of the capitalist bloc.

The war did have a relatively novel feature, in that a minor capitalist country used *military force* to challenge the hierarchy of states that emerged from the Second World War. Previously this had only been threatened by revolutionary-democratic movements. It fell to the irresponsible and adventurist Argentinian Junta to take the step that the German and Japanese bourgeoisies had only attempted after endless precautions and under cover of the most subtle diplomatic manoeuvres.

The reactionary content of the war determined its reactionary course. In the absence of any democratic popular participation, Argentina and Britain confronted each other as naked capitalist powers, relying solely on the strength of their military apparatuses and the psychological manipulation of the masses.

4. Positions on the War

In all senses, it seems evident to us that a proletarian policy (and even an honest and consistent national-democratic orientation) had to oppose with vigour the Junta's initiative. There was never any possibility of turning this reactionary, expansionist war into the beginnings of an independent, democratic and revolutionary mobilization of the masses. All dreams of such an outcome could not rise above mere subjectivism or, still worse, objective capitulation to the Junta.

There were only two consistent positions: *either* to reject the war and continue the difficult task of working-class reorganization, around a series of basic demands spontaneously arising from the mass movement and the mobilizations against the dictatorship; *or* to support the war, perhaps criticizing the Junta but in practice collaborating with its war effort and the aims of the monopoly–finance bourgeoisie. Unfortunately the bourgeois parties were not the only ones to adopt the second of these alternatives.[25]

In April—June 1982 there were two positions in support of the war, which employed different arguments and proposed formally dissimilar courses of action. And there was one position which, with minor variations, opposed the adventure and denounced its cost for the working class and the Argentinian people. In the first category the CGT, the Multipartidaria alliance and the Argentinian Communist Party pledged full support for the war as such, while the Montoneros, the PST (Socialist Workers Party) and the PO (Workers' Politics) group started from a characterization of the war as 'patriotic' and sought to transform its reactionary methods and objectives into 'revolutionary' methods and objectives. On the other side, a number of groups that we shall mention later rejected the war and gave priority to basic popular and working-class democratic demands.

(a) Unlimited Support

Deolindo Bittel, vice-president and effective leader of the (Peronist) Justicialista Party, set the tone for the pro-war campaign by stating that 'there should be a truce between soldiers and civilians for the sake of national dignity, until the country had pulled through'. Saul Ubaldini, Peronist leader of the CGT—Brasil, echoed: 'As Argentinians and workers we desire peace, but adopt the principle of defending our islands in the South Atlantic. When the conflict ends, the CGT will continue with its plans to oppose the military government.' In the same interview he declined to make any reference to those who had been arrested and subsequently disappeared. 'To keep talking of this now,' he said, 'would be like bleeding something that bleeds by itself, at a time when a British fleet is approaching the country.' Conclusion: the struggle for democracy should be postponed 'for the sake of national dignity'. Carlos Contín, president of the Radical Civic Union: 'Now is the hour to lay aside all domestic questions, to galvanize the unity of all Argentinians.' Antonio Troccoli, of the same party: 'For the time being we have suspended oppositional activity in order to help repair the internal front.' Oscar Alende, self-proclaimed leader of the 'bourgeois left': 'There is a clear national unity around the Armed Forces. They have interpreted the thought and feelings of the nation. They deserve our full support.' Guillermo Estévez Boero, leader of the social-democratic Popular Socialist Party: 'It cannot be doubted that every moment is the right one for the defence of our sovereignty. In this situation it would not be correct to judge the nature and qualities of the government, because there is a unanimous national will to recover the islands.'[26] A special case, if only in name, was that of the Argentinian Communist Party, which not only backed the military initiative but explicitly pledged the support of the USSR and the 'socialist camp'.[27]

This front of political and union leaders was sanctified at the swearing-in of General Menéndez as governor of the Malvinas. Deolindel Bittel, Contín, Ubaldini, even the 'Trotskyist' nationalist Jorge Abelardo Ramos stood shoulder to shoulder with such worthies as General Videla and his fellow-butchers. Leonidas Saadi, leader of the Peronist 'Intransigents' (a populist grouping that still commanded much support at the time), travelled abroad to argue the Argentinian case, repeating the same tune that 'Argentinians had put aside their internal problems in the face of this graver crisis'. In the meantime, the Junta showed its gratitude by dividing the opportunist trade-union bureaucracy and recognizing its more devoted wing (Triacca, Donaires et al.) as the only legal CGT.[28]

(b) From 'Patriotic' to 'Revolutionary' War

A series of forces that distinguish themselves from the party and CGT bureaucracies surrendered disgracefully to the reactionary pro-war nationalism in an attempt to turn it into a dramatic anti-imperialist gesture. This was even the case of currents proclaiming themselves to be revolutionary-Marxist, including the Trotskyist PST and PO.

The Montoneros, it is true, were quite consistent in their positions, even going to the extreme, in Mexico, of singing the national anthem alongside the Argentinian consul. For them it was simply a just war that the dictatorship was unable to wage successfully. They therefore advocated a broad democratic and revolutionary mobilization to make the 'anti-imperialist' war more effective. The heights of absurdity were reached with their ignominious suggestion that the Junta's political prisoners should go to fight with its troops in the Malvinas.[29] But in general their attitude came as no surprise, following a similar line during the conflict with Chile over the Beagle Channel.

As to the main Trotskyist groups, it would be apt to recall Marx's phrase in *The Eighteenth Brumaire* about the burden of inert tradition on the living. Fettered to Trotsky's outdated ideas on the

phenomenon of semi-colonialism, they were unable to understand the new events and joined the march of 10 April in support
of the war.[30]

Both the Montoneros and the Trotskyist groups had their ideas
for changing the methods of combat and even the national
government: 'a plebiscitary government, based upon the Multipartidaria as a multi-sectoral alliance' (Montoneros), or 'a
workers' and farmers' government', as the ultimate guarantee of
immediate elections and the convocation of a Constituent
Assembly (PST). Needless to say, this was pure fantasy: the
Multipartidaria was not in the least interested in bringing down
the dictatorship, while the popular and working-class movement
had not imposed, and could not then impose, a favourable
balance of forces. In reality, then, all these currents supported the
war *tout court*, the rest of their positions being exposed as empty
rhetoric.

(c) Rejection of the War

The highest example of civic and political dignity, of intransigence in the struggle against the Junta for deep democratic
demands, was given by the heroic and selfless Mothers of the
Plaza de Mayo. They were forgotten by the political parties, the
union bureaucracy and the Church hierarchy, cold-shouldered
even by former comrades of their 'missing' children, and harassed
by jingoist currents feeding on the Junta's war.[31] And yet their
response remained crystal-clear throughout. Talks could come
and go, bombs could fly between the two conflicting armies, but
the Mothers continued the demonstrations they had held every
Thursday for five years outside the presidential palace.

A declaration made at the high tide of chauvinist fervour was
remarkable for its calm consistency of purpose. 'The Malvinas are
Argentinian,' it read, 'and so are the missing.' A second statement,
issued when the political and union leaders were holding feverish
talks with the Junta, merely recalled that 'justice is non-
negotiable'. Few yet forceful words. Unlike the speeches of more
experienced militants, both at home and in exile, they remained
firm to the essence of the cause.

The political groups which rejected the war were: the 17th of
October Revolutionary Front, the New Course Group, the
Communist Organization Workers Power, sectors of the Argenti-
nian Socialist Confederation, the Revolutionary Workers Party of

Argentina (a faction of the old PRT–ERP), the Socialist Workers Party (Resistencia), which had split from Nahuel Moreno's PST, the Peace and Justice Service, the Circle for the Formation of an Independent Space, the Independent Movement of Buenos Aires University, and a number of anti-bureaucratic union currents such as the Union of Class Workers and groupings of journalists and railwaymen. In exile a similar position was taken by the TYSAE (based in Mexico, Rome, Stockholm, Paris and other centres), the CADHU, the COSOFAN–Mexico, the Paris journal *Divergencia* and the Madrid-based *Propuesta*, the Forum of the Argentinian Left, and the Movement against the War in the South Atlantic. Adolfo Pérez Esquivel, winner of the Nobel Peace Prize, spoke out clearly against the war, as did a number of other prestigious intellectuals, including Julio Cortazar, Osvaldo Soriano, Osvaldo Bayer, David Vinas and Noe Jitrik.

As to the mood of the masses, we have the evidence of a number of events. On 10 April a demonstration estimated by the press to be three hundred thousand strong seemed to show overwhelming support for the war. A few days earlier, however, the CGT had brought out no more than five thousand for a demonstration that ended with fierce repression, and even these seemed to be in a confused and contradictory state of mind. On 10 April itself relatively few workers put in an appearance at the appointed square, and many of those who did responded more enthusiastically to slogans against the dictatorship than to orchestrated screams of 'Long live the nation!'

At another official demonstration on 10 June, the attendance of five-to-ten thousand clearly marked a sharp decline in the nationalist mood and a growing awareness of the risks of the war. Two days later the Pope's visit brought together a congregation of two million people, from all sections of society, under the same clear sky. 'We want peace' was the universal cry: peace not only with Britain but also within the country itself. The anti-Junta implications were clear to everyone.

Finally, on 15 June the early supporters of the war vented their frustration and disillusionment at the disastrous outcome. They too, when they were faced with repression, raised the explosive demand that the men responsible for the adventure and its resulting deaths and suffering should be placed on trial. 'Galtieri, you butcher, you used the kids like stewing meat' was one of the most expressive slogans heard on that day.

In this contradictory panorama, the obvious silence of the

working class was a factor of enormous importance. During the two months or more of the conflict, there was not a single truly proletarian mass demonstration, not a single pro-war declaration emanating from the rank and file. The workers retreated to their factories and refused to involve themselves in the jingoist fervour. From this front-line trench of the class struggle, they carefully observed the twists and turns of the traditional leaderships, assessing the possibilities for a renewal of the struggle for their own demands.

5

The Malvinas Conflict
and World Politics

Beyond the internal significance of the war for Argentina and
Britain, it had international repercussions within and between the
different state groupings, as well as affecting relations between
the Latin American bourgeoisies and the United States and the
conditions for mass struggle for democracy and socialism on the
American continent. We shall consider each of these dimensions
in turn.

1. The International Context

The Malvinas War broke out at an extremely complex moment
in international relations, characterized by the conjunction of
five relatively new tendencies.

The most general of these, and probably the most important in
explaining the war, is *the deepening depression of the world capitalist
economy*. The 1976-77 upturn which followed the world crisis of
1974-75 was rapidly reversed by the onset of ever sharper
depressive tendencies. Once again the epicentre was in the
industrial heartlands, as it became apparent that the 1974-75 crisis
had been not just a conjunctural phenomenon but the end of the
long post-war period of prosperity. The new epoch would be
characterized by economic stagnation, high unemployment,
falling wages, cuts in social benefits, and a disarticulation of the
multilateral agencies on which the boom had been based (the EEC,
IMF, GATT and OECD).

The accentuation of depressive tendencies was reflected in the
falling value of world trade, together with a sharp decline in the
price of export products (especially raw materials). At the same

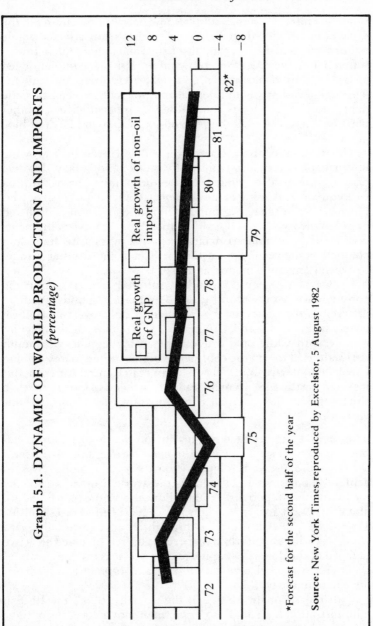

Graph 5.1. DYNAMIC OF WORLD PRODUCTION AND IMPORTS
(percentage)

Real growth of non-oil imports

Real growth of GNP

12 8 4 0 −4 −8

72 73 74 75 76 77 78 79 80 81 82*

*Forecast for the second half of the year

Source: New York Times, reproduced by Excelsior, 5 August 1982

time, real interest rates shot up to new heights; the ending of the cycle of international credit expansion drastically affected whole nations and debt-ridden capitalist firms; and a sharp fall in profits (often below the rate of interest) and in capital accumulation led to a chain of bankruptcies and debt repayment difficulties.[1] Through a variety of commercial and financial mechanisms, the depression tended to be transmitted or intensified in all other parts of the world, including the oil-exporting and Eastern-bloc countries.

This general economic situation was mirrored by a growing internal and external instability of various nation-states. Internal class conflicts also tended to become more acute, with a consequent weakening of the consensual bases of political power. However, against a background of mounting tensions within and between the two blocs, one of the most important developments was a surge of militarism and regional wars (the Iran–Iraq conflict, Franco–Libyan hostility in Chad, the frontier dispute between Peru and Ecuador, and so on).

As we have seen, Argentina suffered acutely from the consequences of the world crisis. The Junta responded with an interventionist policy in the Southern Cone (overt in Bolivia, covert in Paraguay and Uruguay), a sharpening of the frontier dispute with Chile, and a quest for an agreement with South Africa. It tried to win the confidence of the United States, joining it in the counter-revolutionary adventure in Central America. But it also made the USSR its main trading partner and looked to it as a shield against international condemnation of its human rights violations.

The second important tendency in international relations has been *the US reply to the capitalist crisis under the Reagan administration*. Whereas the previous objective of US foreign policy was to achieve a negotiated solution to the world capitalist crisis by means of joint imperialist action followed by some North–South and East–West accord, the new policy has been to re-establish a 1950s-style 'American order', through an adventurist disregard for the existing relationship of forces. This has involved an active defence of the dollar, US capital and its overseas investments, and an attempt to crush democratic and anti-capitalist movements anywhere in the world.[2]

With regard to the USSR and the 'socialist bloc', the Reagan administration has sought to drive them into a corner economically and militarily. The basic reasons for this policy are: the social antagonism between capital or private property and state ownership of the means of production, the Soviet Union's links with revolutionary movements in various parts of the world, and the state-cum-military rivalry between the two 'superpowers'. But in pursuing the goal of hegemony and tightening its alliances with the most reactionary regimes on earth (South Africa, Israel, Taiwan, the Argentinian Junta, the Central American oligarchic governments), Washington has helped to worsen the world economic crisis, aggravated inter-imperialist tensions, strained relations with the Church and the Socialist International, and thrown into turmoil its system of relations with the Eastern bloc (now including China), the Arab world, Black Africa and even Latin America itself.

For the military dictatorship in Argentina, the new North American course brought a period of respite, relieving its international isolation and allowing it to balance its own counter-revolutionary interests with the short-term policy of the main capitalist power. We have already seen that the illusions this gave to the Junta were an important factor in the final decision to occupy the Malvinas.

The third tendency, *the emergence of new regional capitalist powers*, has continued in the context of world recession.[3] The closure of certain export markets, the rising interest rates, the international credit squeeze and the declining prices for raw materials have all weakened their economic bases of reproduction. But far from counteracting previous trends, the new world climate has impelled these countries to strengthen their military potential, to diversify their sources of arms, to increase their influence within international organizations, and to bolster their leading role within the North–South negotiations and the formation of regional blocs. Thus, the militarist Brazilian state has been forging closer economic links with the USSR, Cuba and Nicaragua, lending diplomatic support to Arab countries against Israel and to Black Africa against the apartheid state, and confronting the United States with its resolve to become a new nuclear power.

Argentina is an emergent regional power of a particular kind. Although it has not been successful in developing a vigorous export industry, it has managed to regain a significant role in the world food-grains market and is establishing an export-oriented arms sector. After Brazil, it is perhaps the main exporter of capital in Latin America; while in the military field it has moved towards its goal of acquiring a nuclear capacity and occupying a key position in a South Atlantic alliance. It therefore has relatively broad room for manoeuvre at the international level, and its bourgeoisie is trying to use this to enhance its internal political position.

Against this background in the capitalist world, *the 'socialist bloc' has shown signs of a deepening crisis.* Whereas the twenty-five years from the 1929 Crash to the post-war recovery of the world market were accompanied by the industrialization of the Soviet Union, the period since the 1975 capitalist crisis has not witnessed a convincingly different dynamic in the USSR and Eastern Europe. Indeed, the slowdown of economic growth and the declining efficiency of bureaucratic planning have become more marked in Comecon as a whole. The per capita growth rates are even less impressive, and acute strains have occurred in such vital areas as food production, technology and — to some extent — energy.

As to the Soviet Union's role in the world, its apparently rising influence in a number of very backward countries (Indochina, Ethiopia, Angola, Afghanistan) and its growing military strength since 1960 must be set against the major political breaks with China, Egypt and Iraq. This trend is intimately linked to the relative weakening of the Soviet economy vis-à-vis world capitalism (which registered high growth in the late 1950s and 1960s and a continuing internationalization until the second half of the 1970s), as well as a declining power of economic attraction. The countries which have drawn close to the USSR in recent years are marked by their extreme poverty, weakness and smallness, and by their previous lack of a dynamic, established indigenous bourgeoisie. Generally unable to participate in the post-war boom, they underwent modernizing democratic revolutions — either 'from below' or 'from above', as in the case of Ethiopia and Afghanistan — which formed part of the broader wave of victorious progressive movements. However, more developed countries like Iran and Zimbabwe have joined China, Egypt and Indonesia in distancing themselves from the USSR.

These crucial trends, together with other social and political aspects that we cannot examine here, have given rise to the inter-state conflicts within the 'socialist bloc' (Vietnam— Kampuchea, China—Vietnam), to the adventures in Afghanistan, Eritrea and Cambodia, and to a devastating social and political crisis in Poland. Not so well known is the assertion of centrifugal forces, pulling individual countries towards a separate integration into the world market in order to exploit inter-imperialist contradictions and to obtain alternative sources of supply for key sectors of the economy.[4]

Placed in an essentially defensive position, Moscow has reacted by reinforcing the frontiers of the zone it directly influences, by desperately searching for a military–strategic balance with the West, and by forging new treaties with capitalist states able to offer economic-strategic requirements. Hence its strengthening of diplomatic and trade relations with Argentina and Brazil, West Germany and the Arab world.[5] In the case of Argentina, this involved a straightforward deal whereby a guaranteed supply of food grains was offered in exchange for diplomatic protection of the Junta at the UN and systematic silence on its crimes against the democratic and revolutionary movements.[6]

The four tendencies we have outlined above combined to unleash a wave of militarism and regional wars. State and para-state apparatuses of repression were given a tighter rein over civil society, while the various peoples were stripped of democratic, social and national rights in the name of increasingly meaningless world symbols such as 'the West', 'the Third World', 'actually existing socialism' or simply 'the national interest'. Fortunately for the destiny of humankind, however, new mass movements also developed in all groups of countries, fighting for 'Peace, Bread and Work', political, national and social democracy, and a settling of accounts with the bureaucratic and military forces that chain up the people in the name of bogus national interests. Millions of workers and young people have mobilized against rearmament and unemployment in the imperialist countries, against US imperialism and the bourgeois oligarchs of Central America, against the repressive and economically disastrous dictatorships of South America, against the oppressors of the Palestinian, Eritrean or black South African masses, and against the bureaucratic rulers of the 'socialist bloc'. The ideologies of this multiform movement are still extremely undeveloped, their programmes and methods still more or less rudimentary. But whatever the direction in which they develop, they are today the only real opponents of militarism and war, of imperialist and chauvinist reaction.

2. Political Alignment

In earlier chapters we have discussed the significance of the Malvinas War for the internal political life of Britain and, above all, Argentina. We should now look at the ways in which it affected the international relations of the two countries.

(a) The Role of Britain's Allies

Britain's NATO allies and a majority of Commonwealth countries provided the core of active support for Britain in the war. The United States naturally carried the greatest weight, because of its diplomatic and military role in the Western alliance. But not everyone in the US government supported the British cause, nor was its position expressed in any significant military terms.

The White House's decision was strongly opposed by central figures in the administration, by Republicans and Democrats, and apparently by the army itself. The State Department was deeply divided between the position of the Secretary of State, which eventually prevailed, and the slightly pro-Argentinian neutralism of his assistant for Latin American affairs, Thomas Enders. The US ambassador to the UN, Jeane Kirkpatrick, publicly aired her difference with Alexander Haig, and there can be little doubt that she was pro-Argentinian. Two prominent right-wingers within the Republican Party, Senators Jesse Helms and Howard Baker, explicitly backed the Argentinian cause.[7] And, as we have seen, General Galtieri seemed to be counting on the existence of powerful allies within the US Army.

The Junta's legend that US Army support was key to the outcome of the war does not accord with reality.[8] Military assistance seems to have been confined to four relatively minor areas: intelligence reports (which would have served to detect the *General Belgrano*); auxiliary activities such as transport and the in-flight refuelling of Vulcan bombers used against Argentinian landing strips on the Malvinas; the supply of fuel for the fleet at Ascension Island; and the substitution of US units for British troops temporarily withdrawn from NATO. Other forms of assistance — e.g., permission for British warships to pass through the Panama Canal — played an even less imporant role.[9]

Most of Western Europe supported Britain, although in quite varying degrees. The EEC imposed a trade embargo on Argentina, but Italy and Ireland went their own way and limited their 'solidarity' with Britain to a condemnation of the Argentinian initiative in terms of resolution 502 of the UN Security Council. The French government of François Mitterrand, the most left-wing in the EEC, was Britain's staunchest ally, pledging and practising a policy of unconditional support. In this, however, France was merely demonstrating the consistency of its colonialist orientation in Black Africa, currently threatened by nationalist movements and the emergence of Libya as a rival regional power. For its part Spain, and particularly the far right, tended to side with Argentina. But generally Western Europe did not take a position on the sovereignty issue, and merely followed the Security Council in condemning the use of force. Except in the military sphere, the embargo seems to have been no more than a symbolic political action, since it hardly affected Argentinian exports to the EEC and was sufficiently lax to permit the continuation of exports to Britain itself, with certificates of Uruguayan or Paraguayan origin.[10]

To a greater or lesser extent, Britain enlisted the support of most Commonwealth countries, and even 'Third World' countries like Zaire and Jamaica were in favour of the Security Council resolution. It was precisely the most reactionary and colonialist power in the 'South' — the apartheid regime of South Africa — which assisted Argentina by combining formal neutrality with the maintenance of arms sales.[11]

Japan became the first of Argentina's major creditors to renegotiate a loan at the height of the war ($100m to YPF, on 1 June 1982). The position of Israel was particularly interesting. For although it enjoyed excellent relations with the Conservative Thatcher government, it continued to supply Argentina with Gabriel missiles, similar to the French Exocet, and with spare parts for the Junta's Mirage fighters.

(b) Argentina's Friends and Allies

Apart from the cases we have already mentioned, Argentina was supported by almost all of Latin America, by some Arab, African and Asian countries, and by the 'socialist bloc'. Of course this involved considerable nuances. Whereas Mexico, Uruguay, Brazil and Colombia posed no conditions,[12] Venezuela, Panama, Paraguay, Bolivia and Guatemala tended to limit themselves to recognition of Argentina's claim, condemning both the initial Argentinian action and Britain's use of economic sanctions and military force. (The Caribbean countries, with the exceptions of pro-Argentinian Haiti, Surinam and Dominican Republic, adopted a mildly pro-British neutral position, prompted in part by the fear that the Argentinian example would trigger similar actions against the weak and newly independent states of Belize and Guyana.)

In South America itself, the firmest supporters of Buenos Aires were Peru and Bolivia[13] (which, like Argentina, have outstanding territorial claims against Chile) and the two states traditionally linked to Argentinian capital and diplomacy: Uruguay and Paraguay. A second, informal group of North Andean, Central American and Caribbean countries followed Venezuela in backing Argentina. The crucial factor here seems to have been Venezuela's keenness to win Argentinian diplomatic support for a reported agreement linking Venezuela's claims to the Guyanese Essequibo Basin with Ecuador's claims on parts of Peru and Panama's just demands for US compliance with the Canal treaties.[14] Guatemala, then at the height of a chauvinist campaign against Belize, was an important special case, also perhaps tied to Venezuela's expansionist thrust.

The only country that did not openly take sides in the war, though clearly rejoicing at Argentina's defeat, was Pinochet's Chile. In fact Santiago gave considerable assistance to the British 'task force' by supplying communications facilities and allowing the use of land bases for supply and commando operations (e.g., the attack on the Río Grande base in Tierra del Fuego, reported on British commercial television). It is worth asking oneself whether Pinochet acted merely as a reactionary dictator allied to US imperialism, or as the leader of a national bourgeois class fearful of encirclement and territorial loss.

(c) The 'Socialist Bloc' and Its Friends

It is necessary to make a certain differentiation among the countries in this bloc, even though their basic stances were very similar. The USSR continued its well-established policy towards Argentina, evidently finding a more praiseworthy political justification in the circumstances of war. Yet its support was by no means unlimited, as could already be seen in the fact that it abstained on the Security Council resolution condemning the use of force to recover the Malvinas.

The Cuban position was more interesting, being based upon

general anti-imperialist or anti-US considerations and emphasizing support for the Argentinian people rather than its government. We have already argued that this was an erroneous policy, since the Malvinas War was not a national-popular conflict but a confrontation between two reactionary governments. Nevertheless, there are some grounds for understanding this type of attitude in countries and revolutionary movements that find themselves economically and militarily surrounded by US imperialism, and for which a conflict between Argentina and Britain (or subsequently between Latin America and the United States) could bring a significant respite. This was all the more clear in the case of the Sandinistas or Salvadorean FMLN, which might have benefited from the withdrawal of Argentinian advisers operating against their country. Such factors do not, however, outweigh the harm which the Cuban position did to a democratic, internationalist perspective, or the confusion it served to create among the Argentinian and Latin American peoples.

As to the People's Republic of China, its adoption of a position similar to that of the USSR did not express a left turn in the international sphere, but simply marked a distancing from Washington in protest at the rapprochement with Taiwan and the disregard for commitments to China into which former presidents had entered.

African and Asian countries with the closest links to the Soviet Union took an even more favourable attitude towards Argentina. Indeed, Libya drew alongside Israel as the main source of military supplies during the war. The Non-Aligned Movement recognized Argentinian sovereignty over the islands, condemning Britain and censuring the United States. But as in the case of the OAS and RIAT resolutions, it also refused to endorse the initial recovery of the islands by force.

(d) The International Significance of Argentina's Defeat

For a major part of the international revolutionary movement, including most Trotskyist forces, the defeat of the Argentinian army entailed the strengthening of imperialism and reaction throughout the world. Once again this is a highly impressionable interpretation.

A victory for the Argentinian dictatorship would have had three consequences: the consolidation of the Junta's internal position; the strengthening of its international role in relation to other Latin American bourgeoisies (especially the Mexican and Brazilian); and the extension of its room for counter-revolutionary manoeuvre on the continent (Central America, Bolivia, etc.). Argentina would have emerged as a regional power strongly placed to reach a South Atlantic pact with South Africa and the United States; and it could have set its sights on a war with Chile over the Beagle Channel, dragging in the Peruvian and Bolivian armies on its side and sparking off a war throughout the southern part of the continent. This would not have required it to abandon its grain trade and traditional relationship with the Soviet Union.

The Argentinian defeat had two crucial implications. Firstly, it made considerably harder the eventual recovery of the Malvinas, since the war episode closed the door for a long time to a diplomatic breakthrough. In this sense the adventure (and not the almost inevitable defeat) was a setback for the Argentinian nation that must be blamed squarely on the Junta. Secondly, it decisively weakened both the internal and the international position of the dictatorship. This has benefited Chile by making the possibility of war more remote, and it has also debilitated the reactionary, anti-popular forces in Bolivia sustained by the Junta. In Central America, obstacles have been placed in the way of further Argentinian involvement.

British control of the Malvinas does not intrinsically weaken the Latin American democratic and revolutionary movement, nor does it substantially alter the long-term problem of the islands. London can only hold them at great cost, facing the continual possibility of war in very difficult geographic and strategic conditions. It can neither exploit the oil reserves nor launch an attack on Argentinian territory. Unless it reaches an agreement with countries like Brazil — which seems almost out of the question — it will not find it easy to secure US military support for a joint base.[15]

The role of the United States in Latin America has been weakened as a result of the war, whereas an Argentinian victory might have had the opposite effect by allowing the Junta to re-establish an alliance with the US government. The break-up of the RIAT is beyond doubt, as is the delicate situation within the Inter-American Defence Board.

One possible result of the war, which would be disastrous for the peoples of Latin America, would be the rise of a new, repressive demagogic-nationalist movement fuelling the flames of fratricidal war on the continent.

3. Bourgeois 'Anti-Imperialism' or Militarist Neo-Nationalism?

Many Latin American nationalists see the weakening of the relationship with the United States as a development fraught with revolutionary possibilities in the tradition of Perón, Cárdenas, Vargas, Rómulo Gallegos, Villaroel and Arévalo. Pro-Soviet Communist parties and their blood-brothers are particularly apt to see this as an exceptional conjuncture which could permit the formation of alliances between regional 'progressive' bourgeoisies and the 'socialist bloc'. A kind of anti-imperialist tendency could then be formed, isolating US imperialism, strengthening Cuba and Nicaragua internationally and opening up national-democratic transitions to socialism.

In these cheerful prognoses, pure fantasy is mixed up with a false analysis of real tendencies. Far from there being a historic rupture between the Latin American bourgeoisies and the United States, the temporary rift is due to much more general factors than Washington's position on the Malvinas War. In this context some important events have taken place: the RIAT resolution, the high-sounding statements of some Latin American governments, the refusal of the Brazilian and other armies to participate in the UNITAS 82 exercises, the measures taken by SELA and ALADI in economic support of Argentina, the decision by Venezuela and Colombia to join the Non-Aligned Movement, and the vigorous struggle on the rescheduling of external debts. But none of these has been translated into a diplomatic break, or even a serious attempt to create a new inter-American organization without the presence of the United States. The Inter-American Defence Board is still in existence, and no steps have been taken that threaten the economic interests of the United States.

In the 1930s and 1940s, capitalist development was passing through the stage of deep social and institutional reforms, such as the consolidation of an internal market, the implementation of agrarian reforms, the creation of public financial institutions allowing the state to redistribute productively the mining and agricultural rent, and the establishment of a light consumer-goods industry. This last task did not require large-scale investment, advanced technology, imported raw materials or components, or a highly skilled workforce, because the technical composition of capital was still quite low. The necessary technology was relatively simple and old (as in textiles, cement and basic metallurgy), primary products were produced within the country (wool, cotton, ferrous and non-ferrous minerals), and complex labour skills were not required. These were the parameters of a fundamentally agrarian economic structure, with a family-type industrial and commercial bourgeoisie, a proletariat still linked to the countryside, and a paternalist–reformist state acting essentially in the sphere of the accumulation and distribution of capital.

Although some Latin American countries have not climbed out of this phase, the continental pattern of capitalist development is now very different. We are facing a monopoly–finance capitalism increasingly based upon heavy industry, a high composition of capital, huge injections of sophisticated technology, imported inputs, and a highly skilled workforce. The state has turned into an extremely complex monopolist apparatus, which has assumed the task of developing industry and basic infrastructure in close association with national and foreign monopoly capital. At the same time, there is a growing need for external markets to absorb the products of industry.

The second major change has been in the relationship between national and world economy. If we take the coefficients of external trade, the level of national debt, and the requirement for imported technology, we can see that no Latin American country can develop effectively in isolation. Moreover, the critical world conjuncture (falling value of exports, high rates of interest on a massive external debt, and so on) imposes rigid social and wage constraints on the Latin American bourgeoisies — a marked contrast to the buoyant raw material markets and minimal debt burdens of the 1946-1954 period.[16]

For all these reasons, and whatever the subsequent direction of capitalist development in Latin America, the bourgeoisies cannot lead or even follow a truly progressive or populist course. Since they are also incapable of an anti-imperialist orientation, all they can do is react to the effects of the world crisis and the inflexibility of the United States by trying to strengthen ties both among themselves and with alternative world powers such as Japan, Germany, France, the 'socialist bloc', South Africa, Israel, the Arab world, and—why not?—Britain. But they were already doing this before the war, without making a song and dance about imperialism. The gravity of the crisis could lead some countries to go it alone with more or less radical nationalist policies of a defensive kind, such as the nationalization of the banks in Mexico. However, not only do precedents exist for such a course (the nationalization of Venezuelan oil, the Argentinian and Brazilian nuclear programmes), but it would not decisively alter the external dependence of Latin American countries, nor the nature of their capitalist development.

The Malvinas crisis will almost certainly accelerate the arms race on the continent, already well advanced before the war.[17] Apart from its adverse effect on democratic institutions and mass living standards, this will create an auspicious climate for the new regional powers and their allies to exert bellicose diplomatic pressures on weaker countries and to spin a web of clientelist relations around their electronic weaponry. The new continental 'solidarity' invoked by apologists for cheap nationalism will not put an end to Guatemala's build-up against Belize or Venezuela's threat of force against Guyana.

It is also quite clear that bourgeois Latin American regimes will try to make demagogic use of their contradictions with the United States, and of assorted militarist and chauvinist displays, in order to defuse their socio-economic crises and counter the weakening of their political hegemony. Under these circumstances, some revolutionary states and movements will be able to obtain immediate advantages. (Cuba and Nicaragua, for instance, may widen their economic and diplomatic room for manoeuvre, temporarily undermining the US blockade.) But the arming of bourgeois states in the region would potentially face them with new forms of monopolist–military encirclement, and a further escalation of the military burden their peoples have to bear.

In the important case of Bolivia, a repetition of the General Torres experience could pave the way for a democratic turn by the armed forces. But that would stem from the great weakness of the Bolivian bourgeoisie vis-à-vis the proletariat and the revolutionary left, and from the reduced possibility of intervention by the post-Malvinas Argentinian army. Such a new phase of the Bolivian revolution would be profoundly dissimilar to the nationalist-militarist orientation possible in Argentina, since it would reflect a completely different political and social relationship of forces between the bourgeois state–military apparatus and the democratic mass movement.

In general terms, it could be argued that the new course of the Latin American bourgeoisies, however widespread it proves to be, is located within a more general readjustment of the balance of forces between the old imperialist powers (especially the United States) and the rising regional bourgeoisies. It does not challenge in the least the capitalist exploitation of the working masses or the strength of the world capitalist system, but only the precise participation of Latin American monopoly capital and its various states. In other words, it is a mere dispute between major and minor partners, which implies an attempt to strengthen the repressive bourgeois regimes of Latin America.

The democratic and revolutionary movement must make an effort to grasp the key features of the new period. A working-class policy must remain independent of any jingoist military project, basing itself instead upon the democratic spaces won by the masses, unlimited defence of their social rights and living standards, and a struggle for a new democratic internationalism that opens up broad vistas for the advance to socialism.

6

The Junta's Defeat
and the Prospects for Argentina

The Malvinas defeat completely reversed the prospects and expectations of the Junta and the monopoly-finance bourgeoisie. Instead of consolidation, it brought greater weakness and an explosion of contradictions within and among the three branches of the armed forces and the various bourgeois factions that had directly supported the landing. Instead of being strengthened, its continental position diminished in relation to that of Brazil and Chile; and it lost some of its ground in being recognized as a leading partner in the counter-revolutionary alliance.

1. The Junta's Debacle

With the formal surrender of the Malvinas on 15 June 1982, the Junta sealed its defeat on almost every terrain.

In political and military terms, it spelt disaster for its expansionist external policy, destruction of most of its war machine, a humiliating display of the army's low morale and combat readiness, and the collapse of its project of establishing 'national unity' behind a nationalist current of its own making. In economic terms, it blocked the Junta's grandiose plan for the centralization of capital and a turn to the international monopolies, and forced it to look for alternatives. In the social sphere, where pent-up tensions and contradictions combined with sharp antagonisms between classes and class fractions, a wave of frustration and resentment was unleashed at the cost of the war to the nation and the abrupt clash between objective reality and illusions generated by the Junta's massive propaganda apparatus.

In venting its hatred and complete rejection of the Junta and the monopoly–finance bourgeoisie, the mass movement drove the different military groups into open conflict with one another. As Galtieri's removal began to be debated, three positions emerged within the military apparatus. One sector, led by Galtieri himself, but whose positions had been well prepared by such a lucid cadre of the big bourgeoisie as Lanusse, argued that only one battle had been lost and that the war should continue under Galtieri's leadership. The air force, together with the navy, suggested that power should be immediately transferred to a civilian government. Most of the divisional commanders, however, led by Nicolaides, favoured a kind of 'slow transition' to civilian rule, under an army-dominated Junta. The resulting deadlock led to Galtieri's removal and the appointment of a new president, General Bignone, to head a junta from which the navy and air force had withdrawn.[1] In the unseemly tussle, it was not unknown for a brigadier-general to pass over the head of his commanding officer and to demand Galtieri's resignation. Such a spectacle had not been seen since 1962.[2]

The military principle of a solid and cohesive authoritarian power, sustained by the vertical discipline of the three branches, was beginning to crumble, and with it the subjugation of the mass of civil society (the proletariat, the popular masses, but also the 'opposition' factions of the bourgeoisie itself). Direct and open domination of the monopoly-finance pinnacle could no longer be guaranteed. Even the total inanity of Saint-Jean's interim government showed that a power vacuum was developing.

Why then was the dictatorship not brought down? The essential reason is that the political and union leaderships did not wish such an outcome, preferring a process of reconciliation. The Justicialista Party, the Radical Civic Union and the supposedly tough wing of the union bureaucracy (the CGT–Brasil, led by Ubaldini and Lorenzo Miguel) formed the core of the bloc that agreed to give 'extra time' to the army. Instead of calling for popular mobilization, they entered into corridor deals that promised a return to civilian rule by — March 1984.

Since the organized proletarian opposition was still very weak, the working-class and popular movement remained in the state of watchful alert in which it had been since the beginning of the war. A new kind of military regime emerged, resting upon the army but lacking the support of the other two branches and forced to seek a broad agreement with the Multipartidaria.[3] Behind the dance of successive presidents, promises and negotiations lay the deep-seated elements of a structural crisis. It is these that we must now examine.

2. The Crisis of Argentinian Capitalism

(a) Economic Implications of the Monopoly-Capitalist Defeat

Whatever the future course of events in Argentina, it was clear in June 1982 that the so-called 'process of national reorganization' had ended in political and economic failure.[4] The big landowning and monopoly bourgeoisie and the armed forces had lost the political initiative, and the battered forces of Argentinian populism were temporarily snatching it back. The opening towards elections and traditional forms of social and political organization tended to gain in breadth and momentum.

This tendency will have major social and economic consequences, forcing the government of the hour to temporize with the organizations of employers, unionized workers, small producers and liberal professionals, in a chaotic process that will be extremely difficult to manage. A broad popular campaign will develop against those in the dictatorship responsible for the war, and this cannot fail to split the military institutions and the repressive state apparatuses from top to bottom.

None of the various bourgeois options will be able to circumvent the new correlation of forces, nor to abandon a national–protectionist reorientation of economic policy and international relations along 'third-worldist' and Latin American lines. For the defeat of the Junta's economic project was not just, as the populists believe, a setback for certain fractions of the Argentinian bourgeoisie: it also blocked for the time being a far-ranging attempt to overcome the historic crisis of Argentinian capitalism, evident in the secular economic stagnation and chronic political turmoil of the past thirty years or so. This ambitious drive had, however, represented the only direction congruent with the logic of the capitalist system: namely, the re-establishment of social and political conditions for the valorization, centralization and accumulation of capital, and the effective integration of Argentina into the world capitalist economy.

As we saw in chapter one, the post-war Peronist industrialization spawned a parasitic bureaucratic bourgeoisie, whose profit margins depended more on state subsidy and protection than on its own technological base and the internal generation of surpluses; while the relatively backward technical level of production tended to isolate Argentinian capital from the world and even from the more advanced Latin American countries. Nevertheless, the favourable conditions of external trade allowed the regime to implement a policy of social concessions to the working class. Through the mediation and control of the union bureaucracy, a political front was formed between the 'national' bourgeoisie, the working class and the bloated, paternalist state bureaucracy. The problem was that this pattern generated a historic crisis in agriculture, exports and capital accumulation. It tended to kill the goose that laid the golden eggs, which was ultimately the foundation for Argentina's integration into the world market and the internal financing of all productive activity.

Successive populist regimes generally respected and even intensified this contradictory structure. The military regimes with which they alternated did their best to destroy it, concentrating on the long-term development of Argentinian capitalism and of its most powerful fraction (the Pampas landowners and the big monopoly—finance groups linked to them). The resulting see-saw was in turn closely bound up with the economic conjuncture, as brief periods of expansion led to acute crises in external trade, inflationary explosions and social unrest. The bourgeoisie as a whole would then temporarily regroup around the military to achieve some kind of social and political stability, before a new cycle brought the splintering of the bourgeois front.

In today's conditions, a return to protectionist policies and the subsidization of economic backwardness cannot have any historical prospect. It would impede the modernization and international integration of industry, so that it would be impossible for the agricultural surplus to finance long-term investment without recourse to super-exploitation of the workforce.[5] To this should be added the huge burden of military expenditure, the channelling of funds to the military-industrial complex, the $6bn a year required to service the external debt,[6] a rate of inflation hovering around 200 per cent, the sharpening of depressive tendencies in external trade, and the problem of high interest rates and contraction of credit.

The unviability of populist protectionism does not imply that a conjunctural upturn in production is out of the question. Indeed, the enormous amount of idle productive capacity — due to plummeting output and the boom in machinery and plant imports during the period when the peso was grossly overvalued — suggests that a rapid recovery could take place without a major injection of fixed capital. Moreover, the huge reserve army of labour tends to reduce wages pressure and the general costs of a recovery. The most adverse factor would be the high level of interest rates and corporate debt.

Any orientation to growth would, of course, have to base itself upon broad political support and contain inflation within certain limits. But the present undervaluation of the peso has already created favourable trade conditions and spontaneously erected a new protectionist wall. Argentinian grains and meat have a guaranteed market in the Eastern bloc and the 'Third World', and it may be possible to use export earnings to correct the state of public finances. Nor would it be necessary to rely on Britain and the United States for industrial inputs: iron ore could be imported from Venezuela or Brazil, copper from Peru, plant from Japan, Sweden or Italy, and turbines from the USSR. And yet, such a course would inevitably provoke a fresh and explosive crisis, as soon as idle plant and labour had been absorbed and the full weight of the different classes began to make itself felt. It is quite unthinkable that the agro-export sector would be able to finance both the subsidization of inefficient industry and the servicing of the external debt.[7]

(b) The 'Democratic-Populist' Option

A 'democratic-populist' option, involving the re-establishment of a bourgeois-democratic electoral contest and the return to power of Peronists or Radicals, would inevitably founder on the political, social and economic consequences outlined above. Obviously there are important differences in ideology and social composition between the UCR (Radicals) and the Peronists, since the UCR is the liberal-nationalist party of the traditional petty and middle bourgeoisie, while Peronism is a national-populist force based largely upon the working-class and popular movement and led by marginal sectors of the bourgeoisie in alliance with the union bureaucracy. These differences explain, for example, why the Radicals are more anti-militarist in their ideology than the Justicialista movement, or why they have much less contact with nationalist sectors of the army than the clerical-authoritarian wing of Peronism. At the same time, they have more room for manoeuvre with the generals (particularly on social issues), because they are far less imbricated in the union movement.

Given the structure and critical straits of contemporary Argentinian capitalism, however, both the Peronists and the Radicals have the disadvantage that they cannot govern the country in a non-populist way without splitting the bases of their social and political support. This is partly due to their social composition, which forces them to make continual concessions to the masses in order to preserve their influence.[8] But more generally, bourgeois democracy cannot function as a mechanism of mediation between different social sectors in a climate of extreme crisis and pent-up tensions — or rather, it can only do so in short bursts, rapidly overtaken by the open and direct mobilization of one or all of those sectors.

A return of the Peronists or Radicals would therefore bring a 'Bolivianization' of Argentinian politics: that is to say, an ever quicker alternation of democratic—consensual and authoritarian—repressive forms of rule; the collapse of traditional political parties and state-bureaucratic institutions; and the emergence of a chronic power vacuum. Such a process naturally varies with the relationship between the political parties and the armed forces, between the mass movement and the union bureaucracy. These factors may crucially affect not only the rhythm and scope of 'official' political developments, but also the size of the democratic space opened within society and the political—ideological maturation of the working masses. But the gradual erosion of existing options is an inevitable consequence of an ongoing social and political radicalization of the working-class and popular movement.

(c) The 'National-Corporatist' Alternative

Although the above seems the more likely scenario, one cannot rule out moves towards a 'national-corporatist' solution to the crisis of bourgeois rule. This could temporarily restore a certain consensus and stability of class domination, offering the most to the bourgeoisie and the armed forces and posing the greatest danger to the working people.

A 'national-corporatist' policy would seek to preserve the military tutelage of state and government, either directly through a pseudo-popular 'nationalist' coup, or through a civilian–

military alliance in which the military continued to hold the ultimate reins of power. Like the 'democratic-populist' option, it would involve a 'nationalist' and 'third-worldist' reorientation of internal and external policy, and of the pattern of capital accumulation. Attempts would also be made to integrate major sectors of the bureaucratic bourgeoisie and the union bureaucracy into the ruling bloc. However, it would have a non-populist and much more authoritarian character, nationalist demagogy being used only to manufacture a consensus, to assert corporatist control over the mass movement, and to justify selective repression of its radical, 'unpatriotic' wing. The resumption of hostilities with Britain would be necessary to take advantage of the still strong nationalist feelings among the population and the sense of national frustration. The defeat of June 1982 could then be blamed on a handful of incompetents, and the Malvinas ideal used as cover for the creation of a siege economy and military-style discipline. The end result would be the extension of state capitalism around a strengthened military–industrial complex.

Such a project is viable in economic terms, since it would essentially build upon the earlier programmes of the Junta. Attempts would have to be made to find links with the old populist structures, so that the unity of the bourgeois front could be reconstructed under the hegemony of the new monopolist sector, whose flagship is the Pérez Compac group. But the main aim would still be to effect a radical restructuring of Argentinian industry, inserting it into the new international division of labour in direct association with transnational capital. External policy would share with populism the maintenance of commercial and diplomatic links with the USSR and the 'socialist bloc', the East Coast of Latin America, and some industrial powers such as Japan, Italy and Sweden. But greater emphasis would be placed upon military and geo-political factors pointing towards close relations with Israel and South Africa and the tightening of the circle around Chile.

Whatever the exact political form of such a regime, it would have to implement a rigid policy of wage control and public spending cuts in health, education and social security. Only in this way could the state generate sufficient funds to finance public investment and military expenditure. It would be quite possible to allow an initial rise in wages, later to be reversed by inflation. But even so, all the historical evidence suggests that the working class would not accept a 'national-corporatist' solution, and that the ground would be laid for further *rodrizagos* and *cordobazos*.

3. Prospects for the Mass Movement and the Socialist Left

A number of political contradictions, stemming from the crisis of Argentinian capitalism, indicate a long-term undermining of the various forms of bourgeois political and ideological domination over the mass movement. In order to grasp the prospects for the popular and working-class movement, we must therefore elucidate the nexus of economic, political and ideological problems which it has to face.

(a) The Roots and Survival of State Terrorism

The terrorist authoritarianism of the armed forces has clearly-defined historical roots in Argentina, expressing the interests of the most powerful, dynamic and self-sufficient fraction of the bourgeoisie: the monopoly–finance pinnacle, which grew in close association with big international capital through the direct capitalization of agrarian rent. The evident capacity of this class fraction to organize the economy and state is related to the fact that it could never achieve a social consensus on which to ground a hegemonic ruling bloc. Since its economic dominance cannot be reflected in a constitutional–democratic control of the state apparatus, it is compelled to assure its rule through 'illegal' military coups and suppression of the nation's democratic rights.

At the same time, its ambition to centralize capital, to modernize the productive apparatus and to modify the functions of the state brings it into conflict with a mass of industrial wage-earners, who achieved a high standard of living in decades of near-full employment and powerful trade-union organization.

The 1976 coup was a clear expression of these contradictions. The inhuman savagery of the tortures and 'disappearances' pointed not to intrinsic evil within the military but to a cold and calculated plan to annul the lack of consensus by wiping out all signs of civil society. This imperative has not abated with the Junta's debacle — indeed, it has grown more intense. The present relationship of forces, in which a weak military faces popular loathing and contempt, is a barrier to further immediate blood-letting. But as long as the general crisis remains unresolved, it remains the surest long-term option for the whole of monopoly–finance capital — one that will become viable again if the militarist forces are able to regroup and the masses are plunged into confusion by the sudden collapse of a 'national-popular' alternative.

As a latent possibility, the dictatorial thrust of the monopolist bourgeoisie will try to express itself through continued use of the state's terrorist apparatus and a chain of arbitrary arrests, murders and disappearances. As a longer-term option, it is already preparing itself to cut the Gordian knot of political contradictions. If we think that the Junta's bloody dictatorship was the ultimate horror for the Argentinian people, the conclusion drawn by monopoly–finance capital is that the 1976-82 terror was by no means sufficient. The bloodbath they are beginning to plan will make the 'dirty war' seem like a mere skirmish. In their preparatory work, the repressive apparatuses can count on the vacillation, silence and complicity of the established political and union leaderships. Only a combative and consistently democratic mass movement can prevent a repetition of this tragedy. There can be no truce with the military torturers and murderers.

(b) The Multipartidaria and the Gathering Crisis of Populist Hegemony

The weakness, timidity and capitulatory tendencies of the Multipartidaria, documented in various parts of this book, have a profound objective basis. Unable to satisfy the demands of the mass movement, its component parties find themselves facing a new reality that is at odds with the whole historic trajectory on which their social consensus was based. The Peronists, for example, who have spent their whole political life preaching income redistribution in favour of popular sectors, are now being driven to adopt a blatantly more moderate line.[9]

More generally, the (Peronist) Justicialista Party and the Radical Civic Union — the other main force in the Multipartidaria — are the political expressions of the weakest and hardest-hit sections of the dominant class. No longer inserted into the central structures of the reproduction of capital, the populist bourgeoisie has lost the leadership of its own class and is losing the objective basis for its authority over the mass movement. This material and political decline has in turn led it inexorably to accept the withering of democratic space within society. Already the demagogy and repression of Juan Perón's final government, and *a fortiori* of the Isabel Perón–López Rega tandem, were a far cry from the golden age of Peronism and registered the turn of history's screws for these bourgeois fractions. After Perón's death, they became ever less capable of regenerating their leadership of the masses, or even of producing anything other than a re-hash of the most moth-eaten populist ideas. Within months the *rodrizago* of June–July 1975 underlined their impotence to affect the social struggle, even when they were still able to function as the electoral representatives of a broad spectrum. As time went by, and they kept silent at the height of the butchery, it became clear that they were more frightened of popular action than of the military Junta.

It would be wrong now to expect these parties to take a different position on the burning political issues: the need for a radical break, the exposure of the military's criminal record, the disarticulation of the repressive apparatuses and criminal groups within the police and all three branches of the military, and the satisfaction of the people's democratic and social demands. Rather, under the guise of 'cleaning up' the more intolerable aspects of the past period, they will try to reach a compromise that leaves relatively untouched the principle of 'anti-subversive warfare'. Even as they proffer grudging explanations to the families of the 'missing' and countless promises to the consistently democratic movement of the Mothers of the Plaza de Mayo, they will be moving to protect the personal and professional lives of the officers and policemen responsible for the bloodbath.

Our analysis of the evolution of the populist parties is also applicable to the Peronist union bureaucracy. Although some sections may well shift to the left in response to grassroots pressure and a dawning awareness that the paternalist–populist epoch has come to an end, it is unlikely that the bureaucracy as a whole will play a significant role in the direct and open mobilization of the masses for their social and political rights.[10] Whether or not they still refer to the emblems of Peronism or Radicalism, the leftward-moving young workers will begin to distance themselves from the original political and ideological conceptions of those movements. The dramatic reorientation of social practice will, at most, leave behind an increasingly incongruous subjective nostalgia.

Thus, *the political and consensual crisis of the Multipartidaria harbours in embryo a crisis of bourgeois ideological domination over the mass movement.* There is now an objective possibility that, under the unrelenting pressure of a social and political crisis which none of the bourgeois parties and institutions can resolve, a new set of ideas will come forward to chart a radical transformation of society. In this precise sense, currents like the Peronist *Intransigentes* or the Movement for Renewal and Change within the UCR constitute major advances on their respective orthodoxies and may even produce valuable suggestions for the struggle against political continuity with the dictatorship. But insofar as they remain within the limits of the crisis-ridden populist politics, they are a dead-end for consistent democratic or revolutionary militants, and, worse still, for the popular and working-class movement itself. They form part of the process of dispersal, rupture or reorientation of social practice which may lead either to the demoralization of broad layers or to the overcoming of their inherited political and ideological limitations.

(c) The Situation of the Mass Movement

During the period of resistance to the dictatorship, the working class gradually began to reassemble and reorganize its forces at grassroots level. Together with the many factory and branch strikes, the high-points were the illegal publication of the *Electrum* bulletin by the Córdoba-based Light and Power Union, the underground reorganization of railworkers culminating in the strikes of 1979 and 1980, the production of a huge quantity of hand-printed union leaflets, the election of many 'secret' shop stewards (especially in the Buenos Aires region), the formation of class-struggle groups in the Rosario–Villa Constitución area, and the continuous activity of the Salta Anti-imperialist Class CGT in that province and elsewhere in the north. Naturally this account is far from complete.

Simultaneously, new radical-democratic currents began to develop both within and outside the traditional parties. Apart from the radical youth movements of the Peronists and the old socialists (particularly the Argentinian Socialist Federation), there were the Mothers of the Plaza de Mayo and a variety of democratic-pacifist groups like the CELS and Paz y Justicia. Although these often have a markedly Christian stamp, evident in their 'a-politicism' and their dubious principle of non-violent struggle, they do represent deep currents among the Argentinian people and consistently oppose state repression by the Junta or any other regime cooked up by the monopolies and the armed forces. We should also stress the dignity, sincerity and steadfastness of their democratic struggle, which make them hard to assimilate by any recalcitrant successor to the dictatorship.

A considerable road still has to be travelled before these phenomena can coalesce and mature, and there will have to be much debate on how to integrate the best experiences and traditions of past struggle within the present circumstances. The *defensive* resistance of the masses, and of their democratic and revolutionary detachments, is an objective fact which cannot be reversed in short order. Indeed, the weakness which this implies is one of the few sources of encouragement for the disoriented, desperate and exhausted exploiting class. The mass movement had become stronger on the eve of the war, however, and it will tend to gain momentum at a steady though still unpredictable rate. In particular, we are likely to witness a number of sudden social explosions modifying the relations between classes and class fractions, and these will provide a great apprenticeship for the mass movement, accelerating all the objective and subjective processes in play.

This is not to deny the importance of the present level of mass consciousness. The regime of state terror murdered or drove into exile the core of revolutionaries and worker activists, including nearly all the intellectuals and organizing cadre, that had been built up over the preceding twenty years. These tens of thousands of people embodied an extremely rich socio-political experience of general strikes, factory occupations, grassroots union and neighbourhood democracy, marches, armed struggle, revolutionary organization, electoral victory, and class unions. The military bloodbath therefore struck not only at mass organization but also at the very memory of the movement. Another effect was the appearance of a negative fear or demoralization among sections of the people, above all those hit by unemployment. But although these factors must in no way be underestimated, it is possible to overcome them by utilizing the emergent spaces in the mass movement itself and re-establishing a flow of communication between new activists and revolutionary tradition.

For more than six years the Argentinian people has suffered an almost complete lack of legal, political publications or reasonably honest newspaper reporting. This is particularly striking in the case of students, whose study programmes have involved a total depoliticization. The authorities did not rest at banning the mere mention of Marxism; they drew a line through all forms of democratic and progressive thought. Since the weak revolutionary and socialist groups were unable to organize alternative channels, virtually no underground publications managed to sustain themselves beyond a brief, localized existence. A strong tendency has therefore emerged to ideologize reality according to an essentially Peronist or 'national-populist' world view, so that political events are simplistically reduced to a conflict between the 'people-nation' and 'imperialism-oligarchy'. The Malvinas War exacerbated this trend, adding the dangerous possibility that it could be used to support a 'national-corporatist' military orientation. For these reasons, it is crucially important to engage in democratic and socialist agitation and propaganda, and simply to present objective political information. This will help to overcome ideological backwardness and the jingoist sentiments lurking at the heart of the mass movement.

The most progressive elements in the present situation, constituting a link between the democratic revolutionary traditions of the past and the immensely more powerful movement of the future, are the widespread hatred of the military dictatorship and the armed forces in general, the growing lack of confidence in the traditional parties, and the development of quite advanced forms of organization for clandestine or semi-clandestine union struggle. But if this force is to advance towards something new and higher, it will have to incorporate the essence of previous historical tradition and to respond effectively to the political challenges of the present.

d) The Struggle for Democracy and Peace

Since, as we have seen, the political and ideological structures of military rule have not been truly broken, the democratic struggle against the whole of the Junta's legacy is a fundamental task of the popular and working-class movement. It alone will broaden the democratic space for mass action, dismantle the repressive military apparatus and thwart all manner of reactionary man-oeuvres. More important still, there is no other way to form a mass-based political-revolutionary bloc, independent of the state and the bourgeois parties and able to knit together diverse social demands in a much broader political framework than that of the labour movement alone.[11].

A democratic movement of this kind should assist the development and extension of the proletarian class struggle, linking it to the oppressed and exploited as a whole and raising the possibility that the struggle for formal democratic demands may be transformed into localized struggles for proletarian-popular democracy, at a higher level even than the experiences which preceded the 1976 military coup.

The consistent struggle for democracy must involve firm opposition to any renewal of the adventurist Malvinas War. For its basic function was to strengthen the military institution, to militarize Argentinian society as such, to intensify the economic and social suffering of the people, and to increase the chances of a 'national-corporatist' solution to the crisis. If a war drive sweeps the state and enlists massive support, the working-class and popular movement will be reduced to impotence and find that the most reactionary opportunist and jingoist currents are reinforced within its own ranks.

In order that the struggle against war may be articulated with the broader democratic struggle against all relics of the dictatorship, it must incorporate as a central demand the trial, removal and imprisonment of those who superintended the death of thousands of innocent conscripts and the diversion of war funds — the very same people responsible for state terrorism and the death or 'disappearance' of many more thousands in the years preceding the Malvinas adventure. Such radical-democratic demands will meet with stiff resistance not only from bourgeois politicians and most labour bureaucrats (who will regard them as 'insane' or 'inopportune' obstacles to national reconciliation), but also from broad sectors of the petty bourgeoisie and even the working class, moved by feelings of national frustration at the Malvinas defeat and still imbued with strong nationalist ideas. Since, however, these demands most consistently express the loathing of the dictatorship felt by the majority of workers and the Argentinian people, a profound movement for democracy and peace may spark a historic splintering of bourgeois hegemony over the mass movement and a break-up of chauvinist ideas as a crucial determinant of mass consciousness. To this end, a clear distinction must be drawn between democratic anti-imperialism — which expresses aspirations to national self-determination, international solidarity and the struggle against monopoly capitalism in all nations — and the national chauvinism that seeks unity with the internal exploiters and murderers of the people in pursuit of some spurious national objective.

e) Towards a Class-Struggle Mass Movement and a Socialist Alternative for the Argentinian People

Even the greatest successes in the struggle for democracy will not automatically solve the economic and political crisis that underlies the hunger, employment, state terrorism and war suffered by the Argentinian people. If no bourgeois party has a programme to solve the crisis, this is because it cannot be solved within the limits of capitalism. And unless a global alternative is put forward and achieved, the present period of instability will lead only to another coup, with devastating consequences for the economy and the social and political conditions of the people.

The alternative can only be anti-capitalist and explicitly socialist, based upon the thoroughgoing reorganization of the economic and political institutions of Argentinian society. The key tasks must be to expropriate the main sources of the nation's wealth and place them under democratic popular and working-class control; to attack parasitic consumption at the roots; to promote various forms of social and co-operative ownership; to point culture in a national-democratic and anti-imperialist direction in which the values of solidarity are to the fore; to introduce democratic planning of social and economic development; and to form institutions representing the true, human forces of production. In short, to establish a Democratic Workers Republic.

The basic dividing-line in a mass regroupment around a socialist perspective cannot be that which separates 'national sectors' (including what we have called the 'populist' bourgeoisie) from imperialism and the oligarchy of big landowners and finance capitalists. But nor should it be the primitive class distinction between workers and bosses. The aim should rather be to unite the working masses against national and foreign capital — and in the category 'working masses' we include white and blue-collar workers, agricultural labourers and the unemployed, intellectuals, technicians and students, and those who work on their own behalf (artisans, small shopkeepers, suppliers of various services, market gardeners, small farmers). The springboard to unity should be the demand for a labour democracy, based upon workers' self-management of the big factories, a concentration of small businesses into producers' and traders' co-operatives, and national planning of economic and social development by democratic representative bodies of the world of labour. This principle is radically opposed both to 'money democracy', whether in its purest form (domination of a financial oligarchy) or its Peronist national-bureaucratic variant, and to the 'statist democracy' to which left apparatchiks and union bureaucrats aspire.

Ranged against this socialist alternative are the forces of the bourgeoisie and its institutions of repression and social control, as well as self-styled revolutionary forces like the Montoneros, whose bureaucratic-nationalist political conceptions tend to divide the mass movement and subordinate it to the populist bourgeoisie or new bureaucratic leaderships.[12]. These powerful obstacles underline the fact that an alternative can only mature as part of the radical-democratic movement, as its most resolute and unifying component. The struggle for a new revolutionary workers' power is the logical and natural development from the democratic struggles and demands of the masses.

Such a path implies that the scattered forces of the socialist and class-struggle left[13] will not only attain internal unity but also ally with other revolutionary, socialist and democratic currents emerging from Peronism, Christian organizations and the radical wings of other bourgeois parties. It also presupposes the development of a broad anti-bureaucratic, class-struggle current at the heart of the labour movement, as the essential core and social base of the democratic and socialist movement. Otherwise, it will not be possible to overcome the stage of petty-bourgeois democratism, and the movement will either be deflected by bureaucratic apparatus politics or become a mere appendage of the bourgeois-populist left.

This is by no means a speculative or sectarian fantasy on our part. For a class-struggle current would be a natural sequel to the many dynamic and progressive tendencies revealed in the historic experiences of the labour movement. From the *cordobazo* to the formation of the Salta CGT, from the strikes and mobilizations against the dictatorship to the numerous attempts at rank-and-file union organization, the last decade and a half has often witnessed embryonic tendencies towards class independence, self-organization, alliance with other oppressed layers and the formulation of socialist demands.

The present crisis will spontaneously generate many such tendencies. The challenge facing revolutionary militants is to help them develop and reach maturity, so that a conscious political and organizational plan may weigh decisively in the formation of a democratic socialist bloc of the oppressed and exploited. Then a solid foundation will have been built for a progressive solution to the crisis lashing Argentina.

7

Postscript:
Argentina After the Elections

The collapse of the Military Junta began with the defeat in the Malvinas and ended with the general elections of 30 October 1983, in which the Radical candidates of the UCR won a resounding victory. In this section we shall analyse the process of transition and locate the crucial determinants of the new government's policy and the immediate evolution of Argentinian society. Although there is not yet a mass movement seeking to challenge the social system as such, a deep process of self-examination and moral–intellectual renewal is spreading through the country. We shall therefore begin by assessing the global crisis of Argentina and the stage reached by the mass movement and the various political formations.

1. The Economic Situation

The Argentinian economy has continued to worsen since 1980, and the April–June War had relatively minor or episodic consequences in this respect. The new spur given to the arms drive, for example, was fully within the logic of previous developments; and the resulting drain of foreign currency reserves seems to have had a lesser effect upon the balance of payments than has such factors as under-invoicing and the contraband boom.[1] Gross Domestic Product, which had already fallen by 5.7 per cent in 1981, continued to decline at an annual rate of 5.9 per cent in the first quarter of 1982 and moved further downward in the next year and a half. The rate of inflation, which had risen from 100 per cent in 1980 to 131 per cent in 1981, stood at a monthly average of about 6 per cent during the war and shot up to 16.3 per cent in July 1982. The huge price rises since then would suggest a rate of some 350 per cent for 1983.

General Bignone's assumption of the presidency brought not only the political opening demanded by the bourgeois opposition, but also a turn away from the 'liberal' economic policy of previous years. Under the new economics minister Dagnino Pastore, a team of pragmatic economists bitterly critical of Martínez de Hoz-style monetarism now took charge of policy (D. Cavallo, men like Gottheil, Fraguio or Santirso who were linked to the industrial and agricultural employers' associations). They reimposed the old *dirigiste* formulas, which required a multiple exchange-rate, firm price control or, more fundamentally still, a 'financial reform' to re-establish a regular credit system at strongly negative rates of interest. But although the new policy allowed financial assets to be channelled into the commodities market, temporarily boosting production with the help of import controls and an undervalued peso, the longer-term result was to fuel inflation, speculation in land and physical assets, and the development of smuggling and underinvoicing. Banks saw a third of their deposit funds disappear by the beginning of 1983, since their monthly rate of interest was ten per cent lower than the fifteen-per-cent rate of inflation. The country was on the brink of total chaos by the time that Pastore and Cavallo were replaced by another team consisting of Wehbe and Del Solar.

These unmistakable signs of crisis were compounded by a grave external position which led Argentina to a virtual suspension of international payments. As the second half of 1982 began, the Central Bank found itself facing a bill of $15bn for the rest of the year, including interest payments and the portion of the principal already due or about to become so. Since export earnings amounted to barely half this figure, the authorities had to enter into laborious negotiations with the IMF in order that the big international banks should accept a new repayment schedule. By December 1982 the process was sufficiently far advanced for the Bank of International Settlements and the world's major central and private banks to join the talks. These now centred both on fulfilment of the terms provisionally agreed with the IMF (wage restraint, drastic cuts in the budget deficit and the external current account, a programme to bring down inflation, etc.), and on a set of much thornier problems sometimes with internal political implications, such as the lifting of wartime sanctions on British firms, the pledging of Argentina's gold reserves, a change in the bankruptcy laws that prioritized the claims of internal creditors, and the requirement that Argentina should submit to international law in any disputes over implementation of the agreements. The directly economic demands were also extremely onerous: a system of surcharges and commissions was to raise the effective rate of interest four per cent above 'libor', and public companies requesting new loans were to increase their tariffs according to the model of Aerolineas Argentinas.[2] The whole question of the external debt therefore became an extremely serious economic and political problem for Argentina. The ink had scarcely dried on the first agreements with the IMF when Wehbe launched yet another 'financial reform', in January 1983, which deepened the already major political crisis.

The different branches of the economy were affected with unequal severity: whereas agriculture suffered relatively little, industry producing for the internal market once again received the hardest blows.[3] The new element in the situation was the gradual collapse of the finance sector, publicly seen as the main beneficiary of military rule. According to figures released by the president of the Central Bank, its contribution to GDP fell by 28 per cent between 1981 and 1982, after a decline of 10 per cent between 1980 and 1981. This was essentially due to the fact that the banking sector could neither attract deposits at the officially controlled rate of interest, nor place them at a rate affordable by private business. Between June 1982 (when a credit boom followed Cavallo's financial reform) and May 1983, the flow of bank loans to private business in the main areas of economic activity plunged from 35bn pesos to approximately 20bn pesos (at January 1982 values), and the trading bills discounted by the banks fell in value from 12bn pesos to 6.4bn pesos. According to a report in *Clarín*, the declining role of the bank finance reflected a tendency for major companies to lend short-term liquid assets to one another, at a rate of interest lower than that available on the free market.[4]

Paradoxically, the banking crisis developed just when interest rates were peaking at 19 per cent, when financial speculation was raging together with other forms,[5] and when the outcry was loudest against the 'speculative economy' and the oppression of production by finance. We should bear in mind, however, that the 'finance speculators' of recent years have been not a handful of specialized money capitalists but all sections of capital (industrial, commercial, agrarian and banking), which are often unified in holding companies. Given the rapid devaluation of money and its wild fluctuations in relation to world money and commodity movements, these companies find it much more advantageous to invest their liquid assets in speculation than in production and reproduction. The main actor in this speculative game is precisely big monopoly capital. Whether or not it actually owns banks, it has the largest funds at its disposal, and the best opportunities and networks for speculative activity. In order to avert a total breakdown in the chain of payments, the state intervened to support the banking sector by guaranteeing deposits, providing credits to private banks, raising high-cost external loans, and so forth. These mechanisms naturally had a worsening effect on the fiscal crisis and the rate of inflation.

The main victims of the economic crisis were the wage-earners, whose income diminished month by month and whom the capitalists subjected to lay-offs and redundancies in an attempt to shore up profit margins. Unemployment, both full and partial, steadily rose to the million mark in April 1983. As to real wage levels, the soaring rate of inflation (17.2 per cent in August and 22 per cent in September 1983) and the wide sectoral diversity of working-class strength make it very difficult to give a precise estimate. What is clear, however, is that drastic wage cuts gave rise to a powerful movement of strikes and demonstrations, culminating in the great general strikes of 6 December 1982 and 28 March 1983. In turn, these actions both reflected and deepened the crisis of military rule and the factional splintering of the bourgeois front.

2. The Regime in Crisis

The military dictatorship installed by the coup of March 1976 was the most totalitarian and authoritarian ever seen in Argentina, and perhaps anywhere in Latin America. Unlike the Brazilian military or the Pinochet regime in Chile, the Argentinian Junta could not directly base itself upon any organized civilian force, and therefore had to rely on the army and police themselves in order to construct a new institutional system. The supreme authority resided in the heads of the army, navy and air force, who jointly appointed the president of the Republic and supervised his activity. The rest of the state apparatus was structured around this purely military force, which held in thrall the judiciary, the educational system, the mass media and the various social organizations, and carried decisive weight in provincial and municipal government, and in the main companies and offices depending on the federal government.

Two kinds of civilians took part in the 'Process of National Reorganization': business and finance figures embodying the interests of finance capital; and 'deserters' from the traditional parties. A second line of 'critical' supporters included the different sectors of the big bourgeoisie — which agreed with the general aim of disciplining and restructuring Argentinian society — establishment newspapers such as *La Prensa* or *La Nación,* the core of the greatly weakened conservative parties, and a handful of ideologists of the big liberal bourgeoisie (e.g., Alvaro Alsogaray). The Catholic Church was an important enthusiast of the 1976 coup and, notwithstanding a few moderate criticisms of human rights violations or differences over international policy, it continued to support the Junta until the end.[6] Not a few of the regime's direct collaborators came from the right wing of the Church.

Apart from these cases, then, the great mass of the bourgeoisie and petty bourgeoisie initially considered the Junta as just a lesser evil than subversion, economic collapse and social chaos, while the most corrupt and opportunist trade-union bureaucrats hoped for a 'dialogue' that would allow them to keep control of their apparatuses or to maintain some position in the shade of the military administrators. The kind of support given by both was not at all direct or whole-hearted. It may be possible to talk of a relative social consensus among broad class and institutional layers, particularly in relation to the wild ERP assassination campaign in 1971 and later. But the overwhelming element in the structuring of dictatorial rule was the straightforward application of state terror. The results can be seen in the tens of thousands of dead, missing and imprisoned, and in the hundreds of thousands of people threatened with death or terrified by the disappearance of their relatives, friends or work-mates.

There were two sides to state terror: it was *institutional*, as the Junta finally admitted by describing it as 'action in the line of duty';[7] and it was *clandestine,* in that it involved the old tactic of counter-revolutionary white gangs, operating *incognito* with a large degree of autonomy from the ultimate authority. In order to assure the complicity of their whole branch, the high commands of the armed forces would make all their lower echelons take part in 'dirty' operations. And since these were conducted within a framework that gave wide discretionary powers to every level of the police and military, clandestine terrorist methods were eventually used as a screen for personal theft, revenge and corruption of every kind. The secret, vertical and all-embracing 'dirty war' turned the armed forces into a veritable mafia.

The defeat of this rotten edifice in the Malvinas War immediately triggered a full-scale crisis. As the first soldiers returned home, a torrent of accusations was hurled at the irresponsible, cowardly and incompetent commanders, and at the political-military role of the national government. Former conscripts set up organizations like the Centro de Ex-Combatientes and began to make public the protests of soldiers, democratic organizations, political tendencies, and even the dissident high commands. In fact, the military pinnacle itself split along several lines. The most pro-war faction laid the blame at the door of irresolute officers and generals like Massera or Galtieri himself, while a nationalist tendency typified by General Flouret stressed the bungled political and diplomatic conduct of the war. Rear-Admiral Zarategui and Brigadier Crespi levelled charges against the navy and air force commands respectively; ex-President Viola criticized the actual decision to launch the invasion; and Colonel Cesio and many more used democratic arguments against the dictatorial regime that often resulted in disciplinary arrests. In this context, major changes were made at the top of the three services, particularly in the air force[8], and the Rattembach Commission was given the task of investigating military responsibilities.

As the economic prospects grew bleaker and mass activity developed both qualitatively and quantitatively, the political crisis spread to the whole institutional structure of the dictatorship. Press censorship and control of the arts were reduced to every weaker forms, and increasingly critical positions were set down in print. Two of the many publications that began to appear at this time were *La Voz* (close to Saadi's Intransigencia Peronista) and *Quorum* (which specialized in sensationalist exposures of Massera, the P-2 masonic lodge and the 'verticalist' sector of Peronism). The revolutionary press also reappeared legally, while periodicals like *Humor, Siete Dias, La Semana, Hechos* and *Clarín* all published statements by the human rights organizations. The dictatorship tried to close some of these down, but the judicial power also began to reassert itself by authorizing their continued publication.

The breaking of the military's grip on the judiciary was a crucial element in the crisis of the regime. Although the Supreme Court feebly continued to follow official guidelines, many judges and lower courts ruled against the interests of the government, even ordering investigations of various dignitaries or jailing military personnel in cases of embezzlement, kidnapping, abuse of authority, or economic offences. Among those hauled before the courts were Harguindegy (Videla's minister of the interior), Massera (former commander-in-chief of the navy) and Fiorillo (a commodore who had just been appointed assistant police commissioner for the province of Buenos Aires). The list of civilians included no lesser figures than Martínez de Hoz, Aleman, Cavallo and Ianella (all former economics ministers, or presidents of the central bank). A group of democratic lawyers replaced the right-wing leadership of the Buenos Aires Lawyers Association and, together with the legal workers union and human rights bodies, opened an offensive against the Supreme Court. A special tribunal headed by a member of the Supreme Court removed L. Damianovich de Cerrado from her judge's position on the grounds that she had refused to investigate allegations of torture or to question detainees at the Police Department, rather than in her private office. Similarly, a case was laid against the federal judge Gilletta for a multimillion-peso fraud involving the Oddone Group, and for complicity in the kidnapping and death of a minor, J. A. Polizecki.[9]

In education, the student movement gained in strength and carried out major actions against the anti-democratic university law, rigged entrance examinations and unjust quotas, and the payment of fees. It also threw itself behind the human rights organizations and the most progressive currents within the trade unions and political parties. Some university authorities, such as the Dean of Law and the Academic Council of Medicine at Buenos Aires, tried to reach an accommodation with the students, calling for repeal of the university law, democratic election of rectors, and student representation on faculty boards.

As to the trade unions, any remaining state control collapsed in the face of a wave of mobilizations and rank-and-file organization that systematically breached the Junta's Occupational Association Act. Although strikes remained illegal until 2 June 1983, two general strikes and numerous other stoppages took place before that date.

The question of the *desaparecidos,* and of military and governmental responsibility for known crimes, began to assume greater importance as the prime source of the regime's discomfort. The human rights bodies gained new space and strength, enlisting the support of the student movement and party youth organizations, as well as of minority sections of the labour movement. The issue was even taken up by the Church and the component parties of Multipartidaria, further pressuring the regime to give an answer.

Although divisions remained within the regime, a rough consensus appeared to develop on four lines of action: political retreat to allow for elections; transfer of governmental power to the parties winning a majority; reforging of the cohesion of the armed forces; and a substantial increase in the military capability of all three services.

The handing over of government was decided in two stages. Although a statement of intent was announced on 2 July 1982, it was not until March 1983 that a precise timetable was issued. In the intervening period, attempts were made to impose a conditional electoral agreement on the basis of a prior accord between the military regime and 'representative sectors of the national destiny'. Thus, on 12 November 1982 the Junta called for a national accord on such questions as the struggle against terrorism, the fate of the *desaparecidos,* the Malvinas conflict, the stability of the judicial system, and the constitutional presence of the armed forces in the future government. But since the political parties were opposed to a deal along these lines — opposition echoed by the huge mass mobilization on 16 December — the dictatorship was forced to proceed with elections without attaching formal conditions of any kind.

As to the unity of the military establishment itself, two essential tasks had to be performed. On the one hand, an organic recomposition of the three high commands was accompanied by the removal of officers too deeply compromised in the war, and then by the reintegration of the navy and air force into the Junta. On the other hand, all three branches of the armed forces collaborated in building a new moral and ideological unity around the tradition of the war against subversion. None of the high commands repudiated the past actions of state terror, and indeed new operations began in July 1982 with the full support of the government and the top military brass.[10] Official speeches continually referred to the imminent prospect of a new subversive campaign, and stressed the need to protect the unity and cohesion of the armed forces from the influence of dubious civilian layers. The Junta's 'final document' clearly reaffirmed that, 'should it again become necessary', the same action would be taken as in the past.

This 'final document' on the record of the dictatorship, published on 28 April 1983, characterized the operations of the dirty war as an 'act of duty' and left it to history to judge whether 'unjust methods had been used or innocent people had died'. On 22 September an Amnesty Law cleared of criminal responsibility all members of the repressive forces who had acted within the established institutional framework. However, since the main political parties rejected this law, its main purpose was not so much to provide effective protection for the officers concerned, as to develop the moral and ideological unity of the military caste and to issue civil society with a clear warning for the future. In fact, the law itself did not rule out the possibility of individual prosecutions in cases where 'excesses' had been committed outside the established institutional framework. (The government recognized as much in the trial of Massera, and in July 1983 the Ministry of the Interior informed the political parties that more than two hundred members of the armed forces and the security services were under detention.) What the military authorities really wanted to stress was that they would not allow civilian interference in the judging of their own repressive activities. To a greater or lesser extent, both the major political parties and the Church accepted this basic principle.

If we turn now to the post-Malvinas rearmament, Argentina has either acquired or taken steps to acquire the following material since July 1982:

(a) *Aircraft:* 32 Mirages (including Daggers), making a total of 75;[11] 24 A-4 Skyhawks, purchased from Israel; 14 Super-Etendards; 12 Brazilian Xavantes; 12 French-built AS 332 Super-Puma helicopters, each capable of carrying two Exocets; and 50 Mig-23s, fitted with 30mm cannons.[12] There are also reports of talks to purchase French Alpha-Jets. Altogether, these new supplies considerably exceed the 32 aircraft which Brigadier Lami Dozo admitted lost during the war,[13] or even the 58 aircraft (not including Pucaras) and 18 helicopters which the British claim to have brought down.[14]

(b) *Ships:* 4 German-built frigates ordered before the war; 4 new German TR-1700 submarines; 4 destroyers of unknown origin (according to a report by the scientists Chelala and Westerkamp in the *New York Times*); and possibly two Soviet-built nuclear submarines. It should also be noted that Argentinian shipyards are currently working on frigates and submarines with German licences and equipment. Once again, the new purchases are well in excess of the war losses.

(c) *Missiles:* It has been estimated that some thirty Exocets have been bought from Sudan, and another ten or twenty from other countries.

(d) *Army equipment:* Chelala and Westerkamp mention the purchase of 157 tanks from Austria. Other sources refer to major acquisitions of anti-aircraft matériel, and of infra-red and light-intensification equipment.

(e) *Atom bomb production:* North American and British sources claim that Argentina is on the brink of exploding its first atomic device. Buenos Aires has denied this report, as well as most of the other information about arms purchases.

This wastage of billions of dollars, at a time of acute economic difficulties, met with complete silence on the part of political, union and Church leaders. The political parties, especially the Peronists, also tended towards complicity with the armed forces in the continual talk of a new war over the Malvinas. In the Beagle Channel conflict, however, the politicians generally demanded that the military government accept the papal proposals, for fear that a future constitutional government would be accused by the military of 'betraying the fatherland'.

There were a number of other questions on which the political evolution of the armed forces was far from unanimous. In foreign policy the Non-Aligned meeting in India in March 1983, and the June meeting of UNCTAD in Belgrade, saw General Bignone declare with barefaced cynicism that Argentina was against 'militarism', 'apartheid' and 'outside interference' in Central America,[15] and that it supported the PLO and other such causes. Although these new postures were strongly resisted within the high commands of the armed forces, they seem to have gone down well with middle-ranking officers and the Multipartidaria politicians. Similarly, the ever more nationalist orientation of broad sections of the military — most apparent in the air force's denunciation of the IMF's role and its call for the prosecution of Martínez de Hoz — corresponded to the demands of the main political parties, the union bureaucracies and the Church hierarchy.

It is evident that many of these tendencies pointed to what we have called a 'national-corporatist' solution to the crisis: one that would institutionalize a regime of state terror. But the final outcome depends on a large number of factors, of which the most important is the course of the democratic mass movement.

3. Movements from Below

In the period from the end of the war to March 1983, while the armed forces were wrestling with political and union leaders over the terms of a political opening, the mass movement continued its upward trend already apparent before the second of April. The ex-combatants associations launched their campaign of declarations and protest actions; housewives took to the streets in the Buenos Aires region, Córdoba and Rosario (the shop boycott of 30 July, the 'empty shopping bags' march of 6 August); and local struggles broke out against the poor quality and high cost of municipal services in Greater Buenos Aires. Groups of unemployed workers, centred on the local church or independent bodies such as the Unemployment Committee of La Plata, Berisso and Ensenada, launched major actions which reached a climax on the feast day of Saint Cayetano, patron saint of labour, when hundreds of thousands gathered in Liniers, Quilmes, Rosario and other areas. Labour mobilizations did not reach a high level until the last months of 1982, although there were strikes and other actions in the docks, railways and tramways and the first signs of activity among public employees. On 23 September the CGT–Brasil called a general strike, which was only partially successful, and a protest march brought together some 15,000 people against the feeble concessions being proposed by the dictatorship. In this way the 'hard' wing of the Peronist trade unions temporarily revived the tradition of opposition that had existed before 2 April, strengthening its position within the Justicialista and union movements. At the same time the human rights organizations, headed by the Association of the Mothers of the Plaza de Mayo, intensified their struggle and organized a wide range of actions (demonstrations, leafleting, petitions, trips abroad, court cases, etc.). In campaigning for the reappearance of the missing, the release of political prisoners, the repeal of repressive legislation and the dismantling of the state terrorist apparatus, they were often subjected to harassment or physical assault. But although their struggle was increasingly successful, culminating in the October March for Life, they did not manage to cross the threshold into truly mass actions.

The first party-political rally was held during this period, when the Radical Youth brought together a crowd of seven thousand to listen to Alfonsín in the federal capital. But the parties devoted most of their efforts to a recruitment drive, reaching a phenomenal combined membership of 35 per cent of the electorate around the end of the year. As the Multipartidaria hardened its position against the Junta's manoeuvres, the unions — above all the CGT–Brasil — also stepped up their pressure, and on 6 December the two union federations called for a general strike. The rival CGT–Azopardo had for some time sought official favour by distancing itself in practice from the Peronist movement. But once it saw that this tactic was weakening its base without bringing significant government concessions, it too decided to call for mobilization.[16]

Towards the end of 1982, then, a broad array of social and political forces came together in a 'hot December'.[17] On the fourth of the month veteran conscripts from the Malvinas War staged a veritable act of insubordination by organizing their own ceremony in honour of the dead. Two days later, a general strike called by the two CGTs and supported by the Multipartidaria paralysed virtually the whole of industry, commerce and the service sector, embracing a total of some nine million workers. On 9 and 10 December all the human rights organizations held a Resistance March in the vicinity of the Plaza de Mayo in Buenos Aires, which attracted some ten thousand people and was supported by various youth movements, left-wing organizations and democratic tendencies within the political parties. Finally, on 16 December the Multipartidaria and the union federations mobilized 150,000 to 200,000 in a 'march for democracy'. As the crowd went far beyond the official slogans of the march, venting its accumulated hatred of the dictatorship, the repressive forces intervened and produced a number of deaths, injuries and arrests.

At the level of the state and the dominant classes, this broad mobilization sparked off a temporary crisis by threatening to break the precarious equilibrium within the reconstituted Junta and to cut off its relations with the parties and unions, already considerably more bitter as a result of the introduction of economic austerity measures. At the level of society itself, the 'hot December' deepened the struggle for democratic and other demands, under the impact of the social and political crisis.

Some sections of the military apparatus now tried to discard the conditions set by the Multipartidaria and to insist on a controlled transition or even the reversal of the political opening.[18] However, since the navy and air force and the pro-Nicolaides wing of the army rejected such an approach, a decision was eventually taken to break the deadlock by calling elections for 30 October, scheduling a return to civilian government for 30 January 1984, and appeasing the bourgeoisie with a more flexible credit policy and a reduction in official interest rates. Between March and April 1983 the commanders-in-chief of the navy and army gave an unconditional promise that they would never again try to overthrow a government based on popular sovereignty. When President Bignone added his third-worldist contribution at the New Delhi conference, the politicians and union leaders ended their anti-government campaign and turned their eyes to the forthcoming elections within their own organizations.

The CGT–RA (formerly Brasil) was now accepted by the government as a valid interlocutor, and an alliance was forged between a sector of the army top brass and the '62 Peronist Union Organizations' on which it was based.[19] Paradoxically, it was the CGT–Azopardo which initially called a general strike for 28 March, while the CGT–RA was merely dragged along behind it.

At the same time, the mass movement itself was developing in leaps and bounds: legal, tramway and railway workers, mechanics, electricians, petrol pump attendants, schoolteachers, policemen and public employees all launched strike actions to bring their wages in line with inflation, to reinstate sacked colleagues, to force the repeal of repressive legislation, and so forth. Rank-and-file committees of teachers and rail and state employees began to take independent initiatives, while various anti-bureaucratic tendencies took shape even within the CGT–RA. It was above all the major Volkswagen strike of February–March 1983 which saw the emergence in leading positions of militant, class struggle currents. Similar developments occurred within the most advanced sector of the rail union, particularly the signalmen; old-style bureaucrats were removed from the regional leaderships of the paperworkers and other unions; and shop stewards' committees and other delegate structures were formed in the most important factories of the industrial heartlands of Argentina.

The nation-wide strike movement which developed in August–September 1983 centred above all on the sector of state workers (the most neglected by the various incomes policies of the 'Process of National Reorganization'), and much less on industry proper. Against a background of 17 per cent inflation in August and 22 per cent in September, implying a reduction of nearly 50 per cent in real wages, teachers and lecturers, legal, clerical and customs workers set an example of strike action that was even followed by the police in Buenos Aires, Córdoba, La Pampa and Santa Cruz. At the beginning of September the 1,200 employees of the National Mint also stopped work, creating an acute shortage of banknotes and fiscal and postage stamps. As the situation span out of control, a veritable outcry against the passivity of the union apparatuses forced them to call another national strike for the election month of October.

The consistent democratic movement had also been gaining in strength, and on 21 May thirty thousand people marched through the streets of Buenos Aires to demonstrate their rejection of the Junta's 'final document'. The Association of the Mothers of the Plaza de Mayo and other groups of relatives, Perez Esquivel's Servizio de Paz y Justicia and similar human rights bodies were joined by columns from the PO, MAS, PCA, PSU and several organizations of the independent, *clasista* left, as well as by the Intransigent Party and the left wings of the bourgeois parties (the Peronist Intransigencia y Movilización, the Radical Renovación y Cambio, and the Christian–Democrat Humanismo y Liberación). However, neither the three principal formations of the Multipartidaria nor the two wings of the CGT responded to an express invitation to support the march. From the platform Conte MacDonell, leader of the Humanismo y Liberación current, said: 'We know that behind every missing person, behind every corpse, there is a dossier in the files of those sinister armed forces. When the time comes, the people will be able to use them as evidence'. The Nobel prize winner Adolfo Perez Esquivel added: 'The alternative, liberation or dependence, now means state terrorism or popular democracy... . All the organizations of national political life must incorporate the defence of human rights in their programme... . We will no longer tolerate accomplices.'[20]

This march signalled a considerable advance on the mobilization of 9 and 10 December: not only were the press estimates of the number of demonstrators three times higher, but there was a much better relationship of forces between the radical wing of the democratic movement and the political bloc structured around the Multipartidaria. The human rights organizations were already intensifying their public denunciations of the role of the party apparatuses.[21] And since then, the radical democratic movement seems to have retained its high level of strength and influence, perhaps even extending it in September in the struggle against the Junta's 'self-amnesty' law. The great weakness of 1983, however, was that the rising combativity and independence of the mass movement did not find expression in a global political and social alternative to the policies of the traditional leaderships.

4. The Parties in the Election Campaign

The elections held on 30 October involved a confrontation between the two historical parties and pillars of the Multipartidaria: the Justicialist Party (PJ) or Peronist movement, and the Racical Civic Union (UCR) or Radicals. The Peronists could rely on the massive support of the trade-union movement, politically structured in the '62 Organizations', on their close links with sectors of the major ruling powers (the army, the Church, 'national' business interests), and on their long tradition of electoral participation. Historically the main tendencies of the Peronist movement have been: a right wing with relatively little internal weight, and itself divided between a fascist and a 'moderate' section; a very broad centre grouping the bulk of the union movement and its traditionally dominant current, *vandorismo*;[22] the local political bosses, functionaries of previous Peronist governments and advisers to the union apparatus; and a Left whose strength has varied with the involvement of the youth movement and the political radicalism of the unions. In Perón's lifetime the balance between these forces largely depended on the leader's political twists and turns, so that from 1970 to 1973 he based himself on the pro-Montonero Left and from 1973 until his death on the fascist right. Since he disappeared from the scene, however, the inner logic of the movement has tended to favour the centre.

With the legal reconstitution of the Justicialist Party, the centre acquired decisive weight and was able to impose its own lists of parliamentary, regional and presidential candidates. For the presidential elections it soon became apparent that Luder and Bittel were to be the chosen duo. Italo Argentino Luder is a sixty-six year-old lawyer with a long tradition in the Peronist movement (a deputy in 1949, defence counsel for Perón in 1955, legal adviser to the CGT and UOM, the historical base of *vandorismo*, and then to the Archbishop of Buenos Aires, chairman of the Senate until March 1976 and provisional president in October–November 1975, when he replaced Isabel Perón at the height of the political crisis). Deolindo Bittel is a populist provincial politician who currently occupies the presidency of the PJ, after a long career in the Peronist movement. With strong roots in the Chaco bourgeoisie, he also has close ties to the union apparatus and the Church, as well as to Luder himself.

The structure of the PJ and the composition of its election lists reflect the weight of the political wing of the trade-union movement. Lorenzo Miguel, leader of the majority of the UOM and the '62 Organization', moved on from his victory over the largely a-political CGT–Azopardo to play a key role in the political unification of the movement around the PJ. Moreover, as the backbone of the Peronist movement, Miguel's forces were able to conclude an 'army–union pact' with the faction of officers around Generals Nicolaides and Trimarco, subsequently using it to increase their room for manoeuvre in the ongoing process of trade-union 'normalization' and to bind the military hard-liners to an electoral solution.[23] In order to play this role, *miguelismo* has used the forces particularly of the Peronist Union Youth as a battering ram against the Left and the democratic movement. A series of physical assaults culminated on 8 September in a cowardly attack on a delegation from the Association of Mothers of the Plaza de Mayo, outside the headquarters of the CGT-RA.[24]

Although the 'moderate' wing of Peronism, represented by the CGT–Azopardo and the Matera–Robledo current in the PJ, has suffered a crushing political defeat, the rapprochement between *miguelismo* and the armed forces has indirectly strengthened the positions of the fascist Peronist right. 'Ultra-verticalist' figures have been calling for unconditional allegiance to Estela Martinez de Perón, as the political heir of the Jefe, and there is a grave danger of some accord between the trade-union pinnacle and the remnants of the 'Triple A'. At the same time, the left has been completely marginalized within both the political apparatus and the union section of the Peronist movement. Since it lacks an effective union base and the youth has generally moved away from Peronism, the present expression of the left, the Intransigencia y Movilización current, could not prevent its virtual rout in the internal struggle. Its only victory was in Catamarca province, one of the most backward in the country, where its leader Dr Saadi is the historic leader of the Peronist movement.

The rightward trend of Peronism is clearly reflected in its policy statements and governmental programme, which have a much less populist or nationalist tinge than in the past. At the level of the economy, the main demand has been for a 'Social Pact' between the government and the labour and employer's organizations. The Peronists continue to raise historical banners relating to exchange controls, protectionism, nationalization of bank deposits, negative rates of interest, and incomes policy. But they lay ever greater stress on social discipline and oppose the introduction of price controls, while foregrounding their relations with large-scale industry and the promotion of industrial exports. With regard to foreign capital, their liberal pronouncements speak only of regulation, and their stand on the external debt and relations with the IMF envisages no more than that a constitutional government will be able to negotiate improved terms. At the level of internal politics, the Peronist leadership has used extremely ambiguous terms in charting future relations with the armed forces: they are to be 'recovered for the nation' and removed from the influence of 'anti-national forces'. It has evaded the question of the *desaparecidos*, stressing its firm opposition to any kind of 'Nuremberg justice'. It has remained silent on the new arms drive and spoken against the ending of hostilities in the South Atlantic. Its foreign policy has followed a traditional third-worldist line.

Secondary support for the Justicialist Party has been much weaker than on previous occasions, since traditional allies like the Movement for Integration and Democracy (MID), the Intransigent Peronists and the Christian Democrat Party (PCD) decided to present their own candidates in the elections and to reserve their future position on the electoral college charged with electing the president. In fact the only other support has come from a curious 'left-wing' alliance, the COLINA, and two equally opportunist groups: the FIP and the PPT.

The COLINA embraces the People's Conservative Party (PCP) of Vicente Solano Lima, the People's Socialist Party (PSP), the United Socialist Party (PSU), and the Argentinian Communist Party (PCA).[25] (A split-off from the PCA, the Popular Left Front (FIP) of Jorge Abelardo Ramos, continues to endorse the PJ's policy formulas.) Thus, the alliance comprises a wing of the old oligarchic conservative party (the PCP), two nationalist–social-democratic formations with no mass base, and the traditional party of the pro-Soviet left. For its part, the FIP is a strange amalgam of ostensibly Trotskyist discourse and a right-nationalist political and ideological posture (prostration before the armed forces, agitation for the idea of renewing the Malvinas War, and so on). The Bread and Labour Party (PPT) is the legal cover for what has remained of the Revolutionary Communist Party (PCR) since its protracted nationalist-opportunist degeneration, involving political alignment with Peking and support for the fascist wing of Peronism at the height of the 'Triple A' terror. The PPT describes itself as a 'third-worldist' party and calls for a struggle against 'the two imperialisms'.

The UCR Radicals led by Raul Alfonsín were the only major alternative to the Peronists in the October elections. In their ninety years of political existence, they became the political and ideological expression of the liberal petty bourgeoisie and the middle agrarian bourgeoisie, embodying the most thorough-going programme of bourgeois democracy in Argentina. Howev-er, the *balbinista* old guard had brought the UCR to a position of virtual complicity with state terrorism and military dictatorship, when Alfonsín's victory in the mid-1983 inner-party elections shifted the movement back to more traditional perspectives and drew in sizeable sections of the youth and of the Marxist left of the early seventies. Alfonsín's candidacy in the presidential elections also became a powerful pole of attraction for the petty bourgeoisie as a whole and large sections of the working class. He did not bring any novel ideas, but he was seen as a clear advocate of the old programme of bourgeois democracy. Above all he argued that it was necessary to 'put the military in their place', making them accountable to the law and to civilian authorities elected by the people.

There should be no doubt, however, that Alfonsín's ideas and political perspectives were far from constituting a consistent democratic alternative. He always remained ambivalent towards the human rights movement, and although the Renovation and Change current participated in many of its demonstrations and solidarized with many of its demands, Alfonsín, like Luder, made clear that he was opposed to any 'Nuremberg' or to the dismantling of the organic structure of the armed forces. In June 1983, for example, he drew a distinction between those who had been 'politically' responsible for state terror or committed various 'excesses', and those who had simply carried out orders. This position created a major opportunity for the terrorist apparatus to ensure its future survival, while dividing the struggle of the democratic movement to break up the repressive apparatuses.[26] We should also bear in mind that Alfonsín supported the Malvinas War until defeat was in sight, that he kept silent about the huge expenditure on arms, and that he publicly backed the Church's call for 'national reconciliation'.

As to its economic and social policy, the UCR does not have any very clear differences with the Peronists. It accepts the need for a social pact, and it has virtually identical proposals concerning protection of the internal market, exchange controls and credit policy. It has talked of refusing to pay 'fictitious debts', but has never explained what it understands by this term. Its attacks on the 'oligarchy' and 'financiers' have never been concretized in a proposal for reform, except insofar as it has called for a cut in interest rates. In foreign policy, too, there seems to be a broad measure of agreement with the Peronists.

The UCR candidates attracted virtually no significant secondary support, although the Federal Alliance (AF), a coalition of anti-Peronist provincial conservatives grouped around Francisco Manrique, and the Socialist-Democrat Alliance, a grouping of social-democrats and right-wing liberals, expressed their willingness to support the Radicals in the electoral college.

Alfonsín's tactical plan in the presidential contest was to combine an appeal for peace and democracy, directed at the broadest layers of the population, with a frontal assault on the 'army-union pact' established between Lorenzo Miguel and the Trimarco-Nicolaides military camarilla. His main objectives were: (a) to undermine the PJ electorally: (b) to weaken the 'political' element within the Peronist unions; and (c) to hold out a bridge to forces within the army and navy opposed to any possible national-corporatist orientation. This whole trajectory has widened the gap between Radicalism and Peronism and made any kind of governmental alliance hard to envisage.

By October 1983 a number of parties had not decided what position they would adopt in the electoral college:

The Movement for Integration and Development (MID), with a membership of some 200,000 against the UCR's 1,600,000 and the PJ's 3,000,000, had areas of programmatic agreement with the PJ, but did not support its candidates. For the MID places the stimulation of investment and economic growth higher than the 'social pact', and it is more in favour of encouraging foreign investment.

The Intransigent Party (PI), like the MID, belongs to the old

Radical tradition of bourgeois-nationalist posturing on such issues as the nationalization of the banks and external trade. Of the five components of the Multipartidaria, it was the most firmly opposed to the military dictatorship, and its crucial base is the anti-imperialist youth.

The Christian-Democrat Party has little political importance, its main support coming from liberal sections of the Church. However, its Humanismo y Liberacíon tendency is closely linked to the human rights movement and is quite advanced on social questions. Whereas the PDC leadership left open whether it would support the Peronists in the electoral college, this current stated that if no party won an absolute majority, it would support the one with the largest number of votes.

The Centre Democratic Union (UCD) of Alvaro Alsogaray is the only party which openly hoists the banners of liberal capitalism and free trade. Resolutely anti-statist and anti-populist in character, it condemns the Peronists and Radicals with equal vigour. It is much more doctrinaire than the Federal Alliance, and less inclined to compromise with the provincial bourgeoisies and the social aspirations of the middle layers.

Three left-wing parties also took part in the elections: two Trotskyist (the MAS and PO), and one pro-Chinese. The largest of these is the MAS or Movement for Socialism, which took shape around the old Trotskyist core of Nahuel Moreno's PST, calling for the formation of a single socialist party together with all sections of the old social-democratic movement.[27] It has nearly eighty thousand members and hundreds of local offices. It has built its support on the basis of nationalist positions (support for the Malvinas War, non-payment of the external debt, struggle for a Second Independence) and the slogan 'No bosses, no generals!' Its almost exclusive focus on electoral agitation has further undermined its position in the workers' movement and, to a lesser extent, in the human rights movement.

The Workers Party (PO) is the legal expression of Politica Obrera, the traditional organization of Lambertist Trotskyism in Argentina. Its positions are much more class-oriented than those of the MAS, and it places much greater stress on the struggle for human rights. It ran Rafaël Flores, well-known historical leader of working-class *clasismo,* as its presidential candidate, and Catalina de Guagnani, a prominent leader of the democratic movement, for the position of president. Although it has slightly fewer members than the MAS, and a much **smaller net**work of local offices, it seems to have a stronger presence in the workers' movement. It played a major role in the Volkswagen dispute, for example, but its vanguardist politics contributed to the eventual defeat. In a less opportunist way it also supported the Malvinas adventure and its sectarian style differs from that of the MAS only by its highly doctrinaire inflection.

A number of other Marxist organizations, which did not participate in the elections, are extending their activity in the workers' movement and the various human rights organizations. Perhaps the most important are Nuevo Curso, PST-Resistencia, the OCPO, FR-17, Acción Comunista and Democracía Popular, most of which condemned the Junta's operation in the Malvinas. Finally, there is quite a broad milieu of democratic and class-struggle militants, distributed among small groups, human rights movements, class-struggle union currents, and the more advanced sectors of the bourgeois parties. In the period before the elections the main debate in these layers focused on whether they should support Alfonsín or the MAS and PO, and on the tactics that should be adopted after the elections in order to deepen the process of democratization and the offensive against state terrorism.

Three main processes were apparent in the dynamic of popular mobilization during the election campaign. The first was the polarization of public support between the two historic parties, as could be seen from the various rallies, opinion polls, and so on. The peak of virulence was reached with the Peronists' slanderous attacks on Alfonsín and the frequent assaults on the Radical Youth by the shock brigades of the union bureaucracy. Although the military rulers professed their neutrality towards the two parties, their actual practice tended to favour the Peronists.

The second process was the advance of the Radicals as they began to hold mass rallies in the federal capital and the principal cities. Their end-of-campaign rally drew a crowd of more than half a million in Buenos Aires, most of it consisting of young and enthusiastic supporters. Alfonsín himself played a particularly important role with his anti-dictatorial and often anti-militarist speeches, occasionally promising to reduce military expenditure to two per cent of the national budget or to abolish compulsory military service.

The third process was the decline in support for the Peronists, and the relative weakness of their party rallies. Moreover, a number of historic figures of the movement actually came out in support of Alfonsín's candidacy. As Italo Luder faltered on the campaign trail, the public became aware of the pact with the military, the bullying attitude of the union bosses, and the repugnant blustering of the supporters of Herminio Iglesias, the union bureaucrat selected by the Peronist apparatus to run for the governorship of Buenos Aires Province. In one spectacular incident a roar of booing prevented Lorenzo Miguel from speaking at one of the main Peronist rallies of the campaign. Nevertheless, on the eve of the polls the Peronists were able to draw a crowd of nearly a million, twice more than the attendance at Alfonsín's closing rally. When the last opinion poll was published, it still showed a slight edge for the Peronists, but confirmed the loss of the huge lead they had enjoyed at the beginning of the campaign.

5. Alfonsín's Victory and the Prospects for the New Government

Political observers and even UCR leaders were quite surprised by the results of the 30 October elections. Alfonsín won 52 per cent of the popular vote against the PJ's 40 per cent, securing an overwhelming majority not only in the federal capital — which had been widely expected — but also in Córdoba, Rosario, Avellaneda, San Martín and other industrial areas. The Peronists picked up most of the rural districts, particularly in the smaller, poorer and politically backward parts of the country. The Radicals won an absolute majority in the Chamber of Deputies and the electoral college, so that it will not be necessary for them to undergo a second round of the presidential contest in a more rarefied political environment. Only in the Chamber of Senators and the provincial governorships did they fail to establish a clear supremacy.

The Peronists were, of course, the great losers in the elections. They saw the collapse of their historic majority of sixty per cent or more, and they even lost control of their electoral bastions in the industrial districts of Buenos Aires and Rosario. For the first time in the forty-year history of the movement, not only the Argentinian people but the industrial working class voted against Peronism. Whereas October 1943 witnessed the rise of the Peronist labour movement as the principal political and social force in modern Argentina, October 1983 drew a clear line under a whole period of the country's history.

The 30th of October was also a defeat for the military's desperate attempt to keep a grip on power through its pact with the Peronist union bureaucracy. The blow was all the harsher for its unexpected nature, and it considerably reduced the possibilities for the political restructuring of the armed forces in readiness for another coup and wave of terror.

Alfonsín's victory was not, to be sure, based upon a mass revolutionary process, and still less upon the workers' sudden conversion to the liberal ideology of the Radical Civic Union. First of all, it reflected urban Argentina's resounding rejection of an authoritarian and terrorist type of 'politics' which sharply conflicted with the historical and cultural traditions of the Argentinian people. Social psychologists might simply say that it was an expression of mental health. Secondly, it confirmed the rise of the most modern and proletarianized layers of the urban petty bourgeoisie (the professions, office personnel, students, technicians), already evident in the strike movements among public employees and service workers. These were the forces which openly joined the political struggle and moulded the Alfonsín movement as an alternative to the old Radical party bosses and the political forces associated with military rule. Thirdly, it involved the breakdown of the political unity of the working class, which the Peronist union bureaucracy was no longer capable of holding under its discipline. The most youthful, dynamic and experienced sections of workers voted Radical, as an essentially negative rejection of the military and union bosses. In this sense, the active mobilization of the modern petty bourgeoisie succeeded in structuring and carrying along the still passive rebellion of that section of the working class which seeks a democratic opening in order to reforge its class unity. However, the political recomposition of the working class will open a historical perspective very different from the tragic experience of Peronism and from the present Alfonsín period, which can offer very little in this respect.

The election results virtually excluded other parties from the national political arena, their combined total being slightly under eight per cent in the presidential election and slightly more in the others. The Intransigent Party did win two per cent of the national vote and three per cent in the urban areas, while the Christian Democracy also recorded three per cent in the federal capital, where Conte MacDonell, a well-known leader of the human rights movement, was elected deputy. More moderate forces like the MID and the Federal Alliance, however, which used the campaign to recruit more actively than the PI, were almost completely annihilated at the polls. Only the MID managed to climb above one per cent.

The Left vote was even more interesting. The Argentinian Communist Party (PCA), which had promised to mobilize some 800,000 votes for Luder, won only a little more then 100,000 for itself in the parliamentary elections, and many of these seem to have supported Alfonsín for the presidency. With a total vote three times lower than at its historic peak, the PCA does not have a single deputy. Clearly it is paying the price of its complicity with the military dictatorship, and of its continued support for Peronism at a time when it had played out its historical role and was rushing into the arms of the military. The election result is all the more striking in that the PCA was the only party to preserve its cadres intact during the white terror, even increasing its economic strength through its control of the cooperative bank.

The Popular Left Front, which centred its campaign on the need to relaunch the Malvinas War, was hammered below 0.1 per cent of the vote, even though it met with complaisance on the part of the military government and enjoyed fraternal relations with the Peronists in return for a promise of support in the electoral college. The pro-Chinese Bread and Labour Party, which campaigned under the slogan 'Neither Yankees nor Russians' and was also compromised with the Peronists, received an equally derisory percentage of the vote.

Of the groups linked to international tendencies of the Trotskyist movement, the only one to make any impression at all at the polls was the MAS or Movement for Socialism (between 0.3 and 0.4 per cent, three times higher than the PO vote). Curiously the combined MAS and PO vote was less than half the total membership they had legally recruited in the first quarter of 1983. This discrepancy must be particularly difficult for these groups themselves to explain, since they both described the situation as pre-revolutionary on the eve of the elections. It is clear, however, that although there was an initial wave of sympathy for the various expressions of the anti-dictatorial left, which allowed the MAS and PO to go and recruit in the popular districts, neither group constituted a viable long-term option for the most conscious workers and youth. Whatever their formal affiliation at any point in time, their support was channelled towards Alfonsín and, to a much lesser extent, the PI and DC in Buenos Aires.

The various grouplets of the traditional social-democracy were let off no more lightly than the Trotskyist formations and the rest of the Left. What Adolfo Gilly has trenchantly termed the '10th of April Left' shared in the day of national shame by lending its support to the Junta's Malvinas adventure. And the Argentinian people voted not only against the generals and union bureaucrats, but also for the possibility of a healthier and more consistent Left.

The scale and character of Alfonsín's victory do not require any fundamental alteration of the analysis in chapter six. But we do need to clarify a few points concerning the political prospects for Argentina. With a clear majority behind them, the Radicals now face a shell-shocked army, a divided union bureaucracy whose prestige is on the wane, and a Peronist opposition thrown completely onto the defensive. Moreover, the people has great democratic expectations and is willing to support a government that will open up the space for the workers to democratize the unions, for the students and intellectuals to democratize the universities, and for various sections of society to advance their aspirations towards a democratic renewal of political and social life. In purely political terms, then, the new government will have enough time and space to reorganize the military institutions, to foster a democratic restructuring of the trade unions, universities and judicial system, and to reconstitute the institutions of the state on a bourgeois-democratic basis while containing any immediate social explosions that might threaten its stability. But this alone will not resolve the problems of inflation and external indebtedness; nor will it satisfy the pent-up social demands of the workers, generate new jobs or relieve the acute fiscal pressure on small businessmen and self-employed professionals. Indeed, the democratization of national life will create additional space for such demands to attain an organizational expression and eventually to surface in a wave of social and political conflicts that could only be absorbed in a period of sustained economic growth. Even if inflation is brought under control, and even if an upturn in the world economy and world grain prices allows Argentinian exports to rise to a satisfactory level, the basic structural crisis of the

Argentinian economy cannot fail to take exceptionally acute forms.

At that point the class organs of the Argentinian workers will re-emerge with an objectively anti-capitalist dynamic, and the spectre of counter-revolutionary terror will return in search of ways to restore capitalist order. The course of the conflict, however much affected by trends in the national and world economy, will then ultimately depend on what the democratic interlude has given to the two major political forces of contemporary Argentina: the labour movement and the army.

Within the labour movement a fierce tendency struggle will develop among three forces. While the Peronist bureaucracy will desperately try to maintain its positions and to harass the new government with extensive economic demands, the pro-Alfonsín forces will denounce the privileges of the old discredited leaderships and seek to create a new social-democratic bureaucracy, and the various class-struggle currents will fight to exploit the new democratic space for a perspective that is independent of the state and the union bureaucracy. It seems unlikely that Alfonsín, in the concrete economic and historic conditions of Argentina, will manage to fashion a new bureaucratic leadership along the lines of Acción Democrática in Venezuela. For Argentinian capitalism cannot offer a major rise in working-class living standards, and the workers themselves have retained a memory of past levels through their representative factory committees and inter-union bodies.

The question of the army is more clear-cut. Much will depend on the measures that Alfonsín takes to dismantle the terrorist network at the very heart of the military institutions. His plan seems to involve only the compulsory retirement of existing generals, admirals and commodores (a figure of forty army generals has been mentioned) and the direct subordination of the high commands to the Ministry of Defence. Investigations into the fate of the missing will be left to the judiciary, and Alfonsín seems to be opposed to the idea of a parliamentary commission demanded by the human rights organizations. In general, then, Alfonsín will seek to weaken the fascist camarilla at the top of the armed forces and to replace it with a layer of loyal officers. Since no serious attempt will be made to uproot the terrorist structures within the top and middle echelons of the three armed forces, a crucial role will be played by the human rights organizations and the working-class and popular movement. However much it may be accused of destabilizing the situation, the latter will have to stick to its demands and go well beyond the actions of the government.

The fate of the Alfonsín government will turn on its ability to control the labour movement and the army in a context of economic recovery. However, none of the proposed changes will prevent middle-ranking fascist officers from staging another coup when they think it necessary. A real prospect of long-term democracy will require the development of a very broad revolutionary-democratic movement, linked to the democratic reorganization of the working-class and popular movement along class-struggle lines. The stronger the blows delivered against the military apparatus and the union bureaucracy, the greater will be the chance of a new course for Argentina.

A new revolutionary-democratic movement will not appear out of nothing. It can only arise from a massive convergence of social and political militants which adequately absorbs and builds on the best traditions of struggle. In this process Marxist thought and socialist practice will have to be wedded to the most advanced layers of the Christian, Peronist and Radical movements, and above all to an independent rank-and-file freed of the myths and phantasms of the past.

Alejandro Dabat
10 November 1983

Notes

Notes to Chapter One

1. Our aim here is only to synthesize the theoretical framework of revolutionary Marxism on the national question, before proceeding to a concrete analysis of Argentina. We shall therefore give only the indispensable bibliographical references.

2. See Alejandro Dabat, 'La Economía mundial y los países periféricos a partir de la segunda mitad de la decada de los sesenta', *Teoría y Política* 1, and *Tesis Preliminares Sobre la Evolución del Sistema Capitalista-imperialista Mundial*, CIES, Mexico City 1979.

3. This distinction is made in *Imperialism, the Highest Stage of Capitalism*, as well as in *Notebooks on Imperialism* and other works of the same period. Lenin clearly establishes that the concept of semi-colony refers to what he calls political 'semi-dependence' (the word 'political' referring to the level of the state and not simply to diplomatic or economic dependence). A semi-colony is a particular type of economically dependent country, different both from a 'colony' and from a politically dependent country. This concept has been completely distorted by various Trotskyist authors. Mandel, for instance, defines semi-colonies as financially dependent countries which have reached a 'certain level', quite high, of economic dependence. In this view, they 'only appear when key industries and banks are owned or controlled by foreigners and when, *for this reason*, the state itself essentially protects the interests of the foreign imperialist class at the expense of the domestic bourgeoisie. This is the situation in Greece, Brazil, Ghana and Iran.' ('Las Leyes del Desarrollo desigual', in *Imperialismo Hoy*, Buenos Aires 1971.) According to this conception, Mandel should have begun his list of contemporary countries with Canada or Spain. He should also have made a historical reference to Czarist Russia, whose financial dependence was much greater than that of Brazil or Iran. Foreign capital controlled more than 50 per cent of all capital invested in modern Russian industry before 1913 and 75 per cent of the banking system. (See E. Chambre, *La Unión Soviética y el Desarrollo Económico*, Bilbao 1971; and Lenin, *Imperialism*, ch. 3.) Moreover, Russia's huge external debt, the largest in the world, was more than 500 per cent greater than the value of her already sizeable exports (1.52bn roubles worth of exports in 1913 against a debt of 8bn roubles). Was Russia perhaps a semi-colonial country? How does Mandel reconcile his conceptualization with the fact that all the Bolshevik classics described Czarist Russia as a backward imperialist country?

4. This very important but forgotten idea of Lenin's was systematically developed

between 1913 and 1916 in a harsh polemic with, on the one hand, the 'Bundists' and various nationalist tendencies in the Russian, Polish and West European Left, and, on the other hand, what he called the 'imperialist economism' of Rosa Luxemburg, Piatakov and Bukharin. Whereas the former prioritized the struggle to solve the national problem (autonomy, autonomous national culture, etc.) over the struggle for socialism, the latter denied that the right to self-determination could be separated from socialist revolution. In the course of the argument, Lenin developed the idea that national self-determination was a democratic right of historically viable oppressed nationalities regardless of their economic dependence (which they might or might not exercise, according to their assessment of its desirability), and that socialists of the oppressor nations ought vigorously to support this right while fighting for socialism alongside the rest of the world's workers. See, inter alia, *Critical Notes on the National Problem; On the Right of Nations to Self-Determination; Imperialism, the Highest Stage of Capitalism; On the Nascent Trend of Imperialist Economism; On a Caricature of Marxism and Imperialist Economism;* and *Theses on the Right of Nations to Self-Determination.*

5. The concept of neo-colonialism has two historical roots. The first, which we think is progressive, was formulated by African nationalists in the 1950s inspired by Kwame N'Krumah. This involved the condemnation of semi-colonial ties in countries that had been formally decolonized. The Cairo conference in 1961 examined a number of features which clearly implied relations of political semi-dependence — for example, the imposition of 'puppet governments'; the grouping of states into federations or communities linked to the old imperial power; the creation of fictitious state entities like Katanga, Mauritania or Buganda; the formation of colonial economic blocs; capital investment in the form of 'aid' of a manifestly inequitable kind (and not just the simple fact of foreign investment); direct control over the financial and monetary institutions of the new state; and the establishment of military bases. The second concept, which we think is regressive, confuses these aspects with the very different phenomenon of economic dependence pure and simple, and in particular with direct capital investment by transnationals. Some European and North-American neo-Marxists (e.g., O'Connor, *The Meaning of Economic Imperialism,* and to an extent Jalée, *L'Impérialisme en 1970),* as well as Soviet and Chinese authors writing since the 1950s, have developed a whole theory of 'neo-colonialism' that is very similar to Mandel's 'semi-colonialism'.

6. Lenin argued that 'national culture' *per se* was the culture of the dominant class in each national state. Socialists could never lay claim to more than the democratic, socialist and progressive elements present, albeit in embryonic form, in every culture. The essential task, therefore, was to unite the exploited and oppressed of all nations in the struggle for socialism and democracy, rescuing those elements of the national culture which allowed this unified international struggle to develop. (For an ordered account, see *Critical Notes on the National Problem.)*

7. A total of 3.1bn dollars in foreign capital was invested in Argentina in 1913, sixty per cent of it British. This investment was spread in approximately the following manner: 1.037bn dollars in the railways, another bilion dollars in state debts, and the remaining third in such activities as real-estate (close to a sixth of the total), commerce and public services (tramways, gas, electricity, water, ports). Banking and industrial investments were relatively low, as were those in cattle and land purchases. More than half of the total went into the sphere of

circulation (public debt, external and internal trade, land companies, real-estate credits, etc.) Díaz Alejandro *(Essays on the Economic History of the Argentine Republic,* New Haven 1970) cites calculations that long-term foreign investment constituted 40-50 per cent of total fixed investment in the country. But since a large part of this was indirect, it would seem that there the control of fixed assets was no higher than 25-to-30 per cent.

8. After the defeat of the Indians in 1879, the oligarchic governments were concerned to incorporate sectors of the Patagonian desert into the national economy, encouraging the population with gifts of sheep. An interesting element of its territorial policy was the sponsorship of geographical exploration in Tierra del Fuego and the Antarctic, beginning in 1881 with the joint Italian-Argentinian expedition. Another team later went to the South Orkney and South Shetland Islands, and a scientific station was set up on Laurie Island at the beginning of this century. A whole series of similar ventures led up to the first real Antarctic expedition, in 1942.

9. The mendacious propaganda of the employers' federation, which sought to prove that industrialization in the Oligarchic period was brought about by absolute free trade and 'reverse protectionism', is directly contradicted by serious studies of the period. Díaz Alejandro *(op. cit.)* convincingly shows that: a) from 1910 to 1914 duty-free imports made up less than thirty per cent of the total value of imports, and overwhelmingly comprised means of production and other goods which Argentina did not and could not produce at the time; b) dutiable import items enjoyed an average protection of approximately twenty per cent; c) the level of protection on goods traditionally produced in Argentina (wines, other drinks, sugar, flour, oils, wood and leather goods) varied from 30 to 60 per cent; and d) the level of protection on industrial goods which Argentina had the capacity to mass-produce (textiles, wool and cotton articles, paints and inks) varied from 23 to 40 per cent. These figures were more or less similar to those in the USA, Canada, Australia and Germany, and considerably higher than those which Britain and other imperialist powers imposed with their cannons on semi-colonies such as China and Iran (an average of 5 to 6 per cent). It is also very interesting to note that, except from 1835 to 1840, customs tariffs were much lower in the Rosas period half-a-century before. See Miron Burgin, *Economic Aspects of Argentine Federalism: 1820-1852,* Cambridge, Mass. 1946.

10. The economic policy of the oligarchic governments is extremely interesting not only because of its originality — most advanced capitalist countries took longer to adopt Keynesian-type economic policies — but also because it clearly demonstrates that they were the governments of a politically independent state. While the Oligarchic regime fostered industrialist and statist plans, the Radical and Progressive-Democrat opposition (supposedly anti-imperialist, according to the political mythology of the traditional Argentinian left) stood out for orthodox agrarian and free-trade positions. (See Murmis and Portantiero, *Estudios sobre los origines del Peronismo.)*

11. Murmis and Portantiero maintain that it is wrong to distinguish between a new and an old proletariat in the 1930s and 1940s, since workers were forging a common union and political attitude. We accept the part of their argument concerning the substantive social unity of the class, and we believe that the fusion of the old and new proletariats took place in conditions that determined a general socio-cultural outcome. In the 1930s and 1940s a third of the total labour force (and a much greater part of the annual increments) came from a pre-capitalist or very backward environment. This must have been particularly

important in the fastest-growing industries: textiles or cement in the 1930s, meat in the immediate post-war period. Of course this was but one factor in the composition in the new working class, and we should not exaggerate its importance.

12. The most important studies of foreign, and particularly North American, investment have shown that in the 1930s indirect investment fell sharply and direct investment stagnated. Sommi, for example, holds that betwen 1931 and 1939 loans fell from $500m to $231m and that direct investment rose from $370m to $388m: *Los Capitales Yanquis en la Argentina,* p.79. In Sommi's list of 200 limited companies tied to US capital before 1947, the main investments were made before the 1930s (especially in electricity, meat-packing, automobiles, cement and rubber). From 1933 to 1937, the period of most industrial growth, no important investments were made in industry. For this reason we do not understand Murmis and Portantiero's statement that US investment in particular 'intensified in this period' *(Estudios,* p. 12). What was most striking in those years was the development of a group of industries funded essentially by national capital, in which the oligarchy's investment funds played a major role.

13. Díaz Alejandro *(op. cit.,* p.99) says on this: 'The collapse of free convertibility in the 1930s placed Argentina in a difficult position, as her normal trade pattern involved surpluses with Western Europe and deficits with North America. Therefore, Argentinian commercial policy endeavoured to divert purchases from the United States toward Western Europe, especially Britain, under the slogan: "buy from those who buy from us". By 1938 about sixty per cent of Argentinian imports were made through barter or compensation agreements.'

14. Jorge Schvarzer synthesizes the process which led to Argentinian economic independence' (according to the Peronist interpretation) in the following manner: 'It is well known that from 1938 British business plans for nationalization were submitted to the local authorities almost every two years. To achieve it, the companies entrusted the former Minister of Finance himself, Doctor Pinedo, with a nationalization plan designed to establish operational mechanisms and to convince government officials of their advantages. This was in 1940 — a rather unsuitable time to make such a decision. Later, when British capital wanted to pull out of the railways and realize a handsome profit to boot, a deal was finally made possible by the existence of a mass of credits accumulated by Argentina during the war (from exports of meat not paid by Britain).' 'The wave of nationalizations of British railway companies', he concludes, 'united Argentina, Uruguay and India, among others, with British interests ready to find new business opportunities.' 'Public Enterprises', *Revista Económica de América Latina,* no. 3, p. 54).

15. Under Perón a new fraction of the industrial and commercial bourgeoisie began to differentiate itself increasingly from the traditional fraction that had developed through capitalization of the agrarian rent and personal fusion of landed property and agrarian and industrial capital. This new fraction based itself on the transfer of public funds (preferential imports, subsidized credit and tax exemptions), on the maintenance of high customs tariffs, and on a drastic change in the internal relationship between agricultural and industrial prices. (Between 1936-39 and 1949, industrial prices rose by 45 per cent in relation to agricultural prices, despite the fact that international exchange rates moved in the opposite direction.) The channeling of agrarian rent to industry now took place through a mechanism of state intermediation (ministry officials, IAPI, Central Bank, customs, and so on), which bonded together influential politicians like Juan

Duarte (brother of Eva Perón), state functionaries and thrusting businessmen like Jorge Antonio, Tricerri Villalón or Gelbard. After the overthrow of Perón, this sector linked itself to groups around Rogelio Frigerio and Frondizism, forming the social base of the Radical-Peronist rapprochement of the late fifties.

16. As is already widely known, the Group of the United Officers around Juan Perón, which masterminded the 1943 military coup, was sympathetic to European Fascism. But although such sentiments were more understandable in Egypt or India — whose independence movements had an interest in Britian's defeat — than in the case of Argentina, Peronism can only be defined in terms of its post-war social and ideological evolution, rather than the original ideas of its founders.

17. Between 1940-44 and 1947-49 Argentinian export prices rose by more than 200 per cent. The 50-per-cent improvement in exchange rates during this period also had major consequences for the Argentinian economy. Firstly, it allowed the state to boost its revenue through various fiscal and financial mechanisms, and to use much of the surplus for subsidization of light industry. Secondly, it provided the currency reserves with which to import plant, machinery, raw materials and auxiliary imports for industry.

18. The Argentinian Left was completely isolated in this period. Not only had the Socialist and Communist parties adopted a pro-bourgeois, pro-imperialist policy during the war, but they had systematically opposed union conflicts that might have weakened the war effort. (Although Argentina did not, of course, participate militarily in the conflict, it did provide food for the Allies.) The clearest examples were the open treachery of the union and Communist leaders during the huge metallurgy strikes of 1942 and the meat strikes of 1943, and above all their participation in the 1945 elections in the ranks of the Democratic Union. Government action finished the job: a huge programme of social concessions deprived the Left of an electorate, while repressive drives led to the imprisonment or expulsion of remaining left-wing union leaders. Only a few Trotskyist groups (the Morenoites and the Posadists) existed outside the PS and PCA, and they only ever achieved local bases in the workers movement.

19. The dollar value of the Argentinian wage has been calculated in line with real peso-dollar parities provided by ECLA. The figure for European wages is based on ILO statistics for Britain (45 cents), Belgium (38 cents), France (33 cents), Germany (33 cents), and Italy (26 cents). See A. Emmanuel, *Unequal Exchange*, NLB, London 1972, p.47.

20. Between 1945 and 1954 Argentinian exports fell sharply (to 37 per cent below the pre-depression level), while internal industrial output and world exports both showed a tendency to rise. Thus, Argentina's share of world exports declined as follows between 1934–38 and 1950–54: maize from 64% to 21%, wheat and flour from 19% to 9%, and meat from 40% to 9%. More generally, the share of total world exports fell from 3.1% in 1928 to 0.8% in 1965. (See Díaz Alejandro, *Essays*, p.11.) In addition, from 1948 the external foundation of the post-1945 economic boom began to deteriorate. The trade indices developed from a base of 100 in 1935-39 to 132 in 1948, 110 in 1949, 93 in 1950, 102 in 1951, 70 in 1952, 82 in 1955, 71 in 1956, and 68 in 1957. Per capita output fell in real terms from 3,971 pesos in 1950 to 3,436 pesos in 1953 and 3,477 pesos in 1957. (ECLA, *Estudio Económico de América Latina*, table 99.)

21. Intensive accumulation denotes a process based upon a continual increase in the technical composition of capital and the intensive exploitation of the labour force, and involving a rise in productivity and the use of Taylorist and Fordist

methods. In backward countries it generally follows the initial period of 'extensive' accumulation, in which the proportion of variable capital equals or exceeds that of constant capital. The passage to a new phase of intensive accumulation is not purely a technical question, since it presupposes a global restructuring of capital (expansion of credit and financial capital, modernization of the state, growth of big corporations, greater internationalization of capital, etc.) and a remodelling of labour relations. In other words, there has to be a 'maturing' of capitalism to the point where it acquires its adequate form in modern monopoly capital. With regard to Latin America, see A. Lipietz, 'Towards Global Fordism?', *New Left Review* 132, March-April 1982; A. Dabat, *La Economía Mundial*; Rivera and Gómez, *México: Acumulación*; and Peralta Ramos, *Acumulación de Capital* (although the terminology used there differs from our own).

22. The 1955 coup, called the 'Liberating Revolution' by its supporters, expressed a complex social and political process in which a predominantly anti-working-class and anti-popular orientation combined with the revanchism of social sectors displaced in 1945 (traditional landowning bourgeoisie, various categories of real-estate rentiers, liberal politicians, and so on), the regrouping of the bourgeoisie and the army caused by a fall in capitalist profitability, the deepening of the social and economic crisis, and the desire for renewal and democratization felt by progressive intellectuals and student youth. This complexity can be seen in the fact that the government of General Aramburu combined anti-democratic and repressive measures (the banning of the Peronist movement, intervention in the unions, the shooting of workers) with the re-establishment of university autonomy. Democratic and socialist thought spread among top academics, as the freedom of the press and information was restored (for the Peronists, too, after 1957), anti-communist legislation was repealed, and so on.

23. Chudnovsky, *Comercio Exterior*, July 1982.

24. The economic policy of the Krieger Vasena team led the state to absorb greater quantities of surplus value at the expense particularly of landowners and agrarian capital. Since wages tended to fall, while the tax burden and interest rates were consciously raised, the higher rate of accumulation in the second half of the 1970s had a negative impact on nearly all sections of the population, excluding the financial bourgeoisie and industrial exporters.

25. Argentinian exports grew by an annual average of $3.4bn in the period 1973–76, and by $8.5bn in 1980–81. If agricultural exports registered the greatest increase in value (especially wheat and sorghum), industrial products such as chemicals and textiles showed the fastest rate of growth. By 1978–80 industry accounted for more than half the export total, and metallurgy and chemicals alone for 25 per cent. (See Canitort, *Theory*; Geller, *Las Iniciativas; UN Statistical Trade*).

26. Schvarzer, *Expansión Económica*, Buenos Aires 1980.

27. Schvarzer, *ibid.*

28. Carlos Abalo, in *Argentina 1976–81: Objectivos y resultado de política económica*, cites sources which speak of $30bn of Argentinian investments abroad. The complete figures are to be found in J. M. Quijano's *México: Estado y Banca Privada*, Mexico City 1982.

29. The radicalization of the workers movement developed in two distinct moments. The first (1968–71) was unleashed by great mass actions in the big cities of the interior (the Cordobazo, Rozariazo, etc.). It crystallized in the rise of class unionism, whose epicentre was in Córdoba and the industrial fringe of the

Paraná (North Rosario and the Villa Constitución area), with lesser branches in La Plata-Ensenada, and isolated pockets in the north of Greater Buenos Aires and the northern zone of the country. It was a very radical movement, little influenced by Peronism (although its most advanced tendencies took part), but very isolated from the rest of the country, and particularly from the largest concentration of manufacturing workers, in Greater Buenos Aires. Its political orientations came from a heterogeneous conglomerate of dozens of new revolutionary organizations — Maoist, *clasista*, Trotskyist, Peronist, Guevarist, etc. — which agreed on very little and were grouped into several antagonistic blocs. The strong radical influence of the revolutionary petty bourgeoisie enhanced the isolation of the movement and led it into crushing defeats at Fiat-Córdoba and elsewhere.

The next peak, 1974–75, was much more widespread and national in character, but occurred in a completely different political context. The *clasista* currents had not yet managed to recover from the blows of 1972–73, while the main two militarist formations, the ERP and the Montoneros, had grown substantially. Particularly after the dramatic *Rodrigazo* days of June–July 1974, however, there was a nation-wide surge of rank-and-file union co-ordinating committees. If the broad movement actually fell apart, this was because it lacked a unifying political perspective and an active response to the collapse of the economy. The repressive state apparatus and the union bureaucracy dealt it powerful blows, and the militarist vanguard of the ERP and Montoneros saw it as an opportunity for individual recruitment and a source of haven or logistical support.

30. The external trade of the agro-export countries performed best in the years 1973–74 (part of the international boom starting in 1971). In Argentina's case, export levels doubled (1971-$1,710m; 1972-$1,941m; 1973-$3,269m; 1974-$3,931m; 1975-$3,000m). The wide dispersal of industrial centres supplying plant and technology was another extremely favourable circumstance, to which must be added the development of the Latin American market and the fact that Argentina was largely self-sufficient in oil.

31. At the beginning of June 1975, when Celestino Rodrigo became economics minister and López Rega's right-hand man, he immediately devalued the peso by a hundred per cent. Soaring inflation followed hard on this measure, and the unions demanded wage adjustments in line with price rises. The most important unions did obtain almost complete compensation, but then Isabel Perón's government announced on 28 June that it would not allow wage rises above 50 per cent. Since the Triple A (López Rega's para-military death squad) also began to menace the CGT bureaucracy, it threatened to call a general strike, and Minister of Labour Otero, a metallurgical union leader, resigned from his post. In this climate of political crisis, the Buenos Aires workers launched a huge unofficial strike on 1 July which nearly at once took on national dimensions. The workers organized peaceful demonstrations, taking over city squares and converging on the buildings of the national or regional government. They also began to form regional coordinating bodies, independent of the official union structures. When the country had been paralysed for almost a week, the CGT issued an absurd call for a cessation of activities on 7 and 8 July — but the mass strike continued until 11 July. On that day Isabel Perón gave in to their wage demands and expelled López Rega from the cabinet (appointing him instead to the post of her private secretary). She kept Rodrigo as economics minister, however, only asking for his resignation when a new rash of strikes threatened to break out in mid-April 1976.

32. As yet there is no complete study of the level and targeting of state terror in Argentina. However, one of the most important reports, drawn up by the São-Paulo-based Human Rights Defence Committee of the Southern Cone (CLAMOR), has precise details on 7,291 'disappearances', and it estimates that the real figure is two or three times higher. According to CLAMOR, 48.6 per cent of the missing are workers, 23 per cent students and 20.3 per cent professionals. Most of the disappearances occurred in 1976 (46%), 1977 (36%) and 1978 (11.5%). But this study only examines proven kidnappings and disappearances during the years 1976–1982, excluding similar events in 1974–75 and the killing of people in public operations by the repressive forces. There are serious estimates that a total of ten thousand were definitely killed in the ranks of the people.

33. In 1964 the customs tariffs on imported industrial goods were among the highest in the world. Nominal protection on 125 representative items averaged 131% in Argentina, as opposed to 112% in Colombia, 61% in Mexico and 13% in the EEC. In those days, the average was 107% in the developing countries (See Maddison, *Progreso y política económica*.) After then, however, there seems to have been a general upward trend in Argentina until the advent of the Martínez de Hoz plan. Above all, the most heavily protected industries rose as a proportion of GDP (automobiles up 600%, electric lamps about 300%, televisions more than 200%). The Martínez de Hoz team set out to reduce tariffs on industrial imports by 1982 to an average of 42 per cent and by January 1984 to approximately 20 per cent.

34. The term 'military–industrial complex' refers to the growing integration of the public sector, the armed forces and a broad sector of the bourgeoisie which works as a contractor for state enterprises. The linking of the armed forces with the capitalist class takes place at three levels: institutional leadership of the industrial sector specializing in arms production; military management of the main basic industries (the army being responsible for iron and steel and oil, the navy for atomic energy and shipbuilding, and the airforce for aeroplanes and the giant IME structure); and participation of top retired officers as directors, advisers, public relations agents or even managers of leading capitalist firms.

Military Equipment Plants	Associated Companies
— Fábrica General San Martin (military communications, electronics)	— Petroquímica General Mosconi*
— Fábrica Domingo Matheu (light and heavy automatic rifles, machine guns)	— Hierro Patagónico de Sierra Grande Minera*
— Fábrica San Francisco (ammunition)	— Salta Forestal*
— Fábrica Fray Luis Beltran (ammunition, hand grenades, mines)	— Siderurgia Integrada SA*
	— Aceros Ohler*
— Fábrica Rio Tercero (recoilless cannons, mortars, grenades)	— Zapla Construcciones*
	— IAS*
— Fábrica de Vainas y Conductores Eléctricos ECA (copper wires, shell casings, and other semi-finished products)	— Petroquímica Banía Bianca
	— SOMISA
	— Petroquímica Río Tercero
— Fábrica de Materiales Pirotécnicos (flares, tear gas, and other chemical products)	— Astilleros y Fabricas Navales del Estado
	— Atanor
— Fábrica de Tolueno Sintético (fuels, tar, TNT, and aromatics for private industry)	— Carboquímica Argentina
	— Induclor
— Fábrica de Acido Sulfúrico (sulphuric acid)	— Polisur
— Altos Hornos Zapla (integrated steel works)	— Monómeros Vinílicos
— Fábrica Boulogne (medium-sized tanks)	— Petropol

*Fabricaciones Militares majority shareholding

Source: Reproduced from *Latin America Weekly Report*, 30 November 1979

35. There are now only two ways in which the rate of surplus-value can be raised in Argentina: either the historic level of popular consumption will have to be driven down through a crushing defeat of the proletariat and mass emigration of labour; or the value of labour power will have to be directly reduced through a dramatic cheapening of agricultural and consumer products.

Notes to Chapter Two

1. UN resolution 2065 does not, however, unequivocally recognize Argentina's claim to the islands. In the section dealing with the islanders' rights, it notes that a section of British public opinion would favour granting them independence; whereas the more general UN resolution to which it refers, 1514 (XV), would seem to support Argentina's claim by recognizing the basic principle of territorial integrity.

2. Rear-Admiral Jorge Fraga, retd., has said that in 1968 Argentina was on the point of obtaining British government approval for the purchase of shares in the Falkland Islands Company (or in the major farms — the text is not clear). But 'on that occasion,' he adds, 'someone said that *sovereignty was not negotiable, and there things broke down*'. (See Gregorio Selser, *La Ecuación*.) If it is true that the Argentinian government did not take up the offer to purchase FIC shares for political reasons, this can only be because it had the reactionary aim of consolidating the role of the military in Argentinian society. It was precisely during those years that Fraga's men, Anaya and Massera, drew up the 'Plan Goa' (see Hastings and Jenkins, ch.2).

To understand the full implications, we must realize that the FIC's share value could never have been more than two million pounds, and that the company would have been in no position to turn down an offer of, let us say, £10m. Of the islanders, MP Sir Cyril Osborne said on 12 December 1968: 'I am convinced that if Argentina told them "we are giving you 10m pounds sterling", the islands would be uninhabited in less than twelve months' (cf. Rodolfo Silenzi de Stagni, *Las Malvinas*, p.126).

3. Mrs Thatcher's man in the F.O., Ridley, encouraged the search for an agreement. His alternatives were: a Hong Kong solution (recognition of Argentinian sovereignty plus a leaseback agreement for long-term British administration of the islands); joint ownership; or a freeze on talks on the status of the islands for a certain period of time. On this basis, Whitehall proceeded to consult the divided kelpers. *Between a third and a half of those consulted — the youngest and most 'cosmopolitan' it would seem — favoured one of these proposals for an agreement with Argentina.* Their representatives seem to have shared this position, and in 1981 accompanied Ridley to the annual meeting in New York where Carlos Cavadoli represented Argentina. Britain's offer of a Hong-Kong-type solution, unlike the other two proposals, seems to have met with the Junta's initial sympathy. But talks suddenly broke down at the end of 1981 when Luce replaced Ridley and two of the islanders' more conciliatory representatives were supplanted by anti-Argentinian hard-liners. (See *The Economist*, 19 June 1982.)

4. The above account of the evolution of British government policy owes much to Hastings and Jenkins, *The Battle for the Falklands*, and Anthony Barnett, *Iron Britannia*.

5. Britain spent only £900,000 on the islands in this period, or £40,000 a year. The war would cost nearly a thousand times more than the sum spent on the islands

over 22 years, and approximately two thousand times more than Britain invested in this period. (See *The Economist*, 19 June 1982.)

6. The US Geological Survey published a report by B. Grossling which estimates oil reserves in the Argentinian continental shelf at two hundred billion barrels, or five times more than the North Sea reserves. This is perhaps a little exaggerated, but the possibility of huge deposits is confirmed by the 1976 Shackleton Report and three drilling assays conducted by the USS Glomar Challenger.

7. Silenzi de Stagni, one of Argentina's most famous oil experts and a fervent supporter of the military occupation of the islands, relies on a purely technical argument that the width of the sea-bed deposits (8kms, against 3.5 kms in the North Sea) implies a 'greater probability of finding oil'. See *Las Malvinas y el Petróleo*, ch.5.

8. The fall in international oil prices during 1981–82 is due to three objective tendencies that probably cannot be reversed in the medium or even long term: the international recession (which cannot be reversed without an East–West, North–South international political agreement); the striking economies in oil consumption by the major industrial countries, plus a gradual substitution of gas, coal, nuclear and other energy sources; and the rapid growth of sea-bed exploration. In these circumstances, it is not enough to have oil, however large the deposits. It is also necessary to find export markets, and to keep costs at an internationally competitive level.

9. Several experts agree that the Argentinian and South African governments have been discussing, for more than a decade, a mechanism for naval cooperation in the South Atlantic, and trying to convince both the United States and Brazil of the wisdom of the idea. Carter's opposition to a deal with Buenos Aires and Pretoria combined with Brazil's growing economic and diplomatic links with Black Africa to put the plan on ice. But Reagan's rise to power has revitalized the idea, and a number of meetings have been organized between US, Argentinian, South African, Brazilian, Paraguayan and Uruguayan strategists. The most important of these was held in Buenos Aires in May 1981. (See the *Financial Times* report by Hugh O'Shaughnessy, reprinted in *Contextos*, 10-15 November 1981.) At this meeting there was discussion of a possible SATO alliance, but the Argentinian–South African initiative was once again postponed. For a broader resumé of US debate on Argentina's usefulness in the South Atlantic, see the article by Charles Maechlinger in *Foreign Policy*, January 1982.

10. Shell, which had been awarded one of the YPF contracts for the Rio Gallegos zone, planned in 1981 to bring in two North Sea platforms called 'Interocean II' and 'Epoch'. (See the pamphlet *El Plan Petrolero de la Dictadura Argentina*, edited by the Peronist Technological Council.)

11. See *inter alia* Alfredo Palacios's classic work, *Las Malvinas son Argentinas*; Luis Podesta Costa, *Derecho Internacional Publico*; José Munos Aspiri's book on the Malvinas; and the recent text by Rodolfo Silenzi de Stagni, *Las Malvinas y el Petróleo*. There are also numerous monographs and articles dating back to the last century, like those by Paul Groussac, and the work of early-twentieth-century historians such as Ricardo Callet Bois.

12. Correspondents for major international newspapers concur that the islanders now wish to remain British. But they also report that 'the idea that the islanders would determine the status of the Malvinas is to say the least nominal'. The main (local) personalities interviewed, like Monsignor Spraggan, head of the island's Catholic community, recognize that the options will be defined in London (LAWR, 23-7-82). According to the same source, the most viable British plan

may be to create an independent mini-state in the Malvinas, under its military protection. 'It would be very difficult for London to persuade the islanders that this is in their best interests.'

13. The Bolivian case is extremely interesting because two different aspects are combined. One is the claim to territory that Chile snatched from Bolivia in the 1879 war, and where a number of mining and commercial centres have since been established. Clearly the original injustice cannot be used against the rights of the big Chilean population inhabiting those regions. The second aspect is Bolivia's right to an outlet to the sea — which the Chilean people must certainly recognize in an appropriate manner, although, from a democratic point of view, any solution must involve a bilateral treaty.

14. From the Argentinian point of view, the claim to the Malvinas is a purely territorial demand, in the sense that Britain exercises colonial rule not over a population of Argentinian or Spanish stock, but over territory snatched from Argentina and then populated with people of British origin. When the British occupied the islands, there seem to have been only fourteen people of Argentinian stock on the islands. Even they had been transferred there for military and commercial purposes.

Notes to Chapter Three

1. In constant terms, between 1976–77 and 1979–1980 the value of production fell by 47% for wool, 70% for cotton, 50% for yerba mate and rice, 55% for grapes and olives, and so on. In the Río Negro region, fruit-packing plants closed down or cut back activities. In northeastern and central regions, the bankruptcy of the ultra-modern Ñuñorco plant was matched by numerous closures in Córdoba and Santa Fe; while in Cuyo the collapse of the Greco and Casales groups virtually put an end to viticulture and brought in its wake court actions against the Filippini, Benegas, Yacanta and La Superiora wine-cellars. All this broke up the social structure of the various regions, causing massive migration from rural areas to the already jobless urban centres. See Schaposnik-Vacchino, 'Argentina: fracaso de un ministro o de un sistema?' *Comercio Exterior*, January 1982.

2. Between December 1980 and December 1981, automobile production fell by 39% and commercial vehicles production by almost 47% (*La Nación*, 18 January 1982, quoting the Association of Automobile Factories). The state consciously stimulated the concentration of enterprises (See José Martínez de Hoz, *Bases para una Argentina moderna*, Buenos Aires 1981), and the eight factories were reduced to four. The crisis affecting workers in this sector gave rise to vigorous struggles throughout 1981.

3. These facts are taken from the Swedish-based magazine *En Lucha*, May 1981, which quotes statistics published in *Clarín Económico*. Enrique Koenig estimates in 'Tiempos difíciles para los industriales argentinos', *Contextos*, 3/13, that between December 1976 and November 1981 approximately two hundred companies were calling in the receiver *every month*.

4. BCRA statistics and Koenig, *op.cit*. The National Institute for Statistics and Censuses (INDEC) admitted that between April and May 1982 six per cent of the economically active population was without work. However, it considered as employed anyone who had worked for at least one hour during the week preceding the poll. The Argentinian Business University suggested a figure of 11–12 per cent, while union sources talked of 20–25 per cent. The true figure was

probably about 15 per cent. There are similar problems in assessing wage levels, although there can be no doubt that the 1976–78 period witnessed an alarming decline. (See table 3.3.) The regime was also concerned to foster huge differentials between skilled and unskilled workers, employees of large, medium and small industries, and so on. The link between wages and productivity was, among other things, a way of breaking the social unity of the working class. Guillermo Almeyra makes an interesting study, in 'La clase obrera en la Argentina actual', *Coyoacan* 9, of the structural transformation of the proletariat. However, his research was done before the rise in unemployment, and some of his conclusions should be revised accordingly. See also CIDAMO, 'Económica y Politica en Argentina', *Cuadernos Politicos* 27.

5. Two groups representing monopoly capital fought to have their position prevail within the Junta's economic programme. A clearly recognizable 'Liberal' tendency expressed the interests of big landowners (with holdings in commerce, industry and finance), while another group represented the new layer linked to the military–industrial complex (as suppliers and licensees) and the production of basic goods, energy, steel, petrochemicals, cement, transport and so on. The leading names here were Pérez Companc, Fortabat, Techint, Desaci, Impresit, and Bridas. The main issues of contention were the employment of the agricultural surplus, the level of public spending, the involvement or not of public enterprises and the state bureaucracy in 'efficiency' drives, and the importance of various social and political constraints. As a big landowner and head of the foremost steel company, Martínez de Hoz expressed better than anyone else the fusion of these distinct interests. But it became clear that he was unable to achieve an efficient reconciliation between them.

6. The progressive overvaluation of the peso from 1977 onwards fuelled the 'speculative economy'. At one time there was an eighty-per-cent difference between the trade dollar and the value of the dollar on the financial market. This meant that exporters earned more by hanging on to their foreign currency and speculating with it on the financial market.

7. See the pamphlet published by the Sociedad Rural on 28 March 1981. The Industrial Union's statement is from the same period.

8. Even a politically conservative journalist like Manfred Schonfeld of *La Prensa*, the traditional conservative paper, said of the Multipartidaria that 'a mountain gave birth to a mouse'. The TYSAE Group in Mexico has begun to examine this phase of bourgeois opposition activity.

9. This was a transparent reference to official economic policy. On the 'dirty war' they wrote: 'We must be discerning about the justifications for the anti-guerrilla campaign and the methods used in the struggle. The illegitimate repression also shrouded the nation in mourning.' A truly remarkable text when we consider that many of the bishops present had blessed the weapons of the military at solemn masses!

10. In April 1979 that sector of the union bureaucracy which now heads the CGT–Ubaldini issued a call for a general strike. Although this was heeded in several major industrial centres, the unstable situation of the time meant that it had little impact on national policy. In fact the strike appeal had a frankly regressive ideological content, since it tried to situate itself within official discourse.

11. An assessment made at the Fifth International Conference of the TYSAE, Madrid, September 1981.

12. General Saint Jean, in a move to buy time, promised to legalize political

activity by mid-year and to provide information on the *desaparecidos*, adding, of course, that 'some cases will be impossible to clear up'. A public quarrel ensued in which various currents and ex-members of the Junta governments engaged in mutual recrimination and tried to disclaim responsibility for the 'dirty war'. Even Emilio Massera, a retired admiral and former member of the Junta, commented: 'If there is not a revolution by those in power, then it will come from the streets below... this country will then see a social explosion in which not only the working class and urban or rural businessmen take part, but also the middle class.' *La Nación*, 20 March 1982.

13. General Hector Iglesias, presidential secretary under Galtieri, incisively enumerated 'the three achievements that grant legitimacy to the military process begun in 1976: the defeat of subversion, the recovery of the Malvinas and, as a function of this, the establishment of the foundations for a lasting national political unity' (*La Nación*, 12 April 1982). Colonel Bernardo Menéndez, considered to be one of the military's ideologues, added: 'There have been leaderships with mass support, but such support was also vigorously opposed. The Malvinas are a definite objective, on which a firm policy can be agreed, and our aim is to march forward united.'

14. It is extremely interesting to note how past and present merged in Martínez de Hoz's vision: 'The generation of 1980 was successful and was accorded a place in history because it had a clear awareness of its aims and of the kind of country it wanted... It made this a young and forceful country, which amazed the world at the beginning of the century. It is our task to end this century, which began so brilliantly, but has since undergone so many ups and downs. Today Argentina presents itself to the world as a valid interlocutor, as a country whose presence in the international world is again being recognized... in such a way that it now has everything at hand to rejoin that constellation of countries which are worth something in the world by their active presence and, above all, by their active example' (Martínez de Hoz, 26 March 1980.

15. Both the 'old' and 'new' sectors of the bureaucratic bourgeoisie seemed to share this perspective of monopoly-finance capital. Thus the journal *Estrategia*, edited by retired General Juan Gugliamelli, whose brand of developmentalist populism had a major influence on bourgeois intellectual and managerial strata, attached great importance to the recovery of the Malvinas. In 1976 Guglialmelli himself concluded in a leading article: 'Argentina must not lower it guard. It must insist on a peaceful solution, but without laying aside the extreme alternative. This now requires the preparation of the best strategic conditions. Since the return of the Malvinas is a bilateral issue, the centre of action will be our national power (economic, military, political and psycho-social)... At national level it will be crucial to mobilize all moral, spiritual and material energies.' (*Estrategía* 43-44, November 1976-January 1977.) Bearing in mind the earlier Perón-Gelbard plan and its main ideological underpinnings, we must conclude that the support of the populist parties for the landing involved not so much political surrender as substantial agreement with the Junta.

16. When divergences began to develop with Washington over the Malvinas, all the third-worldists and 'dependency' theorists were desperately forced to discover national-patriotic virtues in Galtieri & Co.

17. This also had an economic dimension, in that the Junta's intervention in Central America was designed to break open future markets for large-scale industry and the plethora of capital which could not be integrated into the productive cycle in Argentina.

18. The 'reactionary ingenuousness' of the Argentinian military was revealed in statements by Brigadier Lami Dozo, Air Force Chief, to Vernon Walters during the Malvinas conflict: 'I don't understand the attitude of the Washington government. Since well before 2 April you knew that you could count on us in all world theatres, and that if the hemisphere had been threatened you could have used not only the islands but also the continental land mass.'

19. There can be few more transparent statements on the link between the Malvinas and the 'great power' ideology than the speech delivered by Admiral Lambruschini in 1981 at the Centre of Strategic Studies of the Escuela Superior de Guerra. It was widely reported in the national press in May of that year. 'We live in turbulent times,' he asserted, 'when respect for the rules of the game of international coexistence is not a general norm... As a sovereign nation we must insert ourselves appropriately into the international arena and consistently fulfil the role that falls on us... Our country is no stranger to the main conflicts of the modern world — it is part of them and will continue to become increasingly part of them, since it now has a clear position to defend, rights to claim and much to offer... The South Atlantic is a vital area to the Republic. Argentina does have political, economic and strategic interests arising from its geography, its history and its future projections, all of which legitimate and require an adequate national presence in the area. If Argentina does not project itself to the extent recommended by its contiguity and opportunities, then other countries will... Any focus on the present situation in the strategic South Atlantic cannot omit the historic imperative of the return of the Malvinas to the nation. They are a key factor in our strategic thinking.' Lambruschini analysed the economic value of Antarctica, and in a passionate defence of the 'Western world' proposed that Argentina should control the region.

20. *La Nación*, 15 January 1982.

21. Despite repeated official denials, it is interesting that once again a certain 'reactionary naivety' led some people to blurt out the truth. Thus, in October 1980 the Paraguayan Minister of Defence admitted that his country had 'for some time' had 'a tacit defence pact' with Argentina. *La Nación*, 2 September 1980.

Notes to Chapter Four

1. A clear example of this happened when Brazil — identified for a long time by dependency theorists as a regional counter-revolutionary gendarme subordinated to the United States — clashed violently with the US government over its independent nuclear programme. Suddenly the lackey acquired anti-imperialist features, and a fierce discussion ensued among standard-bearers of *dependentismo* on the position they should adopt towards the 'unexpected' nationalist turn of the dictatorship.

2. It is true that the proletariat is historically interested in a genuine, democratic peace, based upon the suppression of exploitation. 'The revolutionary proletariat must undertake incessant agitation against war, but without losing sight of the fact that wars will not be suppressed while class domination exists. One cannot help an oppressed class which is not responsible for a bourgeois war between two countries with trivial statements on peace.' Lenin, *Collected Works*, vol. 7, p.44.

3. 'There are wars and wars. We must be clear about the historical conditions which have engendered a war, what class wages it and with what ends in mind. Without understanding this, all our discussion on war will be sterile. All wars are

inseparable from the regime that engenders them.' Lenin, *Collected Works*, vol. 25, p.395.

4. The concept of a 'bourgeois-democratic' revolution (and therefore of 'bourgeois-democratic' war) was coined by the Marxist classics to refer to revolutions which overthrow political obstacles to the free development of capitalism. The concept of 'popular-democratic' revolution was developed after the Second World War in many sectors of the revolutionary left (possibly following the concept of Mao's new democracy) to denote mass revolutions in which political hegemony was not already held by the bourgeoisie, and in which there was an objective chance of uninterrupted transition to socialism. For us the difference between the two lies in their objective and social dynamics. The one develops against autocratic and reactionary states but does not question the capitalist system, while the other challenges the class domination of the bourgeoisie and raises fundamentally anti-capitalist economic and political demands. However, it is not so easy to draw the distinction when one is faced with a 'popular-democratic revolution, on the road to socialism' or the 'democratic phase of the socialist revolution'. The question is particularly relevant in Latin America now, where the existence of capitalist countries with military-autocratic regimes requires a combination of general democratic and socialist aims.

5. Clausewitz already established a link between political objectives and military methods. 'It is true,' he writes, 'that the political element does not sink deep into the details of war... But small as is its influence in this respect, it is great in the formation of a plan for a whole war, or a campaign, and often even for a battle.' *On War*, Harmondsworth 1968, p.404.

6. The fact that the phase of anti-colonial struggle is almost finished does not mean that we should be less indignant about the few remaining colonial situations, nor that the resolution of issues like Puerto Rico and Namibia is not an extremely important democratic task for the American and African masses.

7. We use the term 'socialist bloc' in its customary sense, to refer to the economic and political group of countries with a statized economy articulated around the USSR. We do not wish to imply that they are socialist countries in the strict sense, since a democratic workers' state does not exist in any of them, nor a truly socialized system of economic management and planning, nor a process of transition towards a classless society without social exploitation and oppression. These countries retain certain features of capitalist relations of production, such as the division of labour between planning or management and the actual implementation of tasks, expressed in a despotic organization of labour and an exploitative distribution of the social product between the masses and the controllers of the Plan. Since, however, private ownership of the means of production has been abolished and the market is no longer a basic regulator of economic life, we are faced not with a new stage of the capitalist mode of production, but with a social hybrid lacking long-term historical perspectives and generated by specific socio-historical conditions of the world transition from capitalism to socialism, We might call it proto-socialism or state socialism or bureaucratic socialism.

8. What has to be explained, not in *national* terms but from the point of view of the world working class and its general historic interests, is that the 'socialist bloc' has become increasingly embroiled in bitter controversies that break the bounds of ideology (Stalin anathematizing Tito, Brezhnev, Khrushchev and Mao denigrating each other) and lead to diplomatic and economic confrontations,

frontier tensions, blockades and breaks in relations. There have also been disputes to influence movements in other countries (most dramatically in Angola, where Cuba and the USSR on the one hand , and China, allied to South Africa, on the other, fought each other indirectly through the MPLA and UNITA); military occupation of one 'socialist' country by another (Hungary in 1956 and Czechoslovakia in 1968); and finally open war between China and Vietnam in 1979, not counting the military occupation of Kampuchea by the Vietnamese, which resulted in the overthrow of the terrifying and bloody regime of Pol Pot. For a detailed analysis of these trends, see Adolfo Gilly, 'La Guerra China-Vietnam: socialismo nacional y nacionalismo burocrático', *Coyoacan* 6.

9. According to Gramsci in his *Notes on Machiavelli*, all broad political movements which confront a military power head on are politico-military by their very nature. For they tend to undermine the fighting capacity of the hegemonic power or to disperse it over a large territory. Mass movements like those mentioned in the text cannot therefore be regarded as purely political or social in character.

10. See Fred Halliday, *The Making of the Second Cold War*, Verso/NLB, London 1983, ch. 7.)

11. The statute governing the relationship between the Junta and the president stipulated that the latter could not be an officer on the active list. According to Hastings and Jenkins (op.cit.), a deal was reached between Galtieri and Admiral Anaya in December 1981 to ignore this provision in the preparations for the Malvinas conflict.

12. The agreements between Argentinian hard-liners and the US army were reached between August and November 1981, on the eve of General Viola's removal from power, after visits to Buenos Aires by Meyer and Walters and two return visits to Washington by Galtieri. According to the bi-monthly *US Covert Action Information Bulletin*, secret agreements concluded in September committed the Argentinian military to increase its participation in international counter-insurgency operations and to concede a base on Argentinian territory, among other diplomatic and political concessions, in return for the lifting of the US arms embargo in December of that year. (See *Excelsior*, 11 August 1982.) According to *Cuadernos del Tercer Mundo* (June-July 1982) and other publications, General Walters also agreed at some meetings with Galtieri to 'turn a blind eye' to the Malvinas invasion plan. On 11 December 1981, the Latin American Newsletters political report stated that the Argentinian military attaché in Washington, General Miguel Mallea Gil, had been discussing a price of some $126bn for the installation of a US military base in Patagonia. In the same month, the US press reported that Salvadorean intelligence officers had been seconded some two years before to courses in Argentina on 'aspects of organization, infiltration and integration' and that Argentinian counter-insurgency experts were '*already to be found* in El Salvador, Guatemala and Honduras'.

13. Argentina already has a nuclear reactor, built with West German collaboration in 1974, called Atucha I. A second reactor, at an advanced stage of construction, will come into operation in 1984, and a third reactor will be built in 1983 with Canadian help. The Junta also planned to instal a 40-megawatt reactor using heavy water and natural uranium to produce the plutonium for nuclear bombs. Another plant on the outskirts of Buenos Aires can already separate plutonium and uranium and nuclear fuel. The Junta refused to sign the Non-Proliferation Treaty and the Tlatelolco Treaty of Latin America, or to allow IAEA inspection of work in progress with West Germany and the USSR. All this

led military experts througout the world to speculate that Argentina would have domestically manufactured nuclear weapons towards December 1982.

14. See *Boletín de Coyuntura* 4, CELA, FCYS and UNAM sources, and the yearly report of the London-based International Institute for Strategic Studies.

15. In hindsight a crucial aspect was that the Argentinian air force did not try to purchase the US bomb-priming manual until it had fallen under the embargo (Hastings and Jenkins, *The Battle*).

16. According to one of the most serious military accounts of the war by British experts who were personally involved (Hastings and Jenkins), the 'task force' would have faced disaster if any of the aircraft-carriers had been sunk. The Argentinian high command claimed that it had 'seriously damaged' the *Hermes*, and there are reports (*Sunday Times*, quoted in LAWR, 29 July 1983) that HMS *Invincible* was hit by torpedoes from an Argentinian submarine, the *San Luis*, which failed to explode. The British High Command does not accept these claims.

17. *Excelsior*, 23 May 1982.

18. *Excelsior*, 17 April 1982.

19. This is the list of ships hit issued by the Argentinian Joint Chiefs of Staff: the detroyers 'Brilliant', 'Sheffield' and 'Coventry', the frigates 'Antelope', 'Ardent' and 'Atlantic Conveyor' were all sunk; the cruiser 'Glamorgan', the destroyer 'Battleaxe', the frigates 'Arrow', 'Active', 'Ariadne', 'Aurora', 'Euryalus', 'Plymouth' and 'Argonaut', the support ship 'Stena Seaspred' and 'Norlan', a troop transport, were all damaged, while the aircraft carrier 'Hermes', on which information is contradictory, the destroyer 'Broadsword', the frigate 'Dido' and the pleasure vessel 'Canberra' were all seriously damaged. With some exceptions, these claims were directly or indirectly corroborated by British military sources. (See *Malvinas*, official story of the war, published by Latin American Newsletters.) Information on air force casualties differed a great deal, but once again the British undoubtedly suffered serious losses, while the cost paid by Argentina was two-thirds of its air force put out of action.

20.The United States and the USSR placed six-to-eight spy satellites in geo-stationary orbit over the battle area. 'The USSR needs to obtain the maximum amount of details to assess the progress made by the NATO allies,' explained General Georges Buiz, considered to be France's foremost stategist. It is important to remember that one of the most impressive successes of the new electronic weapons was the Exocet missile, which, launched from a 'Super Etendard' aircraft, sunk an extremely advanced destroyer, the 'Sheffield'. (After this demonstration of its efficiency the Exocet leapt in price from $150,000 to $1m.) One of the more general results of the conflict will probably be the replacement of the large, heavy ships of the British fleet by much smaller, lighter and quicker units, fully equipped with electronic mechanisms of attack and defence.

21. On 15 May, at the height of the second phase of the conflict, British strategists believed that Argentina's greatly superior air resources would inflict serious losses (*Excelsior*, 16 May). See also the more general declarations about Britain's weakness by Sir Christopher Foxley-Norris, RAF Chief Marshal in the Second World War: *Excelsior*, 6 June 1982.

22. *Latin America Weekly Report.*

23. These elements were all recognised by the openly pro-war weekly of the Argentinian Communist Party: *Que Pasa?* See in particular, its edition of 29 June 1982. Hastings and Jenkins mention the fact that the Argentinian garrison had

only stored a month's supply of provisions, which it then had to ration.
24. In *Iron Britannia*, Anthony Barnett correctly defines the Malvinas conflict as a conventional war between two bourgeois states to consolidate their unpopular democratic regimes. However, his argument that Argentinian expansionism cannot be regarded as an imperialist trend since it is limited to neighbouring countries, is much more open to question. Indeed, precisely this limited character of the thrust marked the early imperialist drive of the pre-1914 United States, Czarist Russia or Imperial Japan.
25. Many tendencies on the Argentinian and Latin American left argued that it would have been to 'play at politics' to set themselves against the broad mass mobilization. But not only did this view misread the mood of the masses; it involved acceptance of all or some of the arguments and manoeuvres of the class enemy. In April it was doubtless extremely difficult to fly in the face of the national chauvinists. But that was the only possible contribution to any durable self-education of the masses. Although it would probably have had no immediate effect, it was the only perspective that could have helped the mass movement to advance and to overcome bourgeois ideology.
26. All these quotations are taken from leading Argentinian papers such as *La Nación* and *Clarín*. There was more than one chink in the consensus, however: CGT leader Ubaldini and Ricardo Pérez of the Truckdrivers Union initially opposed the line of near-total support for the military initiative. Ubaldini even went so far as to say that this 'would make a gift of all we won on the 30th' (i.e., the demonstration of 30th March). In the end, Lorenzo Miguel seems to have been the one who forced through the majority line of the union bureaucracy, although a few men like Juan José Taccone of the Light and Power Union still refused to propagandize at home or abroad on behalf of the Junta.
27. The PCA's position on the war was a supreme example of its quest for an 'external contradiction' that will mask class conflict within the country. Since the Junta expressed this 'contradiction' with US imperialism by trading with the USSR and embarking upon the Malvinas operation, it was legitimate to give it full support in the recovery of the islands. See Athos Fava, 'Malvinas: batalla por une nueva Argentina', PCA pamphlet, June 1982.
28. The split in the CGT took place in the middle of May — as a union delegation was being drawn up for the annual meeting of the ILO — and consummated at a plenary session of union leaders called by the Ministry of Labour.
29. See the Montoneros statement of 28 April 1982.
30. 'Britain is an imperialist country. Argentina is a semi-colonial country. We workers fight on the side of the colonized in any confrontation between an imperialist country and a semi-colonial country' (document of the PST-A, cited by a party member in *Unomasuno*, 29 June 1982). The PST-A position was echoed by another Trotskyist group, the PO, and by the United Secretariat of the Fourth International. It should be pointed out, however, that some comrades from this tendency not only opposed the war but also developed practical tasks against it. Outstanding examples are Adolfo Gilly, whose position became more precise in the course of the conflict, a group of revolutionary Marxists comprising well-known and experienced militants of the Argentinian left (Daniel Peyrera, Guillermo Almayra, Angel Fanjul, among others), and the New Course group actually inside Argentina.
31. One example of such harassment is this quotation from a printed leaflet: 'All together except the little mothers (*madrecitas*). Those who said their sons had "disappeared" now want the English to smash up other people's sons for defending the Malvinas.'

Notes to Chapter Five

1. In the United States, the number of bankruptcies per ten thousand firms rose from 42 in 1980 to 61 in 1981 and 82 in 1982 (a projection from June 1982), as against 44 in 1975 at the height of the earlier crisis. By March 1982 the following countries were failing to maintain their debt repayment schedule: Turkey, Pakistan, Poland, Romania, Sudan, Zaire, Senegal, Sierra Leone, Liberia, Uganda, Jamaica, Nicaragua, Costa Rica and Bolivia (*The Economist*, 20 March 1982). Since then they have been joined by almost all the debtor countries, with an exceptionally acute crisis in the case of the world's largest debtor, Brazil.
2. The US position in the world economy was severely eroded between 1950 and 1980 by Japanese and West European competition. Its share of world industrial production and international trade fell by more than 55% and 33% respectively to 35% and 17% approximately. Moreover, the United States has suffered a relative decline in its military superiority over the USSR, as well as an obvious undermining of its diplomatic pre-eminence. See Halliday, *op.cit.*
3. The main tendencies of Marxist thought are beginning to tackle this crucial problem with new concepts such as 'medium-developed capitalist countries' (E. Semo), 'sub-imperialist powers' (R.M. Marini), and 'semi-colonial autonomous finance capital' (E. Mandel). However, these theories are still extremely limited, because they are based upon either the traditional eclecticism of the West European Communist parties (Semo), or the dependency analyses of imperialist 'gendarmes' supported by regional 'subgendarmes' (Marini), or a theoretical compromise with third worldism, as in Mandel's theory of semi-colonies. See Dabat, 'La Economía Mundial y los países dependientes a partir de la segunda decada del sesenta', *Teoría y Política* 1.
4. The best-known case is Hungary, which applied to join the IMF in 1981 and apparently succeeded in obtaining greater flexibility towards the West at the July 1982 meeting of Comecon. Significantly Cuba, at the peak of an advertising campaign to promote tourism, decreed in February 1982 a law authorizing the direct investment of foreign capital and the formation of joint companies with the state. Angola is another thought-provoking case. Despite its links with Comecon, it conducts 85 per cent of its external trade with capitalist countries, and is promoting new investment by transnational mining companies.
5. A debate organized in Moscow by the Latin America Institute brought together leading Soviet specialists in 1981. The proceedings were published in the Soviet magazine, *Latin America*, and summarized in LAWR, 15 January 1982. 'The Soviets,' it said, 'prefer to have relations with stable capitalist states which have reached a certain level of development, rather than assume responsibility for fragile states of a progressive bent.' The roles of Brazil and Argentina were analysed most thoroughly during the debate. Typical ideas were that 'Brazil is on the way to becoming a developed capitalist power like Canada'; or that 'Argentina is capable of demonstrating a greater degree of independence in external policy than Brazil'; or that the tendency towards autonomy in the external policy of these countries is due to the emergence of 'state-monopolist structures'. Another interesting aspect was the recognition by one of the participants that 'Argentinian industry, except enterprises attached to the military-industrial complex, is moving to Brazil'.
6. This stance was also expressed in symbolic actions such as the decoration of Galtieri during General Braiko's visit in August 1979, and the support given to the Junta by the Argentinian and other Latin American Communist parties.

7. This information was fully reported in such newspapers as *Excelsior, Time, Business Week* and *The Economist.*

8. Hastings and Jenkins (*op.cit.*) think differently. In their view, the Pentagon gave the British all they asked for, except the famous long-range AWACS airborne surveillance systems. The main areas of aid were: communications facilities, Sidewinder air-to-air and Shrike air-to-ground missiles, and fuel supplies. However, since these authors do not assess the role of such assistance in the final outcome, their judgement can hardly be regarded as definitive.

9. International military experts have pointed out that the weaponry used most by the British on land — Lynx helicopters, light tanks such as the 'Scorpion' and 'Scimitar', 'Rapier' and 'Blowpipe' ground-to-air missiles — was certainly in their possession well before the war. Besides, Argentinian batteries were themselves provided with electronic and heat-sensor devices on their new artillery. If the Argentinians did not field other British 'innovations', this was because of incompetence or failure to improvise; such equipment was incomparably cheaper and easier to acquire than Exocet missiles. According to Hastings and Jenkins, the fully automatic Argentinian FN rifles were more powerful than the British SRLs; their night-vision equipment was more efficient; and there was no appreciable difference in field-artillery.

10. Argentinian exports to the European Community have been barely affected by the embargo and continue to be sheltered by contracts signed before 15 April or by later agreements on which the earlier date is stamped.

11. The South African regime became an important military force in the 1960s, and had a military budget of more than \$2bn by 1978. It developed its own weapons industry in this period, producing a version of the Mirage-F1 jetfighter and, in collaboration with Israel, a version of the Exocet missile called the Gabriel. Pretoria did not immediately forge a solid political-military alliance with the Argentinian dictatorship, but it did agree to collaborate in certain areas (despatch of Argentinian military advisers for work with the repressive forces in South Africa and Namibia, progress on a South Atlantic defence pact, and so on). According to *South*, July 1982, South Africa sent Gabriel missiles to Argentina during the Malvinas War.

12. At first Brazil maintained a neutral stance, slightly tilted towards Britain. (Foreign Minister Ramiro Saraiva Guerreiro declared that his country would allow British warships to moor in sight of the coast.) But opposition from Brazilian officers led him to change his position (see LAWR, 9 April 1982). Brazil began to support Argentina in the second stage of the war and sent a number of 'Bandeirante' aeroplanes, although these do not seem to have played a significant role. Well-informed international sources maintain that Brazil changed its stance because Itamaraty feared the Southern Cone would be politically destabilized by an Argentinian defeat, in view of the strong dependence of the Uruguayan, Paraguayan and Bolivian governments on Argentina (see *The Economist*, 8 June 1982). In any case, Brazil has emerged as one of the great beneficiaries from the war: its prestige has been enhanced in Latin America and overseas; it represented Argentina in London after the breaking off of diplomatic relations; it replaced EEC countries as Argentina's main supplier in several export lines, at a time when Brazilian global exports fell by 7 per cent; it can now increase its influence in the smaller countries of the Southern Cone without fear of a major conflict with post-Malvinas Argentina; and it has the chance to replace Argentina as the exporter of sheep-meat and other products to the EEC (the position adopted by the Association of Meat Producers in Río Grande do Sul). *Colombia* was the only

country in Latin America which adopted a more ambiguous position than Chile. This seems to have been due to the fact that it, together with Chile, has the largest number of acute border disputes: one with Chile itself, another with Venezuela to the east, yet another with Peru to the south, and even one in the Caribbean with Nicaragua (San Andres Islands). Not only might an Argentinian victory have fuelled such disputes, but it could also have strengthened the Caracas–Buenos Aires axis, with the subsequent formation of a powerful military encirclement by Peru and Venezuela supported by Buenos Aires.

13. According to a report recently published by *Excelsior* in Mexico, undisclosed Ecuadorean sources leaked the existence of a secret mutual assistance pact between Argentina, Peru and Bolivia to support their claims against Chile. According to the terms of this agreement, which was apparently signed during the Malvinas conflict, Argentina would be assured of hegemony in the South Atlantic and of control over the Magellan, Beagle and Drake passages; Peruvian hegemony in the South-East Pacific would be guaranteed and its territorial demands on Chile, Ecuador and Colombia would receive support; and Bolivia would be granted an exit to the sea between the 23rd and the 25th parellels (which would involve acquisition of the northern part of the Chilean province of Antofagasta, containing Chile's fourth largest city, and the whole of Tarapacá). This tragic plan for forcible territorial gain also had a comic aspect: Bolivia would have to recognize Argentina's right to use the Chilean ports of Tocopilla, Antofagasta and Taltal.

14. According to the source quoted in the previous note, an agreement of this type was made at the first Colombian congress of diplomatic and international studies. We do not know of any other sources, nor whether this agreement has an inter-state expression.

15. The British government had planned to offer the Malvinas for a US military base complementary to the one on the Ascension Islands. If this had happened, another extremely dangerous factor would have threatened the future of democratic and progressive struggles in the Southern Cone.

16. This golden decade was followed by a sharp worsening of the terms of trade that produced what CEPAL has called the 'economic strangulation' of Latin America. The enormous political and economic consequences underlay the development of populist experiences in Brazil, Argentina, Chile, and so on.

17. Chile doubled its military spending in real terms between 1977 and 1980. Argentina's expenditure rose by 55 per cent, its troop levels by a third, and police and paramilitary forces by a hundred per cent. Peru has doubled the size of its armed forces in the last decade, while Mexican expenditure rose by a 'mere' 22 per cent in real terms in 1980. As to the arms industry, Brazil now has 350 plants with a total workforce of 100,000, producing sixty per cent of its requirements and exporting to 32 countries. The Argentinian industry employs 50,000 (including ancillary workers) and is also becoming a major exporter. Chile makes its own patrol launches and landing craft and has begun to manufacture armoured cars and to assemble imported aircraft. Mexico is now producing its own patrol boats and armoured cars. LAWR, 28 May 1982.

Notes to Chapter Six

1. Those officers who wanted a return to civilian rule were concerned to prevent the further erosion of military power, so that withdrawal to barracks might gain

time for the rebuilding of monolithic control and allow the opposition to demonstrate its disunity, contradictions and weakness. Above all, a deal with the Multipartidaria would guarantee immunity from examination of events under the dictatorship (the 'dirty war', the Malvinas War itself). It is even possible that the air force chief, Lami Dozo, hoped that the prestige of his service and his advocacy of 'democratic advance' would eventually make it possible for him to stand for the elected civilian presidency. At the same time, the faction headed by Nicolaides had no real confidence that a civilian government could pilot through the storms of the transition period. He preferred the army to keep the reins of power, using the underlying threat of a new bloodbath.

2. In 1962 a long period of clashes betwen different sectors of the armed forces culminated in the triumph of the *azul* wing, led by Onganía, over the *colorado* wing. Basing themselves on a strictly professional army, with no deliberation at any level and complete obedience to the commander-in-chief, the victors tried to establish the closest ties between the top military commanders and the monopoly bourgeoisie, or between the industrial sector under military control and big private capital. The present crisis has for the first time seriously dented this model, opening up at least a temporary possibility that internal contradictions will multiply and weaken the military's capacity as a repressive apparatus.

3. The Multipartidaria, after issuing confused statements, agreed to see Bignone. At the meeting the parties sought the lifting of the state of siege, the return of normal status to the unions, and the release of political prisoners held without trial. This involved recognition of the Junta's tribunals, since all prisoners who had passed before them and all sentences it handed down had been related to subversion. Nor did they once mention the dramatic problem of the 'missing', either at the meeting or in the document issued on that day. At the end of the talks Carlos Contín said: 'General Bignone is a convinced democrat'. That this was not an isolated opinion is confirmed by the statement of A. Robledo, a Peronist leader: 'I applaud the gesture of calling the political parties to a meeting.'

4. It is not so easy to draw a more detailed balance-sheet of the dictatorship. From its own point of view, it seems to have achieved major successes in the development of production, agroexports, transport, energy and communications infrastructure; and to have made less clear advances in the centralization of capital, the raising of productivity, and the restructuring of the labour market. On the other hand, its anti-inflation drive was a resounding failure, as were its attempts to develop a capital market articulated with an efficient banking system, to cut the cost of the state apparatus, and radically to restructure industry along more efficient and competitive lines strongly rooted in the new international division of labour. These failures in such important areas prevented it from overcoming the essentially destructive nature of the Junta. Nor did it ever move beyond its essentially destructive tasks to a global restructuring of capital articulated around finance capital, state finance and competitive world markets. This above all else sets it apart from the Brazilian experience.

5. In Argentina there has been a major gap between the standard of living of the working class at its highest (1948–1951, 1958, 1965–66, 1974–75) and at its lowest (1956–1963, 1976 onwards) — perhaps as much as 35 or even 50 per cent. Thus, whenever the process of accumulation restores full employment — which it does quite rapidly, given the lack of a sizeable reserve army of labour — the social strength of the working class soon pushes wages up to what it regards as the historic level. The bourgeoisie must then have recourse to military coups in

order to drive down the price of labour power through a process of super-exploitation.

6. *Clarín Económico*, 4 August 1983. Nearly 70 per cent of export earnings ($5bn out of $8.5-9bn) have been chanelled into repayments on the Argentinian external debt. This coefficient, the highest in the world, is particularly serious since Argentina lacks other major sources of foreign currency such as tourism or remittances from nationals abroad, and it suffers from a strong tendency to capital flight. In these circumstances the only way to service the external debt is to force imports below 3bn dollars. But even then it would be necessary to maintain the volume of exports — an almost impossible task given the decline in world trade and the heavy subsidization of the principal export lines. Furthermore, the post-Malvinas rearmament drive and modernization of the military apparatus threatens to devour scarce foreign-exchange reserves and further to limit the capacity of import essential goods.

7. It should be added that capital accumulation in industry subtracts ever greater resources from the agricultural sector, providing industry with equivalent resources (inputs of equipment at decreasing costs). It therefore progressively discourages the flow of capital to the countryside, affecting not only agrarian profit levels but also the profits made by the weakest links in the chain of Pampas production. This factor, together with the wages cycle already mentioned above, accounts for the characteristically short and sharp oscillations of the economic conjuncture in Argentina.

8. Frondizi managed to contain the mass upsurge in 1958-59, but he thereby lost all his political prestige and was forced to make major concessions to the bureaucratic leadership of the union movement. Illia did not dare to repeat this in 1965-66, and therefore paved the way for the military coup.

9. See the closing statement of the 'First Stages of Social Economy' event organized by the Justicialist Party in 1981: 'Justicialism preaches... the spread of popular savings, labour productivity and consumer austerity as the basis for national capitalization... Social discipline for economic development freely assumed by all.' Earlier there had been talk of 'incomes policies agreed between labour, capital and the state which tend to increase the participation of wages in profits linked to productivity increases' (*Controversia* 11–12) — a far cry from the distributionist demagogy of previous Peronist governments. Any official economist could have given a similar speech.

10. Historically the union bureaucracy has been linked to one of the bourgeois sectors we have analysed. In better times, when it was still possible to follow a policy of high employment and good wages, the bureaucracy appeared to the masses as an effective negotiator of improvements. It also helped to manipulate and contain struggles. But in the present crisis the most it can do is to bargain for miserable crumbs. The bureaucratic union leadership is fundamentally weakened by the decline of the populist bourgeoisie. Crisis in the latter means crisis in the former.

This does not mean that a body like CGT-Ubaldini is of no account, since it can act indirectly as a unitary point of reference for broad sectors of the class. However, it was formed 'from above' by leaders whose representative capacity was fiercely challenged in Isabel Perón's time (some eight years ago) and who have retained their positions largely as a consequence of the paralysis of union life during the dictatorship. Nor should it be overlooked that most of these leaders were long opposed to mobilizations for class democracy and independence, and that the crisis and contradictions in the Multipartidaria can only accentuate the underlying historical tendencies.

16. It is very important that radical democratic demands should not be separated from the social demands of the workers and the people. The most important of these are: the recovery and maintenance of wage levels; social security for the unemployed; price controls with popular participation; strict legislation against capitalist speculators, loan sharks and foreign-exchange hoarders; expropriation under workers' control of enterprises acting against the national and popular economy; a sharp reduction in military expenditure and in the salaries and assorted perks of state, military and judicial functionaries; and an emergency tax on big capital and landowners.

12. The role of the Argentinian Communist Party (PCA) is perhaps worthy of a footnote. After recovering from the blows of the 1967–68 military government, it was able to reach an agreement with the 1976 Junta and to continue operating freely in the worst years of repression. Its chain of co-operatives and its Institute for the Mobilization of Cooperative Funds allowed it to take advantage of the 1977 banking legislation and to begin functioning in the manner of the big banks. It was thus able to weather the 1979–1980 financial crisis and to consolidate its position in the capital market. It is common knowledge that the PCA now uses its banking system to recruit small and medium-sized capitalists and all kinds of people desperate for credit.

This banking structure, together with other major industrial and commercial enterprises associated with the Party, is a not insignificant force within Argentinian capital. At the same time, the PCA has continued to lose ground in the working class, although it is still able to recruit young people because of its formal left-wing stance and its huge economic and cultural apparatus. It is perhaps the only legal channel linked to the 'left' which young intellectuals or artists can join if they want to further their career, go on tours, travel abroad, and so forth. But it no longer has much to do with the proletariat.

13. 'The Socialist Left' was an important tendency within the Argentinian revolutionary movement. It was formed between 1969 and 1972 by several groups based in the main industrial centres of the country. It did not manage to form a unified organization, and was scattered by repression after a serious political crisis over tactics for the 1972–73 election, the military strategy of the mass struggle and the characterization of the ERP and Montoneros. Nevertheless, it emerged as the most advanced expression of the combative sectors of the working-class and popular movement, putting forward a series of ideas that constituted a radical attempt to break from the traditional left (the PCA, the Maoist or Trotskyist groups, and the pro-Cuban tendencies). Among these were its characterization of Argentina as a politically independent state; its definition of the social nature of the Argentinian revolution; its call for a democratic, class-struggle practice within the workers movement; and its (unrealized) goal of forming a proletarian party. It also tended to adopt an independent position on international questions, and a majority were critical of the bureaucratic experience in socialist-bloc countries.

The Socialist Left sank quite deep roots in the more radical proletarian sectors, jointly leading some of the major experiences of 1971-75 (*clasista* unions in Córdoba and Paraná province, the general strike at Villa Constitución, the more progressive Intersindicales movement of 1974–75, etc.). It also gained considerable influence within the student movement, and won the leadership in Córdoba and other key parts of the country. Throughout this period it worked closely with the more advanced Peronist currents (the Peronismo de Base, the FR-17 groups) and with progressive elements of the FAL and MRA armed organizations. But it was never able to cohere as an organic structure or to make an adequate political response to Perón's return, the development of a broad political struggle and the rise of militarism led by the ERP and the Montoneros. At present there are a number of groups inside and outside the country which see themselves as part of this historic tendency.

Notes to Chapter Seven: Postscript

1. During 1982 contraband exports and under-invoicing reached a phenomenal level. *Business Week* (20 September 1982) reported that ten per cent of Argentina's soya crop was being sold on the black market in Brazil and Paraguay, after crossing the border on lorries or small boats plying the River Paraná. According to World Bank experts quoted in the *Latin American Weekly Report* (15 June 1983), under-invoicing allowed an extra 1,800 million dollars to leave the country in 1982. Despite this drain of wealth, and despite the worse conditions in the world economy, exports reached a value of $7.8bn, considerably less than the 1981 record but only slightly down on the 1980 figure.

2. The almost usurious financial conditions imposed on Argentina were repeated in other Latin American countries. See the *Latin America Weekly Report* of 13 May 1983.

3. Industrial exports continued to enjoy preferential treatment in 1982: reimbursements of approximately 15 per cent plus a supplement above a certain level; interest-free export credits granted by the Central Bank for a commission charge of one per cent (see the BCRA circulars RF 99 and RF 153); an assured supply of foreign currency; and automatic tax-exemption, until July 1983, on temporary imports of industrial inputs. Industrial exporters also benefited from the successive devaluations of the peso after 1981.

4. For a detailed analysis of the banking collapse, see the 'Economic Supplement' to *Clarín*, 7 August 1983.

5. A leading Argentinian periodical described the situation in late 1982 and early 1983 as follows: 'The market for land and real estate, for example, was affected by speculative buying... In some cases it was possible to acquire land of high agricultural potential or buildings in the most expensive areas for a quarter of their historic value or a tenth of their dollar value of three years before.' *El Trimestre* no. 7, 'Temas'. According to the *Latin America Weekly Report* of 15 July 1983, 'capital left the trusts to acquire real estate, capital goods, consumer durables, shares and strong currencies'.

6. In 1979 the Church started a campaign for 'national reconciliation' which ended in April 1983 with its support for the Junta's 'final document' on the *desaparecidos*. See Ruben Dri, *Obispos argentinos justifican a la Junta Militar sobre los desaparecidos*, CENCOS, Mexico City 1973. The only serious political differences with the Junta were over the impending war with Chile in 1978 and during the somewhat fraught period between May 1981 and the beginning of the war in April 1982.

7. For a juridical analysis of 'global parallelism', see Dr Emillo F. Mignone, *El Caso argentino: desapariciones como instrumento básico y generalizado de una politica*, CAS, Mexico City 1981.

8. On 16 July General Nicolaides announced a reorganization of the army high command which involved the removal of Generals J. B. Menéndez, Jofre, Parada

and Daher (all commanders of the Malvinas operation), the reallocation of Colonels Aguiar, Chimeno, Mambraga and Ali Seineldin, and a request for the retirement of General J. O. García, head of the Fifth Army Corps and organizer of the landing on the Malvinas. In August Brigadier Hugue replaced Lami Dozo as head of the air force. By the end of the year *Ambito Financiero* (25 November 1982) could report that sixteen brigadiers had been retired and that another seven would join them in the next month. In September the reorganization of the naval command began with the replacement of Anaya by Admiral Franco.

9. For a more detailed account, see the CISEA publication, *El Bimestre Politico y Económico*, Buenos Aires, nos. 4 and 9.

10. After 2 July the following persons were kidnapped and killed: the journalist Dupont, the workers Lopez Cassani and Del Plá, the political militants Moreno, Cambiasso, Pereyra Rossi and Jagger, and the student Khairallah. Human rights organizations also reported the 'suicide' of six political prisoners accused of subversion. There were innumerable accounts of torture, and more than a dozen judges were subjected to threats or physical attacks. The Mothers of the Plaza de Mayo were also assaulted or insulted. The police killed people attending demonstrations. In the cases of Cambiasso and Pereyra Rossi, the Buenos Aires district police chief, General Verplaetsen, took full responsibility for their killing. Faced with subversion, he said, 'there can be no dialogue, no armistice, no laying down of weapons, no resignation, no cease-fire, no gentlemen's agreement, no raising of the white flag'. 'Each member of our police force has taken his decision, and no one will tread softly in discharging his duty.' *El Bimestre* no. 9, p.88. The commander-in-chief of the army expressed his full solidarity with General Verplaetsen.

11. According to J. Deprès in *Le Monde*.

12. *Latin America Weekly Report*, quoting *Defence and Foreign Affairs*.

13. *El Bimestre*, quoting *Hechos*, 7 July 1982.

14. See Hastings and Jenkins, *op. cit.*

15. In the same period, Argentina was entertaining close relations with South Africa (see the declarations by General Calvi, and the visit by the South African President Marais Viljoin in September 1983) and maintained a military presence alongside the anti-Sandinista forces in Honduras. See, for example, the statement by Raul Alfonsín on 9 November 1982. In its June 1983 issue (pp. 62-63), *El Bimestre* published a statement by *La Voz* to the effect that Fabricaciones Militares had sent war matériel worth $4m to the anti-Sandinistas in December 1982. It also mentioned the testimony of peasants who had fled a *somocista* camp that Argentinian advisers were giving courses to some three hundred contras in Tegucigalpa.

16. The fact that the main state and service-sector unions belonged to the CGT–Azopardo must have affected its positions when they became the epicentre of the strike movement. However, it began to lose strength very quickly in the second half of 1982, and at the beginning of January 1983 the so-called 'non-aligned unions' returned to the CGT–Brasil.

17. The term is taken from Adolfo Gilly, 'El Diciembre Caliente', *Coyoacan*, January–June 1983.

18. Although the exact line-up is far from clear, we should mention the statement issued on 13 February by retd.-General F. Toranzo Montero, chairman of the Officers Centre of the Armed Forces. He called on the government to 'make a swift and drastic change in its political conduct, in order to assure the survival of the Republic and its armed forces'.

19. It would seem that the 'army–union pact' was backed by Generals Nicolaides, Trimarco and Suarez Nelson. Raul Alfonsín publicly denounced it on 26 April, using reports provided to him by the sympathetic Reston–Cerda faction within the army. According to the *Prensa* journalist Iglesias Rouco, the pact would have been known to, and perhaps endorsed by, members of the fascist current within Peronism such as retd-Col. Prémoli, the politician Deheza and the Croat General Vogelich (a Nazi who had joined Perón while living under Trujillo's protection in the Dominican Republic).

20. *El Bimestre* 9, 1983, p. 51.

21. On the occasion of the murder of Cambiasso and Pereyra Rossi, the head of CELS Conte MacDonell asked whether the Mutipartidaria would continue to remain silent, as it had done when the first unmarked graves were discovered and relatives of the missing were being intimidated. *La Prensa*, 19 June 1982.

22. Vandorism is the main current within the Peronist union movement. It took shape in the struggle to regain control of the unions after the 1955 coup, gathered strength through the pact with President Frondizi (1959–60) and achieved full legality by means of an Occupational Associations Act which bestowed great privileges on the unions and their leaders. It then became the axis of the political reorganization of Peronism, even challenging Perón himself, and it reached an agreement with the military in 1966 to bring down President Illía. When the trade-union movement was repressed by the Onganía dictatorship, it became the pillar of the Peronist centre, opposed both to *dialoguismo* and to the so-called 'liberation unionism' of Raimundo Ongaro that preached a combative, revolutionary Peronism. Vandor himself was assassinated by the Montoneros.

23. The pact involved support for Miguel's forces at the elections supervised by the Junta. This aspect of the accord, which was publicly denounced by the CGT–Azopardo, seems to have been implemented by General Suarez Nelson.

24. In Avellaneda the Peronist Union Youth (JSP) supported the bureaucratic removal of A. García from the CGT–Brasil regional office, accusing him of 'using labour movement funds to facilitate Marxist infiltration'. (García belonged to the Integration and Renewal tendency and had links with combative sectors of the striking Volkswagen workforce.) At a rally on 16 April, called by human rights organizations in Buenos Aires, the JSP shouted provocative slogans such as: 'Let us disown the murderers of Argentinians [a reference to the Montoneros], the infiltrators of the Peronist movement, and the saboteurs of the

25. Having supported liberal forces within the Radicals until the whole UCR moved to the left, the PCA electorally supported the Peronists at a time when they were moving to the right. The posture of the PCA is consistent with its unswerving support for Miguel and its distance from the Peronist Left. In the student movement the PCA tends to form joint lists with the official Peronists against the Left and the Radicals.

26. Old Supreme Court rulings laid down that no subordinate could be freed of guilt because he committed a crime on orders from a superior. This is a universal legal principle accepted by the United Nations and the Nuremberg Tribunal. Alfonsín's position implied that child-murderers, rapists, torturers, thieves and psychopaths should be cleared of blame if they had acted in a context which made them consider their actions to be legitimate.

27. In 1982 the MAS called for unification of all sections of the old Socialist Party, a Bernsteinian formation founded by Juan B. Justo in the 1890s. This reformist party, which supported the Liberating Revolution of 1955 and other military adventures, has lost all touch with the working class in the last forty years. The

opportunism of the MAS goes so far that it has tried to negotiate recognition by the Socialist International.

Selected Bibliography

Books and Articles

Abalo, Carlos, 'Argentina, 1976-1981, objetivos y resultados de la política económica', *Comercio Exterior*, Mexico City, June–August 1981;
——, 'Notas sobre el carácter actual del capitalismo argentino', *Cuadernos de Marcha* No. 2, Mexico City.
Almeyra, Guillermo, 'La clase obrera en la Argentina actual', *Coyoacan* No. 9, Mexico City.
Arancibia y Pérez, 'La política en torno de las empresas públicas en América Latina', *Economía de América Latina*, CIDE, Mexico City 1980.

Barnett, Anthony, *Iron Britannia*, London 1982.
Bausualdo, E., 'Tendencias a la transnacionalización de América Latina durante el decenio de los setenta', *Comercio Exterior*, July 1982.
Burgin, Nyron, *Aspectos económicos del federalismo argentino*, Buenos Aires 1960.

Cabrera, Guillermo, 'La nueva izquierda comunista latinoamericana y los problemas del mundo actual', *Teoría y Política* No. 3, Mexico City.
Canitrot, Adolfo, 'Teoría y práctica del liberalismo. Política anti-inflacionaria y apertura económica de la Argentina', *Desarrollo Económico*, Buenos Aires.
Capocci, Daniel, 'El proletariado y la amenaza de la guerra fratricida', *Debate Proletario* Nos. 5-6, Buenos Aires 1980.
Castillo, Carlos, 'Los dilemas de la posguerra', *Cuadernos del Tercer Mundo* No. 53, Mexico City 1982.
Chambre, Henry, *La Unión Soviética y el desarrollo económico*, Bilbao 1972.
CIDANO, 'Economía y política en la Argentina', *Cuadernos Políticos* No. 27.
Circulos para la formación de un espacio independiente, *La verdad o la mística nacional*, Buenos Aires 1982.
Claudín, Fernando, *The Communist Movement*, Harmondsworth 1975.
Comité Editorial de Debate Proletario, 'Declaración sobre la guerra China-Vietnam y su significado histórico y político', *Debate Proletario*, 1979.
Conferencia Episcopal Argentina, *Iglesia y Comunidad Nacional*, Buenos Aires, May 1981.
Consejo Tecnológico Peronista, *El plan petrolero de la dictadura argentina*, Cuadernos CTP, New York 1981.

Dabat, Alejandro, 'La economía mundial y los países periféricos a partir de la segunda mitad de la década de los sesenta', *Teoría y Política* No. 1, Mexico City 1980;
——, 'Tesis preliminares sobre la evolución del sistema capitalista-imperialista mundial', duplicated paper, CIES, Mexico City 1979;
——, 'Intelectuales, proletarios y déspotas', *Teoría y Política* No. 4.
Díaz Alejandro, Carlos F., *Ensayos sobre la historia económica argentina*, Buenos Aires 1974.
Drí, Rubén, 'Obispos argentinos justifican a la junta militar sobre los desaparecidos', *Cencos: Suplemento Iglesias*, Mexico City 1983.

Emmanuel, Arghiri, *Unequal Exchange*, NLB, London 1971.

Fava, Athos, *Malvinas: batalla por una nueva Argentina*, Buenos Aires 1982.
Ferrer, Aldo, 'La economía política del peronismo', *El Trimestre Económico*, Jan.–Mar. 1977, Mexico City.

Geller, Lucio, 'Las iniciativas en el sector externo de la oligarquía financiera argentina', *Teoría y Política* No. 3.
Gilly, Adolfo, 'Las Malvinas, una guerra del capital', *Cuadernos Politícos* No. 35; ——, 'La guerra chino-vietnam: socialismo nacional y nacionalismo burocrático', *Coyoacan* No. 6.
Gómez y Rivera, 'México: acumulación de capital y crisis en la década del setenta', *Teoría y Política* No. 2.
Gramsci, Antonio, *Selections from the Priston Notebooks*, London 1971.
Guglielmilli, Juan A., 'Las negociaciones por las Malvinas en una nueva etapa?' *Estrategía* Nos. 43-44, Buenos Aires 1977.

Halliday, Fred, *The Making of the Second Cold War*, Verso/NLB, London 1983; ——, 'The Sources of the New Cold War', in *Exterminism and Cold War*, Verso/NLB, London 1982.
Hardy, Marcos Armando, *Esquema del Estado Justicialista*, Buenos Aires 1977.
Hastings, Max, and Jenkins, Simon, *The Battle for the Falklands*, London 1983.
Hodges, Donald C., *Argentina 1943-76: The National Revolution and Resistance*, Alburquerque, NM, 1976.

Jalée, Pierre, *L'Impérialisme en 1970*, Paris 1970.

Koening, Enrique, 'Tiempos dificiles para los industriales argentinos', *Contextos* No. 13, Mexico City.
Kon, Daniel, *Los chicos de la guerra*, Buenos Aires 1982.

Lambruschini, Armando, 'Speech of 5 August 1978 at the Centre for Strategic Studies of the Escuela Superior de Guerra', *La Prensa*.
Latin American Newsletters, *Malvinas: The Official History of the War*, London 1983.
Lenin, V.I., *Imperialism: The Highest Stage of Capitalism*, Moscow 1966; ——, 'Notebooks on Imperialism', *Collected Works* (CW), vol. 39, Moscow 1968; ——, 'Critical Notes on the National Question', *CW* 15; ——,'Theses on the Right of Nations to Self-Determination', *CW* 21.
Lipietz, Alain, 'Towards Global Fordism?' *New Left Review* No. 132.

Maddison, Angus, *Economic Progress and Policy in Developing Countries*, London 1970.
Mandel, Ernest, 'Las leyes del desarrollo desigual', in *Imperialismo Hoy*, Buenos Aires 1971.
Mandel and Jaber, *Estudios sobre el capital financiero semicolonial*, Buenos Aires 1977.
Mao Tse-tung, 'On the New Democracy', in *Selected Works* Vol. 4, Peking 1963; ——, 'On the People's Democratic Dictatorship', *SW* 4.
Marini, Ruy Mauro, 'Estado y crisis en Brasil', *Cuadernos Politicos* No. 9.
Martínez de Hoz, José, *Bases para una Argentina moderna*, Buenos Aires 1981; ——, speech delivered on 26 March 1980, Ministerio de Economía, Buenos Aires 1980.
Marx and Engels, *On Ireland*, London 1970; ——, *Selected Correspondence*, Moscow 1975; ——, *Karl Marx on Colonialism and Modernization* (ed., S. Avineri), New York 1980.

Montoneros, 'Declaracíon del 9 de abril sobre la guerra de las Malvinas', Mexico City 1982.

Murmis and Portantiero, *Estudio sobre los orígenes del peronismo*, Buenos Aires 1971.

O'Connor, James, 'Sobre el significado del imperialismo económico', in *Imperialismo Hoy*, Buenos Aires 1971.

Ortiz, Ricardo, *El ferrocarril en la economía argentina*, Buenos Aires 1958.

Pēna, Polit and Testa, 'Industrialización, burguesía industrial y marxismo', *Fichas* Nos. 4–8, Buenos Aires, Dec. 1964–Dec. 1975.

Peralta Ramos, Mónica, *Acumulación de capital y crisis política en la Argentina: 1930-1974*, Mexico City 1978.

Phipps, Colin B., *Belize and the Falklands: The Impact of Oil*, London 1980.

Prebisch, Raúl, 'Informe preliminar acerca de la situación económica', in *Memorias del Banco Central de la Republica Argentina*, Buenos Aires 1955.

Quijano, José Manuel, *Mexico: Estado y Banco privada*, Mexico City 1982.

Real de Azua, Mario F., 'La convención de Nutka de 1970 y la recuperación de las Islas Malvinas', *Cuadernos de Marcha*, Nov.–Dec. 1982.

Rivera, Miguel A., 'La política exterior de México: expansionismo y demagogía', *Teoría y Política* No. 5.

Rouquie, Alain, 'Hegemonía militar, estado y dominación social', in Rouquie et al., *Argentina Hoy*, Mexico City 1982.

Schmidt, Lorenz, *Países en desarrollo*, Mexico City 1982.

Schwartzer, Jorge, *Expansión económica del estado subsidiario*, Buenos Aires 1980.

Schwarzer, Jorge, 'Empresas publicas y desarrollo industrial en la Argentina', *Economía de América Latina* No. 3, Mexico City 1979.

Schasposnick-Vacchino, 'Fracaso de un ministro o de un sistema?' *Comercio Exterior*, January 1982, Mexico City.

Selser, Gregorio, 'La sensación expansionista tras la recuperación de las Malvinas', *Cuadernos de Marcha*, Nov.–Dec. 1981.

Semo, Enrique, *La crisis actual del capitalismo*, Mexico City 1976.

Silenzi de Stagni, José, *Las Malvinas y el Petróleo*, Buenos Aires 1982.

Sommi, Luis, *Las inversiones yanquis en la Argentina*, Buenos Aires 1949.

Spagnolo and Esteso, 'Argentina y las Malvinas: sueños de potencia y resistencia popular', *Cuadernos Políticos* No. 32.

Trotsky, Leon, 'Por los Estados Unidos Socialistas de América Latina', in *Obras* vol. 15, Mexico City 1973.

TYSAE (Mexico), *Argentina: Avanza la Resistencia*, Mexico City 1981.

TYSAE (Mexico), *A 19 años de la masacre de 19 combatientes populares en Trelew: la lucha continua*, Mexico City 1981.

Wakasman Shinca, Daniel, 'Lo que está en juego: una inmensa reserva de recursos energeticos y alimentarios', *Cuadernos del Tercer Mundo* No. 25, Mexico City 1978.

Bulletins and Yearbooks

ALN, *Informe Latinoamericano*, London.

BCRA, *Boletín*, Buenos Aires.

CELA, *Boletín de Coyuntura*, Mexico City.

CEPAL, *Informe Económico de América Latina*, New York.
CISEA, *El Bimestre Político y Económico*, Buenos Aires.
IIEE, *Anuario*, London.
IMF Bulletin, New York.
SIPRI, *World Military and Social Expenditures*, Stockholm.
UNO, *Statistical Trade Yearbook*, New York.

News Magazines and Political Journals

Business Week International, New York.
Contextos, Mexico City.
Divergencia, Paris.
El Economista, Buenos Aires.
En Lucha, Sweden.
Estrategía, Buenos Aires.
Foreign Policy, New York.
Le Monde Diplomatique (Spanish edition), Mexico City.
L'Expansion, Paris.
Mercado, Buenos Aires.
Propuesta, Madrid.
Que Pasa, Buenos Aires.
Socialist Review, London.
South, London.

Daily papers

Clarín, Buenos Aires.
El Dia, Mexico City.
Excelsior, Mexico City.
Financial Times, London.
La Nación, Buenos Aires.
La Prensa, Buenos Aires.
Le Monde, Paris.
Los Angeles Times.
New York Times.
The Economist, London.
Uno mas Uno, Mexico City.

Index